British Literary Manuscripts

Series I
from 800 to 1800

Catalogue by
VERLYN KLINKENBORG

Checklist by
HERBERT CAHOON

Introduction by
CHARLES RYSKAMP

THE PIERPONT MORGAN LIBRARY
in association with
DOVER PUBLICATIONS, INC.
NEW YORK

The preparation of this work was made possible through a grant from the Research Resources Program in the Division of Research Programs of the National Endowment for the Humanities, a Federal agency.

Published in Canada by General Publishing Company, Ltd., 30 Lesmill Road, Don Mills, Toronto, Ontario.
Published in the United Kingdom by Constable and Company, Ltd., 10 Orange Street, London WC2H 7EG.

British Literary Manuscripts/Series I: From 800 to 1800 is a new work, first published by Dover Publications, Inc., in 1981 in association with The Pierpont Morgan Library.

International Standard Book Number: 0-486-24124-6
Library of Congress Catalog Card Number: 80-71101

Manufactured in the United States of America
Dover Publications, Inc.
180 Varick Street
New York, N.Y. 10014

Introduction

This first volume of *British Literary Manuscripts* illustrates the course of English literature over a thousand-year period through a series of reproductions of manuscripts of literary works (mostly autograph), autograph letters and a few inscriptions in books or signed documents, receipts or notes. It begins just before the year 800 with a manuscript fragment of the monumental work by the Venerable Bede, *Historia Ecclesiastica;* it ends about 1800 with autographs of Blake and Burns. The second volume covers British literary manuscripts from 1800 to World War I.

A companion volume, *American Literary Autographs from Washington Irving to Henry James*, was published by The Pierpont Morgan Library in association with Dover Publications in 1977. A checklist, similar to the one in that book, is located at the end of the second volume of the present publication, in this case showing all of the British literary manuscript holdings, from the sixteenth century to the present, in the Morgan Library. This will afford scholars and other libraries a ready reference to one of the three or four most important collections of British literary autographs in the world.

Our aim is to present a popular guide to this subject. Most surveys of historical or literary autographs are expensive books, often in several volumes. This guide, however, should be within the reach of any school or college library, young students and beginning collectors. The two volumes cover a wider range of time and of genres, and a larger number of authors, than such distinguished books on the subject as W. W. Greg (editor), *English Literary Autographs 1550–1650* (Oxford, 1925, 1928, 1932); P. J. Croft, *Autograph Poetry in the English Language: Facsimiles of Original Manuscripts from the Fourteenth to the Twentieth Century* (London, 1973); and Anthony G. Petti, *English Literary Hands from Chaucer to Dryden* (London, 1977). Unlike those volumes, these two have more to do with literary values and the author's reputation than with technical aspects of manuscripts. We have not tried to present a palaeographical survey, nor have we analyzed any of the handwritings. We have not provided principles of textual study, nor methods of identifying hands and editing manuscripts.

Each entry in the present volumes briefly describes the manuscript from which the illustration is taken and relevant aspects of the life and work of the author. There are comments on the particular leaf or leaves chosen and the importance of the work or the letter from which it came. We have also attempted to list the major manuscript resources for many of the authors so that those who wish to pursue their studies further will be able to do so easily, and the reproductions given may help in identifying holograph material of the leading British writers.

It is remarkable how many important literary holographs have been discovered only recently; for example, the poetical autograph manuscripts now known of Sir Philip Sidney and his brother Robert, and those by Donne, Herrick, Chalkhill, Denham and Dryden. There are still no autographs known of Langland, Gower, Lydgate, Malory or the *Gawain* poet; for Chaucer there is as yet only a possibility of a prose treatise in his hand; for Spenser, only documents; for Shakespeare, six signatures and (plausibly ascribed) three pages of the manuscript of the play *Sir Thomas More;* for Marlowe, a signature; for many of the other Elizabethan and Jacobean dramatists, nothing at all; for Bunyan, only a document or two and some signatures have been found.

Before 1700, British literary holographs are indeed rare. Milton stands alone among the writers of the first nine hundred years of English literature in that significant autograph manuscripts survive for him, perhaps, as P. J. Croft has written, because "they were consciously preserved as literary relics *ab initio:* the idea is in keeping with Milton's solemn dedication of himself to the Muse . . . ." The star piece in the present volume is the illustration of a page from

Book I of *Paradise Lost*, the sole remnant of the manuscript dictated by Milton, corrected under his supervision and used as copy by his printer. It is the most important literary manuscript in the Morgan Library and one of the most celebrated English literary manuscripts in existence.

For the early centuries there are nevertheless other manuscripts in the Morgan Library of extraordinary importance: what is in all likelihood the most significant text for one of the greatest narrative poems in English, Chaucer's *Troilus and Criseyde;* the only substantial literary autograph manuscript of Sir Philip Sidney, his *Defence of the Earl of Leicester;* the only complete manuscript (containing one of the two known pages in his handwriting) of Crashaw's most famous poem, his "Hymn to St. Teresa"; three wonderful letters from the largest collection of Dryden's autograph manuscripts; a manuscript of Locke's *Essay concerning Humane Understanding;* and Sir Isaac Newton's youthful notebook.

From the eighteenth century there are such important manuscripts as Swift's cover letter, copied by Gay, sent to the publishers with the anonymous transcript of *Gulliver's Travels*, and the autograph manuscripts of Pope's *Essay on Man*, Fielding's receipt for the purchase of copyright of *Tom Jones*, Johnson's "Life of Pope," Sterne's initial attempt (in all probability) in the method of writing *Tristram Shandy*, Gray's ode "On the Death of a favourite Cat," notes for Gibbon's *Decline and Fall of the Roman Empire*, Mrs. Thrale's *Anecdotes of the late Samuel Johnson*, Blake's "Auguries of Innocence" and Burns's "Auld Lang Syne."

All of these literary manuscripts are in the Morgan Library; in fact, all of the 129 entries for 111 authors in this first volume have been selected from the collections of the Morgan Library except eight which were chosen from private libraries in the United States. We are deeply grateful to all of those who permitted their manuscripts to be used and are especially indebted to Mrs. Donald F. Hyde, a Trustee of the Library, for allowing us to show four manuscripts from her collection.

It is generally recognized that of the great American collectors who were active at the end of the nineteenth century and the first part of this, J. Pierpont Morgan (1837–1913) "was the most catholic in his tastes." We think of his collecting above all in relation to many kinds of art from many thousands of years. The same is true of the written records which he gathered together, from the earliest tablets and papyri to books and manuscripts of his own contemporaries. He began by collecting autographs, specimens of the handwriting of the principal figures of his day. When still a schoolboy, before he was fifteen, he had acquired the autograph of President Millard Fillmore and, in response to Morgan's request, six letters from bishops of the Protestant Episcopal Church. The collection of autographs is, therefore, the cornerstone of all of the Morgan collections: at The Pierpont Morgan Library, The Metropolitan Museum of Art and throughout the United States and the world.

By 1883, Morgan had a library with only a few fine books, but many more excellent autographs: letters of Robert Burns, Alexander Hamilton and George Washington, and one of the finest collections of autographs of the signers of the Declaration of Independence. Morgan's passion for collecting literary and historical manuscripts never abated, and it was very strong also in his son, J. P. Morgan (1867–1943). In the course of time, owing to the dazzling collections of medieval and Renaissance manuscripts, early printed books and drawings, and the wealth of European materials in The Pierpont Morgan Library, the importance of the English and American collections of manuscripts, both literary and historical, has been diminished in the public eye. Yet in both fields, the collections of autograph manuscripts are among the finest in the world.

The foundation of the Morgan collection of British literary manuscripts was the purchase a century ago, in 1881, by Junius Spencer Morgan, father of Pierpont, of the original manuscript of Sir Walter Scott's *Guy Mannering*. Junius later gave it to his son. But not until after his father's death in 1890 did Pierpont begin to buy on a large scale, which he continued to do for nearly a quarter century, to the time of his death in 1913. He was aided and stimulated by his nephew, Junius S. Morgan, by his brilliant young librarian, Miss Belle da Costa Greene, and by many dealers, of whom the firm of J. Pearson & Co. in London was the most important. Those were the years during which the notable manuscripts of Burns, Byron, Dickens, Keats, Ruskin and Scott came to the Library. The manuscript of Book I of Milton's *Paradise Lost* was acquired by Mr. Morgan after it had been offered for sale at an auction devoted only to this manuscript held at Sotheby's in London, 25 January 1904, but had been bought in by the owner.

After Pierpont Morgan's death, his son, J. P. Morgan, added many fine British literary manuscripts to the collection, including Thackeray's *The Rose and the Ring* and letters and manuscripts of John Locke, Jane Austen and the Brownings, among others. The collection has continued to grow since the death of J. P. Morgan in 1943 through purchases, gifts from the Fellows of the Library and individual donations. Sir Philip Sidney, Sir Francis Bacon, Coleridge, Wordsworth, the Brontës, Ruskin and Gilbert & Sullivan are among the many authors now represented by letters and manuscripts of the first rank.

Since this guide and the checklist at the end of the second volume may call the attention of scholars to manuscripts in the Morgan Library which they may wish to see, inquire about or have copied photographically, it should be noted that applications for cards of admission to the Reading Room are made on forms provided for the purpose; cards are readily issued to qualified and accredited scholars. Graduate students and scholars having no institutional affiliation are expected to present with their applications suitable references concerning their fitness to handle rare manuscript materials. Prior notification of visits by those from out of town is advisable in order to insure the availability of the manuscripts desired, but it is not insisted upon. The Reading Room is open from Monday through Friday, 9:30–4:45, except holidays.

In the past three years we have recatalogued all of the English literary manuscripts in The Pierpont Morgan Library. This project was made possible by a generous grant from the National Endowment for the Humanities. The work was carried out by Mr. Verlyn Klinkenborg under the supervision of Mr. Herbert Cahoon, Curator of Autograph Manuscripts in the Library. These two volumes of British literary manuscripts are also chiefly due to their work, and in particular to the efforts of Mr. Klinkenborg, who deserves great credit for his diligent research and for his lively and graceful skill in preparing all of the entries. The photographs were prepared by Mr. Charles V. Passela, assisted by Mr. C. Mitchell Carl. We also owe thanks to Mr. Reginald Allen, Mrs. Ronnie Boriskin, Miss Deborah Evetts, Mrs. Sara Feldman Guérin, Dr. Paul Needham, Mrs. Patricia Reyes and Mr. J. Rigbie Turner of the staff of the Library, as well as to Mr. Roger W. Barrett, Mrs. Donald F. Hyde and the anonymous owners of manuscripts not in the Morgan Library which were used in this publication. The Firestone Library of Princeton University was invaluable in providing many reference and research materials. At Dover Publications, Mr. Hayward Cirker and Mr. Stanley Appelbaum were of special help in preparing this volume.

CHARLES RYSKAMP
Director
The Pierpont Morgan Library

Contents

The dates are those of the particular manuscripts being reproduced.

Alphabetical List of Authors

The numbers are those of the 129 specimens reproduced.

British Literary Manuscripts

Series I

from 800 to 1800

1

BEDE
673?–735

Manuscript of "Historia Ecclesiastica Gentis Anglorum," part of Chapters xxix and xxx of Book III, on vellum. Written in a pointed insular script with slight polychrome decoration, end of the VIIIth century. 1 leaf. 302 x 233 mm. M 826.

Though the Venerable Bede's *Historia Ecclesiastica* was not written in English, it is nonetheless a peculiarly English work, the first great historical creation by an insular writer. Beginning with a brief characterization of the island Britannia—"placed right in manner under the north pole"—it relates the history of the English church from its foundation in the sixth century to the time of the composition of this text—about 731, just before the author's death. A Northumbrian monk at Wearmouth and Jarrow and a Saxon, Bede was close to the fount of Celtic christianity, an ascetic model best represented by monastic cells in the Orkney Islands; but his life was spent in a Benedictine monastery with strong ties to Rome. Placed thus at the juncture between two worlds, Bede brought to his work a profound understanding of both traditions and a narrative ability that gives his stories, fabulous and credible alike, permanent interest. The passage shown here is the conclusion of Book III, chapter xxix, part of a letter from Wighard at Rome to Oswy, king of the Saxons, about 667. Among other things he writes that he has sent to Oswy's "Lady and bedfelowe" "a crosse of golde having in it a nayle taken out of the most holy chaines of the blessed Apostles Peter and Paule." [Thomas Stapleton translation, 1565.]

Only five eighth-century manuscripts of *Historia Ecclesiastica* survive, of which this fragment is one. It was removed from a binding and was owned for many years by Sir Thomas Phillipps, the great Victorian collector. It belongs to the same textual tradition as the oldest text of *Historia Ecclesiastica*, the Moore Bede at Cambridge, completed just after Bede's death.

[Section beginning two-thirds down in first column:] Nam et coniugi uræ nostræ spĩtali filiæ direximus ꝑ p̃fatos gerulos crucem clavem auream habentem de sacratissimis vinculis beatoꝝ petri et pauli apostoloꝝ;

De cuius pio studio cognoscentes tantũ cuncta sedis apostolica una nobiscũ lætetur quantũ eius pia opera corã dõ flagrant et vernant. . . .

[...] epistula [...]
beato principi apostolorum
directa pastorali [...] memoria
suscepimus; gratias [...] ac
pro vestra incolumitate iugiter Dominum
deprecabimur cum Christi clero.

Itaque qui haec obtulit minister
de hac luce subtractus est, statusque
ad limina apostolorum, pro quo valde
sumus contristati, cum hic esset defunctus.

Verumtamen gerulis harum
litterarum nostrarum vestris missis
benedictionis, sanctorum, hoc est reliquias
beatorum apostolorum Petri et Pauli
et sanctorum martyrum Iohannis
et Pauli, Laurentii et Gregorii
atque Pancratii [...] dari
vestrae excellentiae profecto
omnes contradendas.

Nam et coniugi vestrae nostrae
spiritali filiae direximus per praefatos
gerulos crucem clavem auream
habentem de sacratissimis vinculis
beatorum Petri et Pauli apostolorum;

de cuius pio studio cognoscentes,
tantum cuncta sedes apostolica
una nobiscum laetatur, quantum
eius pia opera coram Deo fragrant
et vernant.

celsitudo
Festinet igitur, quaesumus, vestra
ut optamus, totam suam insulam
[Deo Christo dicare.]

Profecto enim habet protectorem humani
generis redemptorem Dominum nostrum
Iesum Christum, qui ei cuncta prospera
impertiet, ut novum Christi populum
coacervet, catholicam ibi et
apostolicam constituens fidem.

Scriptum est enim: Quaerite primum
regnum Dei et iustitiam eius, et haec
omnia adicientur vobis.

Nimirum quaerit et impetrabit
et omnes suae insulae, ut
optamus, subdentur.

Paterno itaque affectu salutantes
vestram excellentiam divinam precamur
iugiter clementiam, quae vos
vestrosque omnes in operibus
omnibus bonis auxiliari dignetur,
ut cum Christo in futuro regnetis saeculo.

Incolumem excellentiam vestram
gratia superna custodiat.

Quis sane pro Wighardo suscepto
ac dedicato episcopo sit
libro sequenti oportunius dicetur.

XXX. [...] Orientalium Saxonum

Eodem tempore praefuere
post Suidhelmum, de quo supra
diximus, provinciae reges Sigheri
et Sebbi, quamvis ipsi regi
Merciorum Vulfhere subiecti.

Quae videlicet provincia

AELFRIC, ABBOT OF EYNSHAM
ca. 955–1025?

Fragment of "Exodus" translated into Anglo-Saxon. Written in a minuscule script on vellum in England, mid-XIth century. 4 ff. 280 x 185 mm. Glazier 63.

Aelfric was the most prolific prose writer in the century before the Norman Conquest, but little is known about his life. He is associated with three monasteries: Winchester, where he was a pupil; Cerne Abbas, in Dorset, to which he came as an instructor about 987; and Eynsham, near Oxford, of which he was made the first abbot in 1005. Aelfric's writings are both pedagogical and homiletic; although *The Lives of the Saints* and *Homilies* are his most important works, the main purpose of his life was to preserve and improve the quality of monastic education. To this end he wrote both a grammar, derived in large part from the Roman grammarian Priscian, and his *Colloquium*, a series of Latin dialogues with Anglo-Saxon glosses to assist the student. He began his paraphrase of the *Heptateuch* (the first seven books of the Bible) near the end of the tenth century. All that survives of this manuscript of the *Heptateuch* are sections of *Exodus* that concern the gift of manna, Moses striking water from the rock and his ascent of Mount Sinai, as well as sections of the laws.

The primary texts for Aelfric's rendering of the *Heptateuch* are in the British Library (Cotton Claudius B IV) and the Bodleian Library, Oxford (Laud Misc. 509).

[First seven lines (Exodus 23:8–12)]: þu lác þa ablendað gleawne. & awendað rihtwisra word. Ne beo þu elþeodigũ grã. forþã ðe ge wæron elþeodige on egypta lande. Saw VI gear þin land & gadera his wæstmas & læt hit restan on þã seofoðan ꝥ ðearfon eton þær of & wildeor. do þu on þinũ wingearde & on þinũ elebeamon. wyrc VI dagas geswic on þã VII foðan ꝥ þin oxa & þin assan hi gereston & ꝥ þynre wylne sunu sy gehyrt & se utan cymena. . . .

þu lac þa ablendað gleawne. ⁊ awendað riht wisra word. Ne beo
þu elþeodigum gram. forþam ðe ge wæron elþeodige on egypta lan
de. Saw .vi. gear þin land ⁊ gadera his wæstmas ⁊ læt hit res
tan on þam seofoðan þæt ðearfan eton þær of ⁊ wildeor. do
þu on þinum wingearde ⁊ on þinum elebeamon. wyrc .vi. dagas.
⁊ gereste on þam .vii. seofoðan þæt þin oxa ⁊ þin assan hi gereston ⁊ þæt
þinre wylne sunu sy gehyrt. ⁊ se utan cymena. Healdað ealle
þing þe ic eow secge. ⁊ ne swerige ge þurh utan cymena goda
naman. Ðriwa on geara ge wurþiað minne freols. þu ytst
þeorf symbel. vii. dagas ge etað þeorf. swa ic þe bebead. on þæs
monþes tid niwra wæstma. þa þu ut fore of egypta lande. ne
cymst þu butan ælmyssan on mine gesihðe. heald þa symbel
tide þæs monðes frumsceatta þines weorces. þe ðu on lande sæwst.
⁊ on geares utgange þonne þu gegaderast þine wæstmas togædere.
þr. iii. on geare ælc wæpned man ætywð beforan drihtne. ne
offra þu þinre onsægednysse blod uppan beorman. ne wysle
[illegible] lifð oð merigen. Bring þine frumsceattas to godes huse
na ic sende minne engel þæt ðe læde into þære stowe þe ic ge
gearwode. gym his ⁊ gehyr his stemne. forþam þe he forgyfð
þonne ge syngiað ⁊ min nama is on him. Ic beo þinra feonda
feond ⁊ þe inn gelæde to amoreus lande. ne geeadmed þu
hyra godas ac tobrec hyra anlicnyssa. Þeowiað drihtne
ic blætsige eow ⁊ do ælce untrumnysse eow fram. ⁊ ge ice eower
dagas. ⁊ aflyme þine fynd beforan þe. ⁊ ic asende hyrnetta
þe aflymað eveum ⁊ chananeum ⁊ ethel monþum ær þu infare.

3

JOHN GOWER
1325?–1408

Illuminated manuscript of "Confessio Amantis," on vellum. Written and illuminated in England by an Anglo-Flemish artist, second half of the XVth century. 212 ff. 436 x 320 mm. M 126.

Gower's *Confessio Amantis* is a protracted cure for the lover's wounds. Like Robert Burton's *Anatomy of Melancholy*, it ranges from heaven to earth, past to present, in search of consolation and includes within its scope a compendium of mythological tales, astrology and conventional advice. *Confessio Amantis* was written at the request of Richard II, who encountered Gower rowing on the Thames, and the first version of it was completed by 1390. A lover, walking forth in May, falls to the ground in anguish and pleads to the King and Queen of Love for solace; pitilessly, the King of Love thrusts a fiery lance into his heart, but the Queen (who asks Gower at the end of his work to "grete well chaucer whan ye mete") sends her priest, Genius, to shrive him. This framework established, the confessor draws from the assembled lore of ages past the stories that illustrate his advice. The leaf shown here (f. 146[a]) is the beginning of the tale of Nectanabus, who, by his guile and sorcery, begat upon Olympyas, wife of King Philip, the baby who grew up to be Alexander the Great. The reward of Nectanabus' deceit was to be killed by his own son. The miniature illustrates King Philip (who doubted his wife's story of impregnation by a god in the form of a dragon), Queen Olympyas and Nectanabus as a dragon and an eagle. Nectanabus appeared before Philip in these forms to convince him of Olympyas' innocence.

This manuscript, one of forty-nine in English, belongs to an intermediate form of the first version of *Confessio Amantis* (in later versions, Gower dropped the familiar allusion to Richard II in the prologue and added a dedication to Richard's enemy, Henry of Lancaster, later Henry IV). It also has a distinguished provenance, having been owned by the English antiquarians Peter Le Neve and Sir Andrew Fountaine (a close friend of Swift). In the late eighteenth century nine miniatures (including the one shown here) were cut from the manuscript but they have since been restored to their proper places.

[Starting with column 2, line 9:] He axeth thanne and herd telle/ How that the kyng was out go/ Upon a werre and hadde tho/ But in that Cite thanne was/ The quene which olympyas/ Was hote and with solempnyte/ The feste of hir natyvyte/ As it bifel was thanne holde/ And for hir lust to be behold/ And preised of the peple aboute/ She shope hir for to ryden oute/ At after mete openly/ A noon were al men redy/ And that was in the monthe of Maij/ The lusti Quene in good aray/ Was set upon a mule white/ To seen it was a gret delyte/ The Joie that the Cite made/ With freisshe thingis and with glade/ The noble toun was al be honged/ And ev̄y wight was sore alonged/ To se this lusty Lady ryde/ Ther was gret merthe on al syde/ Where as she passeth by the strete/ Ther was ful many a tymber bete/ And many a mayde carolyng/ And thus thurghout the toun pleyng/ This Quene unto a pleyn rode/ Wher that she hoved and abood/ To se diverse game pleie/ This lusti folk iust and turneye/ An so forth every other man/ Which pleie couthe his pley began/ To plese with this nobil quene ...

Hic narrat exemplum super eodem qua
liter Nectanabus ab Egipto in Mace
donia fugitivus Olimpiadem Philippi re
gis ibidem tunc absentis uxorem arte ma
gica decipiens cum ipsa concubuit, magnum
que ex ea Alexandrum sortilegus genuit
qui natus postea cum ad erudiendum sub cu
stodia Nectanabi patrem suum ab altitudine
cuiusdam turris in fossam profundam pro
iciens interfecit. Et sic sortilegus ex suo
sortilegio infortunium sortem sortitus est.

The hihe creatour of thinges
Which is the kyng of alle kynges
Ful many a wonder worldes chance
Let slide under his suffrance
Ther wot noman the cause why
But he the which is al mighty
And that was proved whilom thus
Whan that the kyng Nectanabus
Which had Egipt for to lede
But for he sih tofore the dede
Thurgh magique of his sorcerie
Wherof he couthe a gret partie
His enemyes to him comende
Fro whom he might him not defende
Out of his owne lond he fledde
And in the wise that he him dredde
It fel for al his wycche craft
So that Egipt him was beraft
And he desguised fledde awere
Be ship and held the right weie
To Macedoyne wher that he
Aryveth at the chef Cite
Thre yemen of his chambre there
Al only for to serve him were
The which he trusteth wonder wel
For thei were trewe as eny steel
And hapneth that thei with him ladde
Part of the beste good he hadde
Thei took logginge in the toun
After the disposicion
Wher as him thought best to dwelle
He axeth thanne and herd telle
How that the kyng was out go
Upon a werre and hadde tho
But in that Cite thanne was
The queene which Olympyas
Was hote and with solempnyte
The feste of hir natyvyte
As it bifel was thanne holde
And for hir lust to be beholde
And preised of the peple aboute
She shope hir for to riden oute
At after mete openly
Anoon were al men redy
And that was in the monthe of May
The lusti queene in good array
Was set upon a mule white
To seen it was a gret delyte
The joie that the Cite made
With fresshe thinges and with glade
The noble toun was al behonged
And every wight was sore alonged
To se this lusty lady ryde
Ther was gret merthe on al syde
Where as she passeth by the strete
Ther was ful many a tymber bete
And many a mayde carolynge
And thus thurghout the toun pleyinge
This queene unto a pleyn rode
Wher that she hoved and abod
To se diverse game pleie
The lusti folk just and tourneie
An so forth every other man
Which pleie couthe his pley began
To plese with this nobil queene
Nectanabus cam to the grene
Amonge other and drogh him nigh
But whan that he this lady sigh
And of hir beaute hiede tooke

Geoffrey Chaucer
1340?–1400

Illuminated manuscript of "Troilus and Criseyde," on vellum. Written in England probably between 1399 and 1413 for presentation to Henry V, whose arms as Prince of Wales appear on the first leaf. 120 ff. 304 x 207 mm. M 817. Lewis Cass Ledyard Fund.

Though he feigned an old Latin source, Chaucer derived the tale of *Troilus and Criseyde* from Boccaccio, who drew the inspiration for his *Filostrato* from medieval versions of the most fruitful of secular narratives, the *Iliad*. Like the *Aeneid, Troilus and Criseyde* amplifies and extends the action of Homer's epic, in this case spinning from a single line of Homer the five books of Chaucer's poem. The rhetorical humility of Chaucer's invocation to Clio, goddess of history, in the proemium to the second book belies the subtlety of Chaucer's craft: "Me nedeth here noon art to use." His claim to "speke of love unfelyngly" masks the comic, Christian irony with which he wrought his story of the tragic love of Troilus for Criseyde. Though almost six hundred years have passed since *Troilus and Criseyde* was completed, it remains, now as then, perhaps the most brilliant narrative poem ever written in the English language.

This manuscript of *Troilus and Criseyde* was written throughout in a single, beautiful hand. A badly stained illustration of Troilus and Criseyde appears on the first leaf; on the final leaf there appear the signatures of members of the Wood family, beginning with Robert Wood, a servant of Cardinal Wolsey. The history of the volume between the first decade of the fifteenth century, when it was probably presented to Henry V, and the second decade of the sixteenth century, when Wood acquired it, is unknown. Just under twenty manuscripts of *Troilus and Criseyde* survive. Of these, the Morgan Library manuscript, formerly known as the Campsall manuscript, is one of the best textual authorities for the poem.

[The special letter for "th" is transcribed as "ȳ":] Owt of ȳese blake wawes for to sayle./ O wynd o wynd ȳe weder gynneth clere./ For yn ȳis see ȳe bot hath swych travaylle./ Of my comynge that unneȳe I it stere./ This see clepe I ȳe tempestous matere./ Of desper ȳat Troylus was Inne./ But now of hope ȳe kalendes bygynne.

O lady myn ȳat called art Cleo./ Thow be my sped fro ȳis forth and my muse./ To ryme wel ȳis book til I have do./ Me nedeth here noon art to use./ For whi to every lovere I me excuse./ That of no sentement I ȳis endite./ But out of latyn in my tunge it write.

Wherefore I nel have neyȳer ȳank ne blame./ Of al ȳis werk but pray yow mekely./ Disblameth me yf ony word be lame./ For as myn auctor seyde so sey I./ Ek ȳough I speke of love unfelyngly./ No wonder is for it no ȳyng of newe is./ A blynd man ne kan Iuggen wel yn hewys. . . .

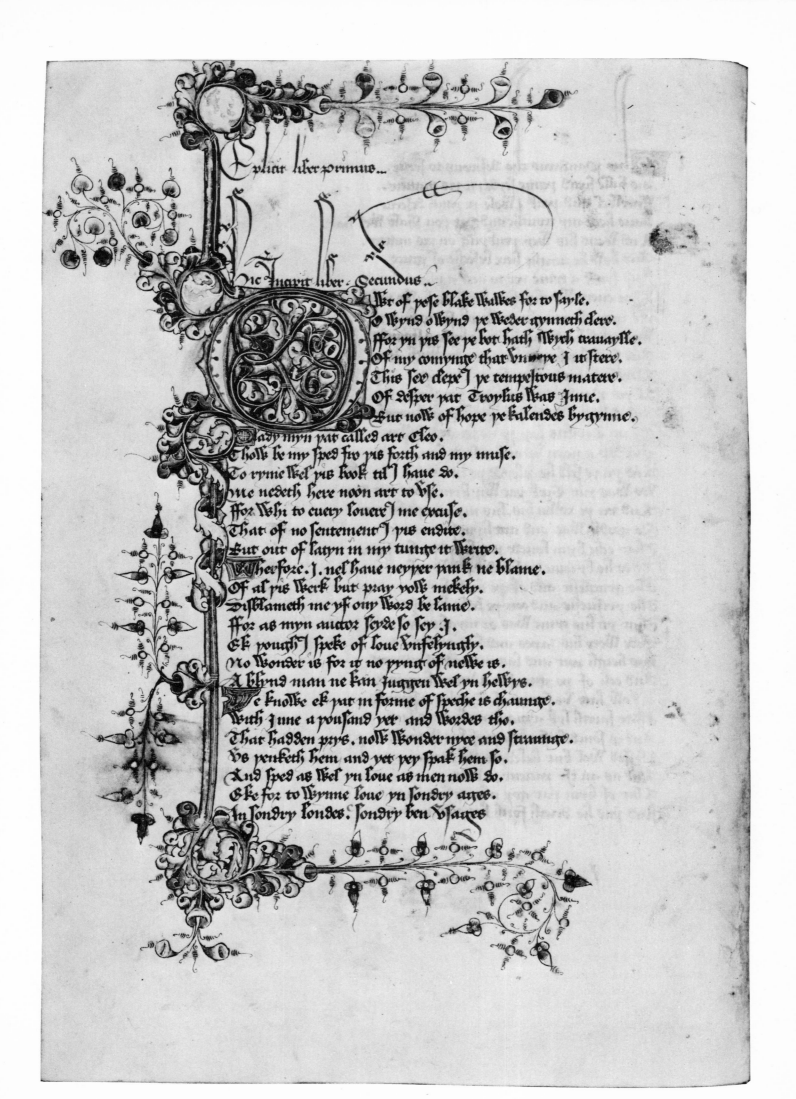

Explicit liber primus.

Incipit liber Secundus.

Owt of þese blake wawes for to sayle.
O wynd o wynd þe weder gynneth clere.
ffor yn þis see þe boot hath swych trauaylle.
Of my connyng that vnneþe I it stere.
This see clepe I þe tempestous matere.
Of desper þat Troylus was Inne.
But now of hope þe kalendes bygynne.
O lady myn þat called art Cleo.
Thow be my sped fro þis forth and my muse.
To ryme wel þis book til I haue do.
Me nedeth here noon art to vse.
ffor why to euery louere I me excuse.
That of no sentement I þis endite.
But out of latyn in my tunge it write.
Wherfore. I. nel haue neyþer þank ne blame.
Of al þis werk but pray yow mekely.
Disblameth me yf ony word be lame.
ffor as myn auctor seyde so sey .I.
Ek þough I speke of loue vnfelyngly.
No wonder is for it no þyng of newe is.
A blynd man ne kan juggen wel yn hewys.
Ye knowe ek þat in forme of speche is chaunge.
With Inne a þousand yer and wordes tho.
That hadden prys. now wonder nyce and straunge.
Vs þenketh hem and yet þey spak hem so.
And sped as wel yn loue as men now do.
Eke for to wynne loue yn sondry ages.
In sondry londes. sondry ben vsages

GEOFFREY CHAUCER

Manuscript of "The Canterbury Tales," on vellum. Written in England, first half of the XVth century. 275 ff. 292 x 190 mm. M 249.

The Canterbury Tales is the work of Chaucer's full maturity, not only the greatest Middle English poem, but also the most textually complex. The Host's suggestion that each pilgrim tell four tales, two on the way to Canterbury, two on the return trip, was never fulfilled and, though several links between tales exist, there is no clear indication of Chaucer's preferred sequence for his poem. The textual relations between the numerous manuscripts of *The Canterbury Tales* thus become doubly confused. This manuscript, formerly one of three in the Ashburnham collection, belongs to what is called the Petworth group, itself a subdivision of a group entitled Corpus-7333. All the usual tales survive in this manuscript, but it lacks a number of links, notably that between the Tale of Melibee and the Monk's Tale. Shown here is the Prologue to the Tale of the Clerk of Oxenford. With his customary raillery, the Host invites the laconic student to contribute his tale:

> Sire clerk of Oxenford oure host saide
> Ye ride as stille and coy as doth a mayde
> Were newe spoused sittynge atte bord
> This day ne herde I of youre mouthe a word.

The clerk agrees and tells the story of patient Griselda, which he had learned from Petrarch, "the laureat poete . . . whos rethorik swete/ Enlumyned al lumbardie of poetrie."

The standard textual basis for most editions of *The Canterbury Tales* is the Ellesmere manuscript in the Huntington Library, San Marino, California.

[Caesura divisions omitted in transcription:] Sire clerk of Oxenford oure host saide/ Ye ride as stille and coy as doth a mayde/ Were newe spoused sittynge atte bord/ This day ne herde I of youre mouthe a word/ I trowe that ye studie aboute some sophyme/ But Salamon seith that al thyng hath tyme/ For Goddes sake betth of better chere/ It is no tyme now to studie here/ Tel us some mery tale by youre fay/ For what man is entred into a play/ He nedes mut to that play assente/ But prechethe nougt as Freres done in lente/ To make us for oure olde synnes for to wepe/ Ne that thy tale ne make us not to slepe/ Tel us som mery thyng of aventures/ Youre termes youre figures and youre coloures/ Kepe hem in store until ye luste endite/ Highe stile as men to kynges write/ Speketh so playn at this tyme I you pray/ That we may understonde what ye say . . .

Sire clerk of Oxenford / oure host saide
Ye ride as stille / and coy as doth a mayde
Were newe spoused / sittynge atte bord
This day ne herde I / of youre mouth a word
I trowe that ye studie / aboute some sophyme
But Salamon seith / that al thyng hath tyme
For goddes sake / beeth of better chere
It is no tyme / now to studie here
Tel vs som mery tale / by youre fay
For what man is entred / into a play
He nedes mot / to that play assente
But precheth nought / as freres done in lente
To make vs for oure olde synnes / for to wepe
Ne that thy tale / ne make vs not to slepe
Tel vs som mery thyng / of aventures
Youre termes youre figures / and youre colours
Kepe hem in store / vntil ye lyste endite
High stile / as men to kynges write
Speketh so playn / at this tyme I you pray
That we may vnderstonde / what ye say
¶ This worthy clerk / benignely answerde
Host quod he / I am vnder youre yerde
Ye have as now / of vs the gouernance
And therfore wol I do you obeysance
As fer as reson asketh hardely
I wol you telle a tale / which that I
Lerned at padow / of a worthy clerk
As preued by his wordes / and by his werk
He is now ded / and nayled in his cheste
I pray to god so sende his soule reste
Frauncys petrak / the laureat poete
Highte this clerk / whos rethorik swete
Enlumyned al lumbardie / of poetrie
As lynyan dide / of philosophie
Or lawe or other art particuler
But deth that wol suffre no thyng here
But as it were / in twenkelynge of an eye
Bothe hath he slayn / and alle shull deye /

JOHN LYDGATE
ca. 1370–1450

Illuminated manuscript of "The Siege of Thebes," on vellum. Written in England about the middle of the XVth century. 72 ff. 255 x 165 mm. M 4.

In an act of literary homage to "hym that yf y shall not feyne/ Floure of poetes thurgh all breteyne," the Benedictine monk John Lydgate modeled his *Siege of Thebes* on Chaucer's unfinished *Canterbury Tales*, a framework into which he could easily insert his poem. Chaucer had left his pilgrims on the road to the Canterbury shrine of Thomas à Becket; Lydgate joined them for the return journey through a landscape of considerably flatter dimension. In the prologue to the *Siege of Thebes* (completed about 1421) he described himself to his traveling companions as a "Monke of Burye nye fifty yere of age/ Come to this towne to do my pylgrymage." Apart from time spent in London and Paris, Lydgate's life was consumed writing verses in the great monastery of Bury St. Edmunds near his birthplace of Lydgate in Suffolk and at Hatfield Broadoak in Essex where he was Prior. *The Siege of Thebes* is not a collection of tales, but Lydgate's contribution to the entertainment of the pilgrims, told at the bidding of his host who commanded him to "nod not with thyne hevy bek [heavy nose]." At 4,700 lines, however, *The Siege of Thebes* is far longer than any tale in Chaucer's poem and far duller. The matter of Thebes included the story of Oedipus, whose fortune is told in the passage shown here.

Besides *The Siege of Thebes*, this manuscript also contains several shorter works, among them a minor poem by Chaucer, "The compleynt of Chaucer un to his purse." About twenty-five manuscripts of Lydgate's poem survive; the textual authority of this one has not been established.

[Starting halfway down:] The Curced Constillacion and disposicion of ȳ^e^ heven in the Nativite of Edippus the Kyngs sone/ And ffyneally in conclusion/ They founde Satorne in ȳ^e^ scorpion/ Hevy chered malyncolyc and lothe/ And wode Marse ffurious and wrothe/ Holdynge his Septer in the Cap^i^corne/ The same owre whan the chylde was borne/ Venus deiecte and contrarious/ And depressed in Mercurious house/ That the dome and the Iuggement ffynall/ Off these Clerkes to speke in speciall/ By fatall sorte that may not be withdrawe/ That with his swerde his fader shulde he slawe

Howe the ffate of Edippus disposed was to sle his owne fader and wedde his owne moder

There may no man helpe hit ne excuse/ On whiche thynge the Kynge gan to muse

The selfe owre at his natiuite
Not forgete the hevenly mancions
Clerkely serched smale fraccions
ffurste by secondes terce and eke quartes
On angrym stones and white coartes
Y preved owte by dylygent labour
In tables correcte devoyde off all erroure
Iustely sought and founde owte bothe too
The yeres collecte and the space also
Conciderde eke by gode Inspeccion
Euery houre and constellacion
And eche aspecte and lokes eke dyverse
Whiche were gode and also perverse
Whether they were towarde or ell at debate
Happy wylfull or infortunate

The Cursed constellacion and disposicion off ye heven in the natiuite of Edipp[us] the kyng[es] sone

And ffynally in conclusion
They founde Satorne in ye scorpion
With chered malyncolye and lothe
And wode marse ffurious and wrothe
Holdynge his septer in the Capricorne
The same owre when the chylde was borne
Venus deiecte and contrarious
And depressed in mercurious house
That the dome and the Juggement ffynall
Off these clerkes to speke in speciall
By fatall sorte that may not be withdrawe
That with his swerde his fader shulde be slawe

Howe the state off Edipp[us] disposed was to sle his owne fader and wedde his owne moder

There may no man helpe hit ne excuse
On whiche thynge the kynge gan to muse

7

"A ROYAL HISTORIE OF THE EXCELLENT KNIGHT GENERIDES"

Illuminated manuscript of "Generides," on vellum. Written and partially illuminated in England, second quarter of the XVth century. 152 ff. 398 x 260 mm. M 876. Purchased with the assistance of several of the Fellows.

Translated from a lost French source, the romance of *Generides* survives in two metrical versions, both preserved in unique manuscripts which also contain poems by Lydgate. A splendid setting for the *Troy Book* and *Generides* was obviously intended when this manuscript was designed. Unfortunately, the illumination was never completed and only a few outline drawings and initials and numerous blank spaces indicate how sumptuous a work this might have been. The literary quality of *Generides* is also somewhat sketchy. Through its loosely woven plot set in the East, Generides emerges as a knight of enduring courage and a lover of somewhat unwitting prowess. In the passage shown here he has excited the admiration of Queen Sirenydes (whose name gives a hint of her character). Exile and the numerous adventures that make up the rest of the plot follow when Generides rejects her advances and incurs her disfavor.

The other known manuscript of *Generides* is in the Library of Trinity College, Cambridge.

[Starting one third down first column:] Upoñ a day in somer tide/ The king on huntyng wold ride/ To hunt in a depe forest/ With knightes and squiers of the best/ He lete at home Generides dwell/ The Quene therof anoon herd tell/ She sent aftre him hastelie/ That he shuld come to hir and not tarie/ Unto hir chambre he can goon/ Forto speke with hir anoon/ She leid hir arme about his swere/ She kyssed him with hertie chere/ And seid welcom gentil Generides/ She began discover hir distres/ Entierile ye ar to me welcome/ While my lord is nat at home/ Aftre you now have I sent/ Forto tel you myn entent/ Ye wax goodeli semelie and wise/ And of service ye bere the price/ Of al men that ar in this lond/ Ye ar most goodlie I undrestond/ If god you fortune oones come to elde/ Ye be ful liklie armes to welde/ And ye shal a doughti man bene/ That day I hope shal I seene/ The grettest thing is that longeth to love/ A sovereigne ladie to have: and hir above/ Al othir to serve: than dar I swere/ If ye doo soo: of gretter power/ Shul ye be and more hardie/ And doughtier man of youre bodie/ Above al thing so have I rest/ Of chivalrie love is the best ...

Generides And his maister thoo
Went ageyn ther thei come froo
Thei wer diligent in here seruice
And ful seruiceable in al wise
And thus thei there gan wel
That neuer creature herd othir tell
But that he was grete born
Thei wist noon othir even ne morn
The Quene him loued secretlie
And dalie contynued by and by
On som maner she most nede
To Generides hir folie bede
That suffre lenger she ne might
Such woo to suffre day and night
But if she haue som dele hir will
Hir fals desire shal him spill

Here telleth of the desire of the quene how she desired Generides to haue deceyued the king his fad[er]

[U]pon a day in somer tide
The king on huntyng wold ride
To hunt in a depe forest
With knightes and squiers of the best
He lete at home Generide well
The Quene therof anoon herd tell
She sent aftir him hastelie
That he shuld come to hir and not tarie
Unto hir chambre he can goon
fforto speke with hir anoon
She leid hir arme about his swere
She kyssed him with hertie chere
And seid welcom gentil Generides
She began discouer hir distres
Enterlie ye ar to me welcome
While my lord is nat at home
Aftir you now haue I sent
fforto tel you myn entent
Ye wax goodli semelie and wise
And of seruice ye bere the prise
Of al men that ar in this lond
Ye ar most goodlie I understond
If god you fortune ones come to elde
Ye be ful likelie armes to welde
And ye shal a doughti man bene
That day I hope shal I seene
The grettest thing is that longeth to loue
A souereigne ladie to haue: and hir aboue
Al othir to serue: than day I swere
If ye doo soo of grettir power
Shul ye be and more hardie
And doughtier man of youre bodie
Above al thing so haue I rest
Of chivalrie loue is the best
As men may here in old romaunce
The grete worship and noble chaunce
That fel to knightes that ladies loued
ffor loue here ladies so thei proued
Therfore Generides I counsel you
To loue somwhere for youre prow
And if ye be of loue to seche
To finde a loue I can you teche
To loue a thing that you dooth loue
Me think it were to youre behoue
Than shuld ye loue me the soth to sey
My self I must nedes bewrey
So long I haue loued you stil
Myn dere hert if it be youre will
My loue my hert and my bodie
Here I gyve you feithfullie
At youre wil to be while I lyve
A richer thing can I noon gyve
Though ye were duke outhir king
This profre might be to youre liking
I haue loued and loue you soo
My thoght may nought part you froo
Nouthir by night nor by day
When euer ye list ye may assay
Generides in a studie stode
Him thoght the Quene was tho wode
To make to him such a sermon
Had he know for what encheson
She had for such cause aftir him sent
He nold haue come there to that entent
fful sore abasshed was he there
fforto gyve hir an answere
Ma dame he seid I thank you
ffor the grete loue ye profre me now
But wel ye know oon thing
That my lord is a grete king
He hath me norisshed and furth broght
So wel that me wanteth noght
If I to him did treason or shame
Treulie I were gretelie to blame
I oughte for his grete kindnes
To doo him honour and goodnes
Neuer the les to loue I ne can
Yit neuer to loue I began
And madame if ye haue grete liking
Othir to loue than the king
In this contre is many a fair knight
Goode and curtes of bodie wight
On hem ye might your loue bestow
And on noon so simple nor so low
The Quene his answer understode
And for shame she wax nere wode
Him that she loued for hir delight
Deidlie she hated to se him with sight
She bad him avoide in hast
And began to threte him ful fast
Lewd felow she seid sikir thou be
I shal ful wel be wroken on the

JOHN WYCLIF
d. 1384

Manuscript of the New Testament, translated by Wyclif, revised by Purvey, on vellum. Written and illuminated in the early XVth century, preceded by a Kalendar for East Anglia. 257 ff. 162 x 107 mm. M 362.

The date and exact location of Wyclif's birth remain uncertain, but his county was Yorkshire. From the north he came to Oxford and by 1360 was Master of Balliol College where he taught and preached until 1382. As a philosopher and author of the *Trialogus* (ca. 1382), a preacher of widespread renown and the translator of the first complete English version of the Bible, Wyclif had a profound impact on English theology in the late fourteenth century. In a period of ecclesiastical abuse he attacked the secular interests of the Church and was guided through a consequent maze of convocations and trials by his ally, the powerful John of Gaunt, uncle of Richard II. Wyclif managed to preserve a difficult equanimity at Oxford until two events provoked both civil and ecclesiastical authorities to a more concerted prosecution: the Peasants' Revolt of 1381, widely associated with Wyclif, and his rejection of conventional doctrines of the Eucharist. His followers were effectively barred at Oxford, formerly the center of his influence, and after his death his teachings and his English Bible were proscribed as heretical. In 1428, after the revolutionary effect of his writings had become evident on the Continent in the person of John Huss, Wyclif's body was exhumed and cast into the River Swift.

Almost two hundred manuscripts of Wyclif's Bible, most dating from the early fifteenth century, survive in one of two versions. The first, conventionally ascribed to Wyclif and Nicholas Hereford, was completed about 1382; a revised version prepared by an unknown translator, sometimes attributed to John Purvey, Wyclif's secretary, is far more common. The present copy was owned by the Gerard and Falkner families and contains on its flyleaves the family record of births, deaths and other notable events. Wyclif's New Testament was not printed until 1731, his whole Bible not until 1850.

[Matthew 17:1–9] And after sixe daies ihs̃ took petre and james and jon his broȳir: and ledde hem asidis into an hiʒ hil/ and he was turnyd into a noȳir lyknes bifore hem/ And his face schon as ȳe sũne: and hise cloȳis weren maad whiʒte as snow/ And lo moises and elie apperiden to hym: & spakẽ wiȳ him/ And petre answeride and seide to ihũ/ lord it is good us to be here/ if you wolt: make we here ȳre tabernaclis/ to ȳee oon. to moises oon and oon to elie/ ʒit ȳe while he spak: lo a briʒt cloude. over schadewide hem/ and lo a voice out of ȳe cloude ȳt seide/ ȳis is my derworȳe sone. in whom I have wel plesid to me: here ʒe hym/ and ye disciplis herden & felden doũ on her faces: & dreddẽ greetly/ and ihs̃ cam & touchide hem: And seide to hem/ rise ʒe up and nyle ʒe drede/ and ȳei liften up her iʒen. And siʒen noman but ihũ aloone/ and as ȳei came doũ of ȳe hil: ihs̃ comañdide to hem & seide/ seie ʒe to no man ȳe visioñ: til mannes sone rise aʒen fro deeȳ// . . .

not taste deep: til þei seen mannes
sone comynge in his kyngdom/
. a. And aftir sixe daies þe xvij
ihc took petre and iames
and ion his broþir: and
ledde hem asidis into an hiz
hil/ and he was turnyd into a
noþir lyknes bifore hem/ and
his face schon as þe sunne: and
hise cloþis weren maad whizte
as snow/ and lo moises and
elie apperiden to hym: & spake
wiþ hym/ and petre answerde
ma. 9. and seide to ihu/ lord it is good
lu. 9. us to be here/ if þou wolt: ma
ke we here þre tabernaclis/ to
þee oon. to moises oon and
oon to elie/ zit þe while he sp
ak: lo a brizt cloude. ouer scha
dewide hem/ and lo a voice out
of þe cloude þt seide/ þis is my
derworþe sone. in whom I ha
ue wel plesid to me: heere ze
hym/ and þe disciplis herden &
felden doun on her faces: & dredde
greetly/ and ihc cam & touchide
hem: and seide to hem/ rise ze up
and nyle ze drede/ and þei liften
up her izen. and sizen noman:
but ihu aloone/ and as þei came
doun of þe hil: ihc comaundide to
hem & seide/ seie ze to no man

þe visioun: til mannes sone rise
azen fro deep/ And hise disciplis ii. c.
askiden hym and seiden/ what
þanne seyen þe scribis: þat it
bihoueþ þat elie come first/ he
answerde: and seide to hem/
elie schal come: and he schal mar 9.
restore alle þingis/ and I seie ma. 9.
to zou. þat elie is now comen
and þei knewen hi not: but þei
diden in hym what euere þin
gis þei wolden/ and so mannes
sone schal suffre of hem/ þanne
þe disciplis vndirstonden: þat
he seide to hem of ion baptist/
¶ And whanne he cam to þe pe
ple: a man cam to hym & fel
doun on knees bifore hym and
seide/ lord haue mercy on my so
ne: for he is lunatik & suffriþ
yuel/ for ofte tymes he falliþ
into þe fier: and ofte tymes
into þe watir/ and I brouzte hi
to þi disciplis: and þei myzte
not heele hi/ and ihc answer
de and seide/ a þou generacioun
vnbileueful and weyward:
how longe schal I be wiþ zou/
how longe schal I suffre zou:
bringe ze hym hidir to me/ and
ihc blamyde hym: and þe deuil
wente out fro hym/ and þe child

Reginald Pecock
1395?–1460?

Manuscript of "The Reule of Crysten Religioun," on vellum. Written in England, ca. 1445. 192 ff. 270 x 187 mm. M 519.

In 1457 the Archbishop of Canterbury summoned Reginald Pecock, Bishop of Chichester, to defend himself against a charge of heresy. Given the choice between death and public recantation, Pecock submitted a statement that he had "made wrytten published and sett forthe many and diverse pernitious doctrines bookes workes writinges, heresies, contrary and against the trew catholik and Apostolik faith . . . ." Interestingly, one of the charges he faced was that of writing on doctrinal matters in English. Pecock was a noted anti-Lollard controversialist and his most important work, *Repressor of Over Much Blaming of the Clergy* (ca. 1455), is an able attack on their doctrines. As the martyrologist John Foxe noted, however, even the bishop's mitre and anointing were incapable of preserving Pecock from those ecclesiastical men who "have so many markes, so many eies, so many suspitions." The manuscript shown here, his *Reule of Crysten Religioun*, is probably the earliest of his extant works and forms the first part of a comprehensive theological system. The philosophical "errors" contained in this and successive works on the subject, as well as probable court intrigue, resulted in Pecock's eventual imprisonment in Thorney Abbey in Cambridgeshire. *The Reule of Crysten Religioun* survives only in this manuscript.

[Starting at large initial:] Eche creature in mankynde is maad of a body and of a resonable soule. The firste ꝑtie of ȳis trowȳe, ȳat is to seie, ȳ^{t} ech of us haȳ in beyng a body: we may knowe bi open assay or exꝑience, fforwhi we mowe se it, touche it, and se it worche hise effectis: riȝt as we mowe knowe oȳere bodies deꝑtid from us, ȳat ȳei verrily ben in kynde, and ȳ^{r}fore of ȳis partie is no dout . . .

The End of his Vission

firste trompe/ þe secunde ȝaf þe secunde/ The þridde brouȝte
into me þe .iiij.e and so forþe of oþere ladies and trompis into
þe eende/ And whilis y suffre þe first lady worche as y bifore
biliȝte bi promys & by boond: me þinkiþ y muste nedis write
as now foleweþ and forþ comeþ to myn hond. Here bigyn
neþ þe firste tretice of þis first partie in which tretice is
tauȝt þe firste principal mater of þis book. þat is to seye.
what god is in hise worþi dignitees & persoones of þe godhede/
& of which first matier now bigynneþ of þe first chap. þe first trompe/

j. vitas
corp' & aīa ...

Eche creature in mankynde is maad of a
body and of a resonable soule/ The firste
partie of þis trompe. þat is to seie. þat ech
of vs haþ in beyng a body: we may
knowe bi open assay or experience/ fforwhi
we mowe se it. touche it. and se it worche
hise effectis: riȝt as we mowe knowe o
þere bodies departid from vs. þat þei verrily ben in kynde. and þer
fore of þis partie is no doute/ That ech of vs haþ in his
beyng a resonable soule: we mowe knowe herbi/ Eny body

aīa vegetatiua

þat may wexe or growe. bi takyng of norischyng and turnyng
it into his kynde & into his substaunce. bi manye folde aftre
caiyngis/ as ben drawyngis. defiyngis. þat is to seie depu
ryngis and forþ sendyngis/ and at þe laste into his bodily
substaunce turnyng/ and þerby manye foold chaungis in fi
gure & colour. þouȝ dyuerse partis tansfyng aftir dyuerse tymes:
haþ more þan þat he is a body: for ellis eny body myȝte do
þe same/ And also algatis & alweies whilis þilk body appeeriþ
to oure siȝt: he myȝt do þe same which we knowen evidently
to be vntrewe/ wherfore ech such body haþ a lijf which may
boþe be had and lost/ þe þing þat makiþ lijf in a body is a
soule: wherfore eny such body haþ a soule which is callid þe
growyng soule or þe norischyng soule. which maner of sou

c plant
...bis sit aīa vegetatiua

le is in herbis in plauntis and in trees/ fforwhi in ech of hem
we seen þese worchingis now rehercid. whiche worchingis
witnessen and schewen þat ech of hem haþ lijf: and þerfore
a soule/ ffurþermore eny body which ouer þis þat he

de aīa sensitiua:

may do þese werkis now rehercid may knowe bodili þingis
oþere þan hym silf/ and þat in presence of þo þingis. by eny

[William Dunbar]
1460?–1513?

Contemporary manuscript of "London thow arte the flowre of cytes all," probably written early in the first decade of the XVIth century. 3 pp. 290 x 209 mm. MA 717.

Like many other poets of his time, Dunbar was an extremely obscure figure who greatly admired Chaucer. Aside from the fact that he received a pension from King James IV, little is known about the man who with Robert Henryson and Gavin Douglas brought about the flourishing of Scots poetry around 1500. The attribution of this poem to Dunbar is highly doubtful; the manuscripts merely record that it was written by a "skotte," who remains otherwise nameless. Obviously, this does not narrow the choice of authors very much. Dunbar may have been in London at the time the poem about that city was written, but this fact too is conjectural. "London" may have been composed during Christmas week, 1501, at a reception given by the Lord Mayor of London for a diplomatic mission from Scotland; or, as the manuscript shown here suggests, it may have been intended for the wedding of Prince Arthur (who died in 1502) and Katherine of Aragon on 14 November 1501. In spite of the uncertainty surrounding the poem, "London" nonetheless records in superlative verse the affection of a northerner for the greatest of southern cities.

Of the four existing manuscripts of "London," this may be the earliest. It originally formed the flyleaves in a copy of William Caxton's *Cordiale* (1479), which was bound in that printer's shop. It thus may antedate the manuscript found in the British Library (Vitellius A. XVI), written about 1509. Textually, it differs widely from the other manuscripts, offering a few obviously superior readings and a few obvious corruptions.

A balad mayde at London when my lorde prince Arthur was wed [,] by a skotte havy̅g̅ much money of dyverse lordes for hys Indyty̅g̅—

London thow arte of townes chefe of dygnyte/ And sowerent of all cytes semlyst in syght/ Of hye renowne ryches and eke of ryalte/ Of lordes barons & many goodly knythe/ Of maste delectable lusty & ladys bryghte/ Of famos ꝓlates in habytes clerly all/ Of merchandes of sustans & men of grete myght/ O London thow arte the flowre of cytes all

Now may thow reioy thow lusty Troy meyyte/ Cyte y^t som tyme clepyd was newe Troy/ In all erthe imꝑiall as y^u standythe/ Byrall of cytes of plesure and joye/ A rychere restoryd under crysten roye/ Fore mãly power w^t craftes naturall/ Fore there were no feyerere sythe the flode of Noye/ Londoñ thu art the flo^r of cytes all

Gemme of all joy: jasper of jocundite/ Maste myghty carbuncle of vert[u]es & valour

A balade made at london when my lorde prince Arthur
was wed by a scotte havyng moche money of dyverse
lordes for his endytyng

London thow arte of townes A per se
And soverayn of all Cites semelyest in sight
of hye renowne ryches and ryalte
of lordes barons & many goodly knyghtes
of most delectable lusty ladyes bryghte
of famous prelates in habytis clericall
of merchandes of substaunce & men of grete myght
O london thow arte the flowre of Cites all

Now may thow sey thow lusty troynovaunte
Cite that som tyme cleped was new troy
In all the erthe imperiall as thou standythe
Ryall of Cites of plesure and joye
A rycher restythe under no crysten roye
ffor manly power with craftes naturall
ffortheremore no fayrer sith the flode of noye
london thu art the flour of Cites all

Gemme of all joy Jasper of Jocundite
Most myghty carbuncle of vertue & valour

John Bellenden
1495?–1548?

Manuscript of "The Cronikillis of Scotland . . .," Bellenden's translation of Hector Boece's "Scotorum Historiæ . . ." (Paris: Badius, 1527). Written by David Douglas, ca. 1531. 313 ff. 294 x 190 mm. M 527.

Sometime after 1527 a young Scotsman, John Bellenden, returned from Paris where he had been made Doctor of Theology, bearing with him Hector Boece's *Scotorum Historiæ a prima gentis origine* . . . . Bellenden seems to have garnered a modest reputation as a poet about this time and he was commissioned to translate Boece's work, the first history of Scotland, for his former student, King James V. There is evidence to suggest that the author assisted the translator in preparing this Scottish prose version. As history, *The Cronikillis of Scotland* has somewhat ambiguous merit. Covering the period from the beginnings of Scottish history to the "slauchter" of James I, it relates with equal sobriety the fantastic and the factual. In concluding, for example, Boece observes that during the time of James I there was seen in "Albion" a sword flying through the air to the no less dread than admiration of the people.

This is one of the finest Scottish manuscripts in existence. It offers by far the best text of *The Cronikillis of Scotland* and is the oldest surviving manuscript of Bellenden's translation. This copy was prepared by the "notare public" David Douglas for presentation to the King in the fall of 1531 and is for all intents and purposes the original manuscript of this work. It bears the joint arms of James V and Queen Madeline. The Morgan Library is particularly rich in Scottish materials, especially for Boece: it houses not only this manuscript, but also another important sixteenth-century translation, the Mar Lodge Boece, as well as James V's initialed copy of the first edition of Bellenden's translation, printed on vellum in Edinburgh about 1536 and bound for him with "Iacobus Quintus" stamped on the front.

The translator sayis to his buke, as followis

Now marciall buke pas to ye nobill prince/ King James ye fifte my Soverane maist preclair/ And gif sum tyme you gettis audience/ In humyll wise unto his grace declair/ My walkrife nychtis and my laboure sair/ Quhilk ithandlie has for his pleseir tak/ Quhill goldin Titan with his birnand chare/ Past all ye signis in ye zodiak

Quhill besy Ceres with hir pleuth and harrowis/ Has fillit hir grayngis full of every corne/ And stormy Chiron with his bow and arrowis/ Has all ye clowdis of ye hevynnis schorne/ And schill Triton with his wyndy horne/ Owre quhelmyt all ye flowand oceane/ And phebus turnit under capricorne/ The samyn greis quhare I first began

Sen you art drawin so compendious/ Fra flowand Latyne in to wlgar proiß/ Schew now quhat kingis bene maist viciouß/ And quhay has bene of chevelry ye Roiß/ Quhay has yair realmé in honoure maist reioß/ And with yair blude oure Liberteie has coft/ Regarding noch to de amang yair fois/ Sa yat yai mycht in memory be brocht . . .

The translator sayis to his buke as followis

Thow martiall buke pas to ye nobill prince
King James ye fifte my Souerane maist preclair
And gif sum tyme you gettis audience
In humyll wise vnto his grace declair
My walkrife nychtis and my laboure sair
Quhilk I thandlie hat for his plesoir tak
Quhill goldin Titan with his birnand chare
Past all ye signis in ye zodiak

Quhill besy Ceres with hir pleuth and harrowis
has fillit hir grangis full of euery corne
And stormy chiron with his bow and arrowis
hat all ye flowris of ye hevynnis schorne
And Schill Triton with his wyndy horne
Oure quhelmit all ye flowand occiane
And phebus turnit vnder capricorne
The samyn greis quhare I first began

Sen you art drawin so compendioust
Fra flowand Latyne in to wlgar prois
Schew now quhat kingis bene maist vertuous
And quhay has bene of chevelry ye Rois
Quhay has yair realme in honoure maist rejois
And with yair blude oure libertie hat tost
Jeoparding noth to de amang yair fois
Sa yat yai micht in memory be brocht

Schaw be quhat danger and difficill wayis
Oure antecessouris at yair vttir mychtis
has brocht yis realme with honoure to our dayis
Ay fechtand for yair liberteis and richtis
With Romanis Danis Inglismen and pichtis

12

Sir Thomas More
1477/78–1535

Autograph signature on a lease for Crosby Place, Bishopsgate, dated London, 1 June 1523, on vellum. Also signed by Edward Rest and Roger Pynchestre. 1 p. 205 x 292 mm. MA 311.

Among the many English martyrs who died in the sixteenth century, Sir Thomas More has always retained an unusual hold on the imaginations of subsequent generations. More was the rare sort of man whose life continues to help us define the province of conscience in an oppressively unprincipled world. This was clearly recognized in his own lifetime. In William Roper's *Lyfe of Sir Thomas Moore* (first printed in 1626, though it circulated in manuscript throughout the latter half of the sixteenth century), More is described as "a man of singular vertue and of a cleere unspotted consciens, as witnessethe Erasmus, more pure and white then the whitest snowe, and of such an angelicall witt, as England, he saith, never had the like before, nor never shall againe . . . ." The friendship of Erasmus and More grew out of a shared vision of humanistic scholarship and Christian reformation which led them, because of the peculiar direction of English politics, to seemingly opposed points on the doctrinal spectrum: More died a Catholic martyr; Erasmus made brilliant editorial and polemical contributions to the Protestant cause. The community of their interests and beliefs appears again and again in the course of their friendship, but nowhere more aptly than in the assistance Erasmus gave to the most famous flowering of More's "angelicall witt," *Utopia*, which Erasmus ushered through the press in Louvain in 1516.

In the early 1520s the property known as Crosby Place was in the hands of Sir John Rest, alderman and Lord Mayor of London in 1516. From his executors More purchased the lease for £150. Crosby Place was a residence rich in historical associations, for one of its previous residents had been Richard, Duke of Gloucester, before his coronation as Richard III. (Shakespeare mentions Crosby Place anachronistically three times in *Richard III.*) Among later residents and leaseholders were Antonio Bonvisi, a merchant and old friend to whom More sold the lease, and More's son-in-law and biographer, William Roper.

To alle true cristen people to whom this p̄sent wrytyng indented shall come Edward Rest of London grocer sone & heire to John Rest late of London Alderman Thomas Perpoynt of London draper mary his wyfe Roger Pynchestre of London Grocer & Elizabeth his wyfe doughtere of the seid John Rest & executors of the testament and last wille of the same John Rest/ senden gretyng in our Lord god everlastyng/ knowe ye us the foreseid Edward Rest Thomas Perpoynt mary his wyfe Roger Pynchestre and Elizabeth his wyfe for the some of Cl li sterlynges to us by Sir Thomas More Knyght undertreasourer of England in hande paide wherof we knowlege us wele and truly contented and paide And therof acquyte and discharge the seid Sir Thomas and his executours by these p̄sentes/ of oon assent and consent/ have bargayned and solde and also geven and graunted/ And by these presentes do bargayne and sell and also geve and graunte unto the seid Sir Thomas More alle our interest and termes of yeres whiche we or any of us have due and for to come of and in a great tenement called Crosbyes place . . .

To alle true cristen people to whom this present writyng indented shall come Edward Rest of london grocer sone & heire
to John Rest late of london Alderman Thomas Perpoynt of london draper Mary his wyfe Roger Pynchester of london Grocer
& Elizabeth his wyfe doughters of the seid John Rest & executors of the testament and last wille of the same John Rest /
senden gretyng in our lord god euerlastyng / knowe ye vs the foreseid Edward Rest Thomas Perpoynt Mary his wyfe
Roger Pynchestre and Elizabeth his wyfe for the some of CC li sterlynges to vs by Sir Thomas More knyght
vndertresourer of England in hande paide wherof we knowlege vs wele and truly contented and paide
And therof acquyte and discharge the seid Sir Thomas and his executoures by these presentes / of oon
assent and consent / haue bargayned and solde and also geven and graunted / And by these presentes do
bargayne and sell and also geve and graunte vnto the seid Sir Thomas More alle our interest and
termes of yeres whiche we or any of vs haue due and forto come of and in a great tenement called
Crosbyes place with Sellers solers gardeyn and other their appurtenaunces and of and in vj mesuages therunto
adioynyng sett and beyng in the parisshe of Seint Elyn in Bisshoppesgate strete of london by reason of a lease therof
made vnto oon John Crosby late of london Grocer by the pryores & Couent of Seint Elyn vnder their comen seale for certeyn
termes of yeres / To haue and to holde alle the seid great tenement with houses Sellers solers gardeyn and
other thappurtenaunces and vj other tenementes with their appurtenaunces / togither with alle the interest & termes
of yeres yete due and forto come of and in the same / vnto the seid Sir Thomas More his executours and assignes
from the xij^th day of Aprell next before the date herof / vnto the full ende and accomplisshement of alle
the seid termes of yeres yete forto come / The seid Sir Thomas More therfor yerely yeldyng beryng and
payng vnto the foreseid prioresse and Couent their successoures and assignes alle suche Rent and other
charges as we the seid Edward Rest Thomas Perpoynt Mary his wyfe Roger Pynchestre & Elizabeth
his wyfe by reason of thexecucion of the foreseid testament & last wille stande & be charged to bere yelde
& pay of and for the same / In witnesse wherof aswell the seales of the seid Edward Rest Thomas
Perpoynt Mary his wyfe & Roger Pynchestre & Elizabeth his wyfe / As the seale of the seid Sir Thomas More
to this writyng indented interchaungeably be sett yoven the first day of Iuyn / the xv^th yere of the Reigne
of kyng Henry the viij^th.

per me Edward Rest   per me Tho. More   per me Roger Pynchester

13

THOMAS CRANMER
1489–1556

Autograph letter signed, dated Croydon, 2 November 1539, to Thomas Cromwell, first Lord Cromwell. 1 p. 321 x 218 mm.

Martyrology offers the means not only of interpreting history as a succession of spiritual heroes but also of portraying in graphic terms the will of God. No history accomplishes both these ends more fully than John Foxe's *Actes and Monuments* ... (London, 1562–3). One of the martyrs in this work is Thomas Cranmer, of whom Foxe wrote, "By little & little, he called home and conformed the churches into a more holsom discipline of Christe, and example of the primative churche." In support of his Kings, Henry VIII and Edward VI, Cranmer indeed became the principal agent of religious reformation in England. He consistently advised that the Bible and the church service be translated into English; and his greatest contribution to English literature, *The booke of the common prayer* (London, 1549), is still in use in its revised state. In its preface he sets forth the principle that led him to this work: "There was never anything by the wit of man so well devised, or so surely established, which (in continuance of time) hath not been corrupted." By fixing the divine service in forthright English, Cranmer hoped to restore it to its original purity; he also created a model of liturgical English that has had tremendous influence through the centuries.

When Edward VI died and Mary ascended the throne, restoring Catholicism to England, Cranmer was tried first for treason (for his unwilling support of Lady Jane Grey) and then for heresy, for his conspicuous devotion to the Protestant church. He signed several recantations, but when called upon to make a final oral denunciation of his former faith, he refused, saying: "And for as much as my hande offended, wrytyng contrarie to my harte, my hande shal first be punyshed therfore, for maye I come to the fyre, it shal be first burned."

This letter to Thomas Cromwell concerns the disposition of papers relating to Calais.

My veray synguler good lorde, After my right hartie Comendac$\overline{ons}$ unto yor lordeshype, Thiys shalbe to sygnyfie unto the same, that all suche examynations Inquysitions and other suche wrytyngs as I have concernynge any maters of Calyse be yn the hands and custodye of my Regester Antony Hussey unto whome I have dyrecte my L$\overline{res}$ that he shall w^{t} all expedition repayre unto yor lordeshype w^{t} all such wrytyngs as he hathe concernynge the sayde maters; Thus my lorde ryght hartely fare you well, At Croydon thys ii^{de} of Novembr. Yo^{r} own assured sv^{t} T. Cantu$\overline{arien}$.

My veray syngular good lord, After my right hartie commendacions unto yor lordshippe, Theis shalbe to signyfie unto the same, that all suche examinacions Inquysitions and other suche wrytyngs as I have concernyng the matter of Calys be in the hands and custodye of my Registr Antony Hussey. Unto whome I have wrytten my lettres that he shall w^t all expedition repayre unto yor lordshippe w^t all suche wrytyngs as he hathe concernyng the sayd matters; Thus my lord right hartely fare you well. At Croydon this ij^de of Novembr.

Yo^r owne assured

T. Cantuarien

14

Roger Ascham
1515?–1568

Autograph inscription in Latin and Greek, signed with initials, dated 28 October 1564, to Sir Walter Mildmay, written in a copy of Xenophon's "Cyri Paediae . . ." (Paris: Chrétien Wechel, 1538–9). PML 60841. Lathrop Colgate Harper Trust Fund.

Ascham was the author of few books, but two by him have had profound influence on the shape of English prose: *Toxophilus, the schole of shooting conteyned in two bookes* . . . (1545) and *The Scholemaster* (1570). Educated at the most advanced of the Cambridge colleges, St. John the Evangelist, he created for himself a reputation as a scholar, a penman and an archer. Later in life, as tutor to Princess Elizabeth and as her Latin secretary after she became Queen, he grew to be as familiar with Court as with Cambridge. Both *Toxophilus* and *The Scholemaster* are in a sense the fruit of his pastimes. They emphasize not only the virtues of correct Latin syntax, but also the skills of the gentleman: "I heard myself a good husband at his book once say, that to omit study some time of the day, and some time of the year, made as much for the increase of learning as to let the land lie fallow, maketh for the better increase of corn." Both volumes are important examples of the force of vernacular prose, for in Ascham's writings, the English language acquires a modern voice. "He that will write well in any tongue," he remarks, "must follow this counsel of Aristotle, to speak as the common people do, to think as the wise men do . . ."

This book, one of the loveliest presentation volumes in the Morgan Library, was given to Ascham's friend Sir Walter Mildmay, who was with Ascham "When the great plage was at London, the yeare 1563" and the subject of *The Scholemaster* was first proposed.

Martialis Lib.° 5.°/ Extra fortunam est, quicquid donatur Amicis:/ Quas solas dederis, semper habebis opes.

μοῦνα φίλοις τὰ δοθέντα, τυχῆς ῥόον οὐκ ἀλέσουσι:/ αἶεν ἅπερ δῶκας, ταύτατε κτησόμενος.

R. A. 1564 28 Octob.

Ornatissimo Viro G. Mildmay: Studii literarum amoris μνεμόσυνον.

R. A.

ΞΕΝΟΦΩΝΤΟΣ

ΚΥΡΟΥ ΠΑΙΔΕΙΑΣ ΒΙΒΛΙΑ

ΤΕΤΤΑΡΑ. Α΄. Β΄. Γ΄. Δ΄.

XENOPHONTIS

CYRI PAEDIAE LIBRI

quatuor priores.

Martialis lib°. 5°.

Extra fortunam est, quicquid donatur Amicis:
Quas solas dederis, semper habebis opes.

μοῦνα φίλοις τὰ δοθέντα, τύχης ῥόον οὐχ ἀλέγουσι:
αἰὲν ἅπερ δῶκας, ταῦτά γε χρησόμενος:

R. A.

1564 28 octob.

PARISIIS.

In officina Christiani Wecheli.

M. D. XXXVIII.

Ornatissimo viro G. Mildmay:

Studii literarum &
amoris μνημόσυνον

R. A.

15

Thomas Sackville, First Earl of Dorset 1536–1608

Document signed, dated "From the Court," 6 August 1605, to Sir Richard Verney. 1 p. 302 x 187 mm.

This letter to Sir Richard Verney concerning the nonpayment of loans issued in Warwickshire was written late in Dorset's life, just before or during his entertainment of King James I at Oxford, of which Dorset was the chancellor. The literary portion of Dorset's life had ended some forty-five years earlier when *The Tragedie of Gorboduc*, the last two acts of which were written by Dorset, was staged at the Inner Temple on Twelfth Night 1560/1. A tale of familial rivalry, open rebellion and civil war, *Gorboduc* is generally hailed as the first regular tragedy in English. But Dorset's fame depends much more heavily on an earlier work, *The Myrroure for Magistrates* (1559–63). To this volume, in which the dead narrate their own tragedies and warn the living of Fortune's unsteadiness, Dorset contributed "The complaynt of Henrye duke of Buckingham" and "The Induction," the two most effective sections of the entire work. "The Induction" describes the narrator's meeting with Sorrow, who guides him "to the griesly lake,/ And thence unto the blisfull place of rest," and sets the tone for a visit to hell:

The wrathfull winter proching on a pace,
With blustring blastes had al ybared the treen,
And olde Saturnus with his frosty face
With chilling colde had pearst the tender green:
The mantels rent, wherein enwrapped been
The gladsom groves that nowe laye overthrowen,
The tapets torne, and every blome down blowen.

The manuscript which containes Dorset's contributions to *The Myrroure for Magistrates* is in the library of St. John's College, Cambridge (MS 364).

After my hartie Comendacons. There is some question made amongst such, as have kept the Accompte of ye late loane. Namely touching ye number and pticler names of such as did then refuse to pay having received privie Seales to lend. Wherfore I pray and require you to returne me by yis bearer a certificate in writinge as well of yeir names as refusing to pay, as of ye some wch they were to lend. Omitting only such as upon their humble sute, and iust cause shewed were released either by order from ye 11. of ye Councell, or from ye Lord Leiutenant of ye shire . . . And so I wish you hartely well. From ye Court. ye. 6. of August 1605 Yor very Loving frend. T. Dorset

After my hartie comendacions. There is some question made amongst
such, as have kept the Accompte of the late loane. Namely touching the
number and titles names/ of such as did then refuse to pay/ having received
privie Seales to lend. Wherefore I pray and require you to returne me
by this bearer a Certificate in writinge aswell of their names so refusing to
pay, as of the some wch they were to lend. Omitting only such as upon
their humble sute, and iust cause shewed were released. either by order
from the LL. of the Councell, or from the Lord Leiutenant of the Shire. - -
And so I wish you hartily well. ffrom the Court. the. 6. of -
August. 1606

Yor very loving frend.

T. Dorset

GABRIEL HARVEY
1550?–1631

Autograph signature and notes, dated 8 March 1584, in his copy of "Littletons Tenures in Englishe" (London: Richard Tottel, 1581), f. S8ᵃ. PML 6254.

Gabriel Harvey is the Hobbinol of Edmund Spenser's *Shepheards Calender* (1579) and in this guise was made to speak to Colin Clout (Spenser) words sweeter than he ever wrote himself:

> Colin, to hear thy rymes and roundelayes,
> Which thou wert wont on wastful hylls to singe,
> I more delight than larke in Summer dayes.

Spenser described his friend as a looker-on at life, one who noted "with critique pen,/ The sharpe dislikes of each condition." For Harvey, this was unintentionally ironic praise. He had been checked in his progress at Cambridge by a personal bearing which his peers considered too lofty for the son of a farmer and ropemaker. A thoroughly learned man, widely read in many languages, he made a poor courtier, for he seemed to lack a due sense of decorum, as Thomas Nash (with whom he quarreled throughout the 1590s) observed: when introduced to Queen Elizabeth and Sir Philip Sidney, Harvey was apparently "Haile fellowe well met with those that looke highest." The marks of his "critique pen" are numerous and widely scattered; he freely annotated the volumes he owned, and his commonplace books and marginalia provide a copious record of his literary friendships and opinions. This volume, *Littletons Tenures in Englishe* by Sir Thomas Littleton, was the standard authority on English real-property law at the time that Harvey was preparing for his degree in Civil Law at Cambridge (he eventually took the degree at Oxford). It contains a fine example of his lovely Italian hand.

Relegi duobus diebus, 7º et 8º Martij: 1584. primū, et secundum, 7º: tertium, 8º: qui liber sæpiùs, consideratiusque videbatur prælegendus. Gabriel Harvey.

The Table.

make thee more apt & able to vnderstand, and learne the argumentes and the reasons of the lawe. For by the argumentes and the reasons in the lawe, a man may more sooner come to the certeinte and to the knowledge of the law. Lex plus laudatur quando ratione probatur.

Relegi duobus diebus, 7° et 8° Martij: 1584: primu, et secundum, 7°: tertium, 8°: qui liber saepius, consideratiusq[ue] videbat[ur] perlegendus. Gabriel Haruey.

Imprinted at London in Fletestrete within Temple Barre at the signe of the hand and Starre by Rychard Tottel.

1581.

Perkins.

Grauntes. cap. 1. Faits. cap. 2. Feofments. 3.

Cum priuilegio.

Eschanges. 4. Dower. 5. Tenant per le curtesie. 6. Testament. 7. Deuises. 8. Surrenders. 9. Reseruacion. 10. Condicions. 11.

Loci communes in Esse.

17

William Camden
1551–1623

Autograph letter in Latin, signed, dated Westminster, 4 August 1577, to Abraham Ortelius. 1 p. 286 x 208 mm. MA 2635.

As a child Ben Jonson came to Westminster at the expense of William Camden, to whom he later wrote this tribute, published in *Epigrammes*:

Camden, most reverend head, to whom I owe
All that I am in arts, all that I know.
(How nothing's that?) to whom my countrey owes
The great renowne, and name wherewith shee goes.

Jonson's praise encompasses both halves of Camden's long and honored career. Beginning in 1575, Camden exerted at Westminster a highly respected influence on a succession of England's future poets, scholars and political leaders. During his academic vacations he pursued his lifelong love of antiquarian research, which culminated in three works: *Britannia* (1586), *Remaines concerning Britaine* (1605) and *Annales rerum anglicarum et hibernicarum regnante Elizabetha*... (1615). Each of these contributed to the "great renowne" not only of England, but of Camden, who became a major historian of international reputation. In his *Annales* he provided an interpretation of Elizabeth's reign that has survived to the present day; his *Remaines* record some part of his deep patriotic feeling: Britain, he writes, is "So rich in commodities, so beautifull in situation, so resplendent in all glorie, that if the most Omnipotent had fashioned the world round like a ring, as he did like a globe, it might have been most worthily the only gemme therein."

In this letter to the great mapmaker Ortelius in Antwerp, Camden mentions the coin collection of his patron, Lord Burghley, and Ortelius' forthcoming work, *Synonymia Geographica*.

Ex quo suauissimâ et doctissimâ consuetudine tuâ Londini fruebar, (Doctissime D. Orteli) studio tui incensus sum incredibili, nec meam inde in te observantiam delevit, aut extinxit dies, sed nova potius accessione adauxit, & iam ad summum usque perduxit. meque ad audendum ita proiectum reddidit, ut quamvis planè nihil habeam, quod tuâ intersit, a me scribi; tamen has qualescunque lr̃as ad te dare, & paucis verbis de plurimis beneficiis gratias agere non dubitaverim. Sed cum nullã partem tuorum meritorum referendâ gratiâ consequi possim, ex optima saltem voluntate aliquam tibi relatam gratiam existimes velim. Si non tam subito Londino discessises egregiam antiquitatis supellectilem illic vidisses. Honoratiss. enim Dñs Burghleius, sum̃us Angliæ Thesaurarius, quum ex libello tuo Deorum (quem D. Decanus illi donavit) te antiquis nummis oblectari perspexerat, ex animo optavit, ut, quæ in eius Musæo sunt, antiqua numismata vidisses, et utinam vidisses. ...

(71)

343

Ex quo suauissimâ et doctissimâ consuetudine tuâ Londini fruebar, (Doctissime D. Orteli) studio tui incensus sum incredibili, nec meam inde in te obseruantiam deleuit, aut extinxit dies, sed noua potius accessione adauxit, & iam ad summum usq; perduxit. meq; ad audendum ita proiectum reddidit, ut quamuis planè nihil habeam, quod tuâ intersit, a me scribi; tamen has qualescunq; lr̃as ad te dare, & paucis verbis de plurimis beneficijs gratias agere non dubitauerim. Sed cum nullã partem tuorum meritorum referendâ gratiâ consequi possim, ex optima saltem voluntate aliquam tibi relatam gratiam existimes velim. Si non tam subito Londino discessisses egregiam antiquitatis supellectilem illic vidisses. Honoratiss. enim Dn̄s Burghleius, summus Angliæ Thesaurarius, quum ex libello tuo Deorum (quem D. Decanus illi donauit) te antiquis nummis oblectari perspexerat, ex animo optauit, ut, quæ in eius Musæo sunt, antiqua numismata vidisses. Et utinam vidisses. Latent enim apud illum plurima, & admodum rara Antiquitatis monumenta, et sanè quæcunq;, in Britanniâ sunt, antiquæ memoriæ, ille unus possidet omnia. Est enim vir ille, cum cæteris artibus, quæ tantâ personâ dignæ sunt, excultus singulis, tum post viros nobiles Laurinos venerandæ Antiquitatis perscrutator diligentissimus. Si quis bonus Genius te in Britanniam nostram reduxerit, effecero (uti spero) ut ea omnia videas. Interim quid tuum parturit ingenium scire aueo. Synonymia tua Geographica his nundinis Francfordiensibus auidè expecto, opus n. illud tuo nomine dignum auguror. An restaurator ille antiquitatis D. Hub. Goltzius supremã manũ Thesauro suo (sic n. ut audio, vocat) posuerit, quæso intelligam, et si quod manuscriptum Antonini A. Itinerarium habes, ut Britanniarum itinera mihi describas, te humillimè rogo. sic n. mihi rem longè gratissimã feceris. Vides ut ego qui Antiquitatis admirator sum imperitus, nihil antiquius habeo, quàm tibi de huiusmodi rebus negotium facessere. Sed ignosce quæso, et quicq; ab homine tui studiosissimo expectari potest, a me expectes velim. Dominus Decanus Westmonasteriensis, te quam studiosè, quàmq; ex aio potest, salutat, et tu quæso meo nomine, singulari amico Dn̄o Danieli Rogerio plurimam salutem imperti. Vale. Westmonasterij Pridie Non. Augusti. ∞. CIↃ LXXVII.

Tui studiosiss. Guilielmus
Camdenus.

58

Christopher Marlowe
1564–1593
and Sir Walter Rale(i)gh
1552?–1618

Contemporary manuscript of Marlowe's "The passionate Sheepheard to his love" and Ralegh's "The Nimphs reply to the Sheepheard." 2 pp. 300 x 220 mm.

On the third day of Izaak Walton's *The Compleat Angler* Piscator (the fisherman) and Venator (the hunter) pause from fishing and take shelter under a honeysuckle hedge during a brief rain shower. There Piscator recalls the last time he fished this stream. Crossing into a nearby field, he had found a handsome milkmaid who sang "that Smooth Song which was made by *Kit Marlow*, now at least fifty years ago; and the Milkmaids mother sung an answer to it, which was made by Sir *Walter Raleigh* in his yonger dayes." In these pastoral surroundings Walton prints the fullest text known of Marlowe's poem "The passionate Sheepheard to his love" and Ralegh's response "The Nimphs reply to the Sheepheard," first published in a shorter version in *England's Helicon* in 1600. Only six manuscripts of these poems survive (primarily in the Bodleian and Folger libraries); this is one of the earliest of all, for it dates from the first decade of the seventeenth century. It presents a much shorter text of the poems (Walton prints seven stanzas for each; the Morgan manuscript has four stanzas for Marlowe's lyric, three for Ralegh's response). Textually, it differs considerably from all other versions.

Come live wth me and be my love,/ and we will all the pastimes prove,/ That valleis, mountaines, woods or feld/ or groves, or pleasant pastures yeild

wher we will sitt upon the rock/ and see the Shepherds feede their flock./ By shallow rivers to whose falles/ Melodious bird singe Madrigalls.

wher we will mak the bed of roses/ and a thowsand fragrant poses/ a cappe of flower & a kirtle/ Imbroydred all wth Leaves of mertle.

Her belt of strawe wth Ivy bud/ Corrall clasp & amber Stud./ All this ile give thie mynde to move/ to live wth me and be my Love;

Response/ But if the world & love were sound/ and truth in evry Shepherd found./ Then thes delight[es] might me much move./ To live wth the & be thie love.

Thie belt of Straw thie bed of roses/ thie caps, thie kirtles, & thie poses/ Sone breaks, sone withers, sone forgotten/ wth follie ripe, with reason rotten.

Could youth ~~but~~ long last, & love but feede/ Had tyme no death, nor age no neede/ Then thes delight[es] might my mind move/ to live wth thee & be thie love:

Be it knowne that I have made, assigned, ordeyned, deputed, and in my stead & place have putt & constituted my welbeloved in Christ &c. my true & lawfull attorney, to aske, demaunde, levie, recover & receive for me & in my name, and to my use of &c. his heires &c. and every of them, that somme of &c. which to me they owe, and from me unjustly detayneth, giving and by these presents graunting unto my said attorney full power & aucthoritie to doe, execute, & accomplish, and cause to be done, executed & accomplished by waie of demaund, action, suite, remedies of lawe, and by all other waies & meanes whatsoever all & every acte & actes, thinge & thinges whatsoever, for the levying, getting, acquiring & discharging of the said somme &c. and every parte thereof in such ample, large & beneficiall maner and forme to all intents & purposes as I my selfe might or could doe, if in the premisses I were personally present, ratefying & allowing all & whatsoever my said attorney for me and in my name shall doe or cause to be done in or about the premisses by these presents. In witnes whereof &c.

Poemes written in the Reigne of Queen Elizabeth

Come live with me and be my love.
and we will all the pastimes prove,
that valleis, mountaines, woods or feilde
or groves, or pleasant pastures yelde

where we will sitt upon the rocke
and see the shepherds feed their flocke
by shallow rivers to whose falles
melodious birds singe madrigalls.

where we will make the beds of roses
and a thousand fragrant posies.
a cappe of flowers & a kirtle
3 Imbroydered all with leaves of mirtle. *

A sonnet Madrigal by Sr Philipp Sydney

* The belte of strawe with ivie buds
Corall clasps & amber studs
All theis in [illegible] thee might me move
to live with thee and be thy love.
4

Response

But if the world & love were younge
and truth in every shepherds tounge
Then theis delights might me move
to live with thee & be thie love.

Thie belte of strawe thie bedd of roses
thie cappe, thie kirtle & thie posies
Some breake, some wither, some forgotten
in follie ripe, in reason rotten.

Could youth ~~but~~ long last & love still feede
had tyme no date, nor age no neede
Then theis delights might my mind move
to live with thee & be thie love.

19

SIR WALTER RALE(I)GH

Autograph letter signed, dated 5 October 1610, to Sir Walter Cope. 1 p. 311 x 196 mm.

The active phase of Ralegh's life ended in 1603 when he was unjustly convicted for treason; the contemplative began when he received a stay of execution and was returned to the Tower of London, there to remain until he was released thirteen years later in a final, unsuccessful bid for freedom. The Tower, however, was not a hermitage; Ralegh's wife lived there for a time (in this letter he requests that she "might agayne be m[ade] a prisoner with me") and there he became friend and instructor to Prince Henry, heir to the throne. On his behalf he undertook the writing of *The History of the World*, a work which he did not finish because of the "unspeakable and never enough lamented losse" of the young Prince in 1612. The main burden of this letter concerns the character of Sir Robert Cecil, who was Secretary of State during Ralegh's trial. "It is in his Lordships face & countenance," Ralegh writes, "that I behold all t[t] remaynes to me of comfort, & all the hope I have: & from wch I shall never be beaten, till I see the last of evills & the dispayre wch hath no healp." In his characterization of Cecil, the poet and explorer erred tragically, for Cecil was guilty of what Ralegh calls here "delight in the endles adversitie of an enemie."

S[r] Walter Cope, yow are of my old acquayntance, and were my familier frind for many yeeres, in wch time I hope yow cannot say that ever I used any unkind office towards yow. But our fortunes are now changed, & it may be in your power greatly to bynde me unto yow, if the bynding of a man in my estate be worth any thing.

My desire unto yow is, that you wilbe pleased to move my Lord Treasorer in my behalf, that by his grace my wife might agayne be m[ade] a prisoner with me, as she hath bine for six yeeres last past. Shee being now devided from me, & therby to my great impoverishing I am driven to keip to howses. A miserable sute it is, & yet great to me, who in this wretched estate can hope for no other thing, than peacible sorrow.

It is now, & I call the Lord of all power to wittnes, y[t] I ever have bine & am resolved that it was never in the worthy hart of S[r] Robert Cecyll (what soever a counceler of state, & a Lord Treasorer of Ingland must do) to suffer me to fall, much less to perrish. . . .

Sr Walter Cope, yow are of my old acquayntance, and were my familier frind
for many yeeres, in wch time I hope yow cannot say that ever I vsed any vn=
kind office towards yow. But our fortunes are now changed, & it may
be in your power greatly to bynde me vnto yow, if the bynding of a
man in my estate be worth any thing.
My desire vnto yow is, that yow wilbe pleased to moue my Lord Treasorer
in my behalf, that by his grace my wife might agayne be a
a prisoner with me, as she hath bine for six yeeres last past.
shee being now devided from me, & thereby to my great impoue=
rishing I am driven to keip two howses. A miserable sute it is, & yet
great to me, who in this wretched estate can hope for no other
thing, than peacible sorrow.
It is now, & I call the Lord of all power to wittnes, that I ever hand
bine & am resolued that it was neuer in the worthy hart of
Sr Robert Cecyll (what soeuer a counceler of state, & a Lord
Treasorer of England must do) to suffer me to fall, much less
to perrish. For what soeuer termes it hath pleased his Lord=
ship to vse towards mee, wch might vtterly dispaire any
bodie else, yet I know that he spake them as a counceler, sitting
in councell, & in company of such as would not otherwise haue
bine satisfied. But as God liveth, I would haue bought his
presence att a farr deerer rate than those sharp words, and
these three monoths close imprisonment, for it is in his Lordships
face & countenance that I behold all that remaynes to me of
comfort, & all the hope I haue: & from wch I shall never
be beaten, till I see the last of evills & the dispayre wch hath
no healp. The blessings of God cannot make him cruell that
was never so, nor prosperitie teach ~~[illegible]~~, any man of so great
worth, to delight in the endles aduersitie of an enemie,
much less of him who in his very sowle & nature can never
be such a one towards him.
Sr the matter is of no great importance, (though a cruell destinie
hath made it so to me) to desire that my wife may live with
mee in this vnsavory place, If by your mediation I may
obtayne it I will acknowledg it in the highest degree of
thankfullnes, & rest reddy in trew faith to be commanded
by yow.

W Ralegh

[illegible]
5.

20

Sir Philip Sidney
1554–1586

Autograph manuscript of "The Defence of the Earl of Leicester," undated but written ca. 1584–5. 14 pp. 305 x 215 mm. MA 1475. Purchased with the assistance of the Fellows.

In October 1586 an English military force attacked the town of Zutphen in the Netherlands. "Few of the English perished," Camden records, "but oh! He that countervail'd many men, whose valor paralell'd if not exceeded the best, *Sidney*, his horse being slain, whilst he ascended another, was shot through the thigh, of which wound five and twenty dayes after he dyed, having scarce out-lived his father foure moneths. . . ." The troops in the Netherlands were commanded by Sidney's uncle, Robert Dudley, Earl of Leicester, who for years had been Queen Elizabeth's favorite, in spite of numerous errors of policy on his part. Two years before his nephew's death, Leicester had been attacked in print by the anonymous author of the pamphlet *Leicester's Commonwealth*, which alleged that he had virtually taken the government into his own hands. On behalf of his uncle, Sidney wrote the *Defence of the Earl of Leicester* and circulated it in manuscript among friends and family. (It was not printed until 1746.) The autograph manuscript of the *Defence*, shown here, is the only substantial literary manuscript by Sidney now in existence. He defends his uncle with vehemence, challenging the honor of the pamphlet's author: "So again in any place, wherto thow wilt call me, provyded that the place be such, as a servant of the queenes majestie have free access unto; if I do not, having my lyfe, and liberty, prove this uppon thee, I am content that this ly I have givn thee, return to my own perpetual infamy."

---

of late There hath been printed a book in form of dialog to the de[MS torn] of the Earl of Lester, ~~if at least~~ full of the most vyle repro[MS torn] w^{ch} ~~either~~ a witt used to wicked and filthy thoughtes can imagin in such manner truly y^{t} if the autor had as well fained new names as he doth new matters a man might well have thought his only meaning had been to have givn a lyvely picture of the uttermost degree of railing. A thing contemtible in the doer as proceeding from a base and wretched tong~~e~~ and such a tong as in the speaking dares nor speak his own name. odious to all estates since no man beares a name of wch name how unfitli so ever to the person by an impudent Lyer any thing may not be spokne, by all good Laws sharpli punished and by all civill companies lyke a poisenous serpent avoided. . . .

of late there hath been printed a book in form of dialog to the de[faming]
of the Earl of Lester, ~~if at least~~ full of the most vyle repro[ches]
w[hich] ~~either~~ a witt used to wicked and filthy thoughtes can imagin
in such ma~~tter~~ truly. yt if the autor had as well fained them
names as he doth new matters a man might well have thought his
only meaning had been to have given a lyvely picture of the uttermost
degree of railing. A thing contemtible in the doer as proceeding from
a base and wretched ~~tong~~ and such a tong as in the speaking dares
not speak his own name. odious to all estates since no man
beares a name of which name how unfitli so ever to the person
by an impudent lyer any thing may not be spoken, by all
good laws sharpli punished and by all civill companies lyke a
poysenous serpent avoided. but to the Earl him self in the cis[e]
of any men who with clear iudgmentes can valew thinges a trew
and sound honour grows out of these dishonourable falshods. since he
mey iustly say as ~~with~~ a worthy senatour of Rome one in lyke case
did that no man these twenty yeeres hath born a hatefull
hart to this estate, but that at the same tyme he hath shewd
this enmity to thes Earl ~~doing~~ testefying therebi that singular honour ~~unto~~
~~him~~ as ~~if~~ that his faith is so lynked to her Ma[jes]ties service
that who goes about to ~~one~~ undermyne the one ~~first~~
to overthrow the other. ~~Th~~ old and we think ~~for~~
first that evill contented and evill mynded persons befor[e]
be ryfe for them to shew their hate against the prince or first
vomitt it ~~out~~ against his councelours, nay certainly so stale
a deuyse it is as it is to be mervailed that so fyne witts
whose inventions a fugitive fortune hath sharpned and the air
of Itali perchaunce purified can light uppon no gallanter way
then the ~~or~~ ordinary pretext of the very clownish rebellions.
by name first to publish somthing against the Earl of lester and after when tym[e]
and yet that this is their plott of late by some of their own
served against the queenes majesti
intercepted discourses is made to manifest. He him self in some
places bringes in the examples of Gaveston Earl of Cornwal Robert
Vere Duke of Ireland and Delapool Duke of Suffolk, it is not
my purpose to defend them ~~though perase~~ but I would fain know
whether they that persecuted those councellours when they had
had their will in ruining them whether their rage ceassed
before they had as well destroied the kynges them selves Edward
and Richard the second and Henry the sixt ~~but as I say the~~
~~Earl of lester envy may encreaces great and~~ The old tale testeth
that the wolves yt mean to destroi the flok hate most the trewest and

21

Sir Philip Sidney

Autograph letter signed, undated but written ca. 1586, to Christopher Plantin. 1 p. 314 x 221 mm. MA 409.

The ideal of the courtier-poet was a long time being formed; Sidney gave it the force of actuality by living the life of a literary gentleman and dying a soldier's death. More than any other individual, he gave shape to the poetic ambitions and values of the Elizabethan age. To this day he remains the ablest defender of "ever-praiseworthy Poesie... full of vertue-breeding delightfulnes, and voyde of no gyfte, that oughte to be in the noble name of learning." His *Apologie for Poetrie* (1591; like all his works, printed posthumously) begins with characteristic humility and grace: "in these my not old yeres & idelest times, having slipt into the title of a Poet, [I] am provoked to say something unto you in the defence of that my unelected vocation." Before his argument concludes it swells into a resonant affirmation of poetry's central position among human activities, the point of conjunction between philosophy and history, between man's ambitions and his failures. In his own life Sidney presents one of the finest examples of the humanist credo that the active and contemplative lives must be joined in one.

This letter to the French printer Christopher Plantin was written in the year of Sidney's death, and it may concern the expedition to the Netherlands in which Sidney took part; for he orders Ortelius' *Theatrum Orbis Terrarum*, a book on "les havres de l'europe" entitled *Speculum Nauticum*, and a third work about the description of towns and fortresses.

Most of the extant manuscripts of Sidney's letters are preserved in the British Library and the Public Record Office, London.

Les mappes d'ortelius en la plus nouvelle edition.
Le livre en flaman descripvant les havres de l'europe.
Le description des villes et foreteresses.
Je vous prie Monsr Plantin que ie puisse avoir ces livres, et ne faudray point de vous les rembourser, et en recompense demeure. Vre affectionné ami pour vous faire plaisir et service. Ph. Sidney

Les mappes d'Ortelius en la plus nouvelle edition.

Le livre en flaman descripuant les hauvres de l'Europe.

Le description des villes et forteresses.

Je vous prie Mons.r plantin que ie puisse avoir ces livres, et ne faudray point de vous les remburser, et en recompense demeurer.

vre affectionné ami pour vous faire plaisir et service

Ph. Sidney

Sir Edward Dyer
d. 1607

Autograph letter signed, dated 24 August 1597, to the Governors of the Free School of St. Mary Overey. 1 p. 262 x 194 mm. MA 2415.

During his lifetime, Sir Edward Dyer published very little, yet he was renowned as one of the best English poets of his age. Like many such reputations, his proved evanescent, much to the bewilderment of the next generation when it tried to collect his poems and found only a small handful. Nevertheless, several good lyrics are attributed to him, among them the poem that begins "My mind to me a kingdom is," and he was an integral member of the finest literary circle of the late sixteenth century. Gabriel Harvey and Edmund Spenser (who called him "in a manner oure onlye Inglishe poett") were his friends, and one rarely sees him mentioned without the accompaniment of Sir Philip Sidney and Fulke Greville, Lord Brooke (when Sidney died, he left his books to be divided between Greville and Dyer). The true source of his reputation may probably be derived from these friendships and from the fact that he had garnered some influence in the court of Queen Elizabeth, though from time to time he fell under the shadow of her displeasure. Certainly, this letter shows him dispensing the benefit of his reputation, for he here recommends a friend, Mr. Fausset, for the position of schoolmaster at the Free School of St. Mary Overey, also known as St. Saviour.

After my verie hartie commendacons. I am moved to disclose unto you, myne opinion off this bearer Mr Fausett, who makth sute unto you to become Schoolmaster of the free school of St Marie Overeye. He is a verie honest & sober man, verie sufficiently learned for that callinge, & much affected to doo good that waye. I think he can not lack the commendacōn of such as yee maye more woorthiely credyt then me: but I, am desirous to ꝑforme the best office to him that herein I maye. Iff it please you to accept of him the rather for my mediation, I shall think I have receaved a token off your good opinions of me, wch I will gratefully acknowledge, & I am sure yee shall fynd the plan verie well furnyshed & to your lyking in the service by him to be doone hereaftir. So fare yee most hartiely well. At my lodging the xxiiii^th^ of Aug: 97 y^r^ verie loving & well assur'd frend Edward Dyer

After my verie hartie commendacons. I am moved
to declare unto you, myne opinion off this bearer Mr
Faucett, who maketh sute unto you to become Scholemaster
of the free schole of St Marie Overye. He is
a verie honest & sober man, verie sufficiently learned
for that callinge, & much affected to doo good that
waye. I think he can not lack the commendacōn
of such as you maye more worthely credyt then me:
but I, am desirous to performe the best office
to him that herin I maye. Iff it please you
to accept of him the rather for my mediation, I
shall think I have receaved a token off your
good opinion of me, wch I will gratefully ac=
=knowledge, & I am sure you shall fynd the place
verie well furnished & to your lyking in
the service by him to be doone hereafter. So
fare you most hartiely well, At my lodging
the xxiiijth of Aug: 97

Yr verie loving & well assured
frend

Edward Dyer

23

Francis Bacon, first Baron Verulam and Viscount St. Albans 1561–1626

Autograph letter signed, dated 16 September 1604, to his half-brother, Sir Nicholas Bacon. 1 p. 305 x 237 mm. MA 1215. Gift of Mr. Roland L. Redmond.

Bacon's *Advancement of Learning* (1605) was partly intended to serve as a present "of affection" for King James I, the monarch under whose aegis he hoped his projected advancement might ensue. With politic flattery, Bacon wondered, "why should a fewe received Authors stand up like *Hercules Columnes*, beyond which, there should be no sayling, or discovering, since wee have so bright and benigne a starre, as youre Ma:[jesty] to conduct and prosper us?" The sentiment expressed in this question is not merely ornamental; it is an appeal to England's highest authority to sustain a systematic attempt to coordinate and extend the communal efforts of man's intellect. In its few pages, the *Advancement of Learning* surveys in outline the entire range of human knowledge and attacks the traditional limitations imposed on the desire for understanding. Bacon optimistically asserts that with the "corrective spice" of charity mixed in, "there is no daunger at all in the proportion or quantitie of knowledge howe large soever. . . ." Despite Bacon's eloquence, James was not prepared to act so vigorous a part nor at first to "prosper" Bacon's political career to the extent of his wishes. At the accession of James in 1603, Bacon had been merely one in a crowd of newly knighted men; at the time the letter illustrated here was written he had just received his patent and pension as King's counsel, the first step in a long, ambitious climb to the position of Lord Chancellor.

In this letter to his half-brother Nicholas (the eldest son of Sir Nicholas Bacon's first marriage), Bacon requests his assistance in the transferral of "the leases, goods, and chattells of Mr Dudly Fortescue," who had recently committed suicide, to Thomas Buchanane and his wife, who was a member of the "Queenes beddechamber." Bacon also apologizes for the quality of the paper on which he writes: "Excuse me I pray you; paper was short at this tyme."

Brother Bacon Whereas it hath pleased the K. to bestowe upon M^{r} Th. Buchanane and his wife being of the Queenes beddechamber, the leases, goods, and chattells of Mr Dudly Fortescue who lately became felo de se, for as much as saved the sending of the Counsells letters, he hath thought good to goe down himself about the busanesse, being intreated by my very good frends to co͞mend his busanesse to yor ayde and favo^{r}, I doe [illegible deletion] very heartily desire you to furder him what you may; I canne assure you it will be very well taken at yor hands, and specially the Q. will thanke you for it, as a pleasure to a ꝑson her majesty doth extraordinarily affect. So I co͞mend you to Goddes goodnesse and remayne Yo^{r} loving brother and frend Fr. Bacon Excuse me I pray you; paper was short at this tyme Court at Wyndsore this 16th of Sep. 1604

Brother Baron whereas it hath pleased the K. to
bestowe upon Mr H. Kirkham and his wife being
of the Queenes beddchamber, the leases, goods and
chattells of Mr Undle Sotherton who lately
became felo de se, for as much as since the
sending of the Counsells letters, he hath thought it
good to goe down himself about the businesse,
being intreated by my verie good frend to commend
his businesse to your ayde and favor, I doe ~~[illegible]~~
hereby desire you to further him what you may,
I cannot assure you it will be verie well
taken at your hands, and specially the K. will
thanke you for it, as a pleasure to a person
who I doe extraordinarilie affect. So
I commend you to Godds goodnesse and
remayne

Excuse me I pray
you; paper was
scant at this tyme

Your loving brother
and frend

Fr. Bacon

Court at Windsore
this 16th of Sep.
1604

JOSUAH SYLVESTER
1563–1618

Autograph poem, "To the worthilie Honored S.ʳ EDWARD LEWIS, Knight," written ca. 1615, tipped into a copy of Sylvester's "The Parliament of Vertues Royal" (London: H. Lownes, 1614–5). 128 x 75 mm. PML 76455.

The eloquent terseness of the Book of Genesis caused Longinus to remark that the simplicity of "Fiat lux" was sublime; at another extreme, it also inspired *La Sepmaine, ou création du monde* (1578), the hexameral epic written by Guillaume de Salluste, seigneur du Bartas, and translated by Josuah Sylvester as *Bartas His Devine Weekes & Workes* (1605). Copious as "eares of Corne in *Autumne* on the Fields," *Devine Weekes* re-expresses the sublimity of Genesis by mirroring the profusion of God's benevolence during the six days of creation. As one of the first and best Protestant treatments of the subject (Du Bartas was a Huguenot), *La Sepmaine* attracted much attention in England when it was published, so much so that the number of notable men who attempted translations of it, including Sir Philip Sidney and King James, somewhat daunted Sylvester when he began his own version. In a prefatory "pyramid" poem, he acknowledged the superior genius of Sidney and rightly wondered "How thẽ shold I, in Wit & Art so shalow,/ Attẽpt the *Task*, which yet none other can?" It is in fact this task which has preserved Sylvester's name over the centuries; though he, following Du Bartas, had a tendency to confuse garrulity and plenitude, Sylvester is more of a poet in *Bartas His Devine Weekes* than he is anywhere else.

Aside from translations, the dedicatory poem seems to have been a genre in which Sylvester also specialized; the bulk of his surviving autograph verse, primarily in the British Library, is in this form and it represents Sylvester at his very worst. The poem shown here is a presentation inscription to Sir Edward Lewis, otherwise unknown, intended to accompany a collection of translations and original poems printed under the title *The Parliament of Vertues Royal*, Sylvester's translation of a work by Jean Bertaut, bishop of Sées.

To the worthilie Honored S.ʳ EDWARD LEWIS, Knight

As like drawes like (by Sympathie)/ Hard Load-stones, Steel; sweet Flow^{rs}, the B[ee;]/ The golden Sun, the Mari-gold:/ Yo^{r} Names & Vertues (Noble Knigh[t),]/ Suiting my Royal SAINCTS so right,/ Attract Us to You, too-too-bold. Among the WORTHIES of the Land,/ That have vouch-saft wth heart & hand/ To wel-come BARTAS Muse & Ours;/ Disdaign not (Sir) wth hand & heart/ To entertain This slender Parte,/ From Him, who vowes him Humbly Yo.^{rs} Josuah Sylvester.

To the worthilie Honored
Sr. EDWARD LEWIS,
Knight.

As like drawes like (by Sympathie)
Hard Load-stones, Steel; sweet fflowers, the
The golden Sun, the Marigold:
Yor Names & Vertues (Noble Knight)
Suiting my Royal SAINCTS so right,
Attract Vs to you, too-too-bold.

Among the WORTHIES of the Land,
That haue vouchsaft wth heart & hand
To wel-come BARTAS Muse & Ours;
Disdaign not (Sir) wth hand & heart
To entertain This slender Parte,
ffrom Him, who vowes him
Humbly Yors.

Josuah Sylvester

25

John Davies of Hereford
1565?–1618

Autograph manuscript of a poem, "Respons," signed, undated but written ca. 1611–2, inscribed in a copy of "Coryats Crudities" (London, 1611). PML 19044.

According to the historian Thomas Fuller, John Davies of Hereford "was the greatest *Master* of the *Pen* that *England* in his age beheld," especially in the skill of "*Fair-writing*, some minutes Consultation being required to decide, whether his lines were written or printed." In his youth, Prince Henry studied with Davies, and later generations followed the examples published in his *Writing Schoolmaster, or the Anatomy of Fair Writing* (1633). Today, however, Davies is best known as the author of numerous rather tedious volumes of poetry, among them: *Mirum in Modum* (1602); *Microcosmos. The Discovery of the Little World* (1603), his most popular work; *The Scourge of Folly* (ca. 1610), which contains an epigram "To our English Terence Mr. Will: Shakespeare"; and *Wits Bedlam* (1617). Several manuscripts by Davies survive, not for the beauty of his verse but for the elegance of his hand.

The four-line "Respons" signed by Davies was inscribed in a copy of *Coryats Crudities* (1611), a travel book written by Thomas Coryat. Fuller observes of this volume: "His book known by the name of *Coriat's Crudities*, *nauceous* to nice Readers, for the *rawnesse* thereof, is not altogether useless though the *porch* be more worth than the *Palace*, I mean the Preface of other mens *mock-commending verses* thereon." Among the authors contributing prefatory poems were John Donne, Thomas Campion, Michael Drayton and Davies. Coryat passed among these men as a learned, witty and merry companion of a lower order. Prince Henry pensioned him and Fuller asserts that "*Sweet-meats* and *Coriat* made up the *last course* at all *Court-entertainments*." In one of many marginal annotations to the text of his copy of *Coryats Crudities*, Davies defends Coryat: "If all the rest had beene no worse exprest then this, thy Poets, Tom, had dispraised them selves, had they not praised thee in ernest."

Respons./ Lo here a Smith, that firiest Witts doth knock,/ With his Witts Hammer gives him self a strok:/ For, here hee iudgeth Tom, and not misdeemes;/ Then hee's his Peere as hee him self esteemes. Jo: Davies.

By thee wise *Coryate* we are taught to know,
Great, with great men which is the way to grow.
For in a new straine thou com'st finely in,
Making thy selfe like those thou meant'st to winne:
Greatnesse to me seem'd euer full of feare,
Which thou found'st false at thy arriuing there,
Of the *Bermudos*, the example such,
Where not a ship vntill this time durst touch;
Kep't as suppos'd by hels infernall dogs,
Our Fleet found their most honest courteous hogs.
Liue vertuous *Coryate*, and for euer be
Lik'd of such wise men, as are most like thee.

Explicit Michael Drayton.

Incipit Nicholas Smith.

TWas much all Country wits to ouershine;
At Court, where there are hundreds iust like thine,
How found they thee? how keepe they thee? except
As Rome being told that onely whilst she kept
The target fall'n from heauen, her state should grow,
Made many like, that none the right might know:
So, to possesse and keepe thee precious man,
They make themselues as like thee as they can.
Hence flow those verses. In this (*Tom*) appears
Thy greatnesse, Thou art iudged by thy *Peers*.

Explicit Nicholas Smith.

FINIS.

Respons.

Lo here a Smith, that firiest Witts doth knock,
With his Witts Hammer giues him self a stroke:
For, here he iudgeth Tom, and not misdeemes,
Then hee's his Peere as hee him self esteemes.

Io: Dauies.

26

Sir Henry Wotton
1568–1639

Autograph letter signed, dated 5 June 1604, to an unidentified recipient (possibly Sir Henry Fanshawe). 2 pp. 308 x 217 mm. MA 2734. Purchased as the gift of Mrs. J. Carter Brown.

In his verse epistle "To Sir *H.W.* at his going Ambassador to *Venice*," John Donne wrote:

> 'Tis therefore well your spirits now are plac'd
> In their last Furnace, in activity;
> Which fits them (Schooles and Courts and Warres o'rpast)
> To touch and test in any best degrees.

No doubt fortified by this assurance, Henry Wotton left London in 1604 and traveled to Venice where he assumed the role of ambassador, a post he occupied for almost twenty years. Before he departed, he paid a visit to the unidentified recipient of this letter (possibly Sir Henry Fanshawe of Ware Park). Here Wotton speaks of the return trip to London and of a servant offered him for his travels abroad. Wotton is best remembered by students of English literature as the friend of Bacon, Donne and Milton, whom Wotton provided with letters of introduction before the poet departed for Italy in 1638. The statesman also wrote verses preserved in *Reliquiæ Wottonianæ* (1651), which contains a prefatory poem by Cowley and a life by Izaak Walton, to whom Wotton was particularly close in later life. Of the "employment of his *time*," Walton commented, "some part of most dayes was usually spent in *Philosophical Conclusions*. Nor did he forget his innate pleasure of Angling, which he would usually call, *his idle time, not idely spent*; saying, he would rather live five *May-months*, than *forty Decembers*."

---

therefore resolve to borrowe him of you for the tyme that I shalbe abroade, and I must needs say that besides ~~youce~~ youre testimonies of him he hath brought me viry good characters in his face which is the first thing that I doe beleeve in any man.

I will now say no more because you promise me so soone the enioying of you agayne: Only lett me beseeche you before youre comming from thense to remember my humble and harty service to youre good Ladie and my most affectionat wishes to ~~youre~~ those sweete ~~children~~ plants that speake about youre boord.

From my chamber this 5 of June 1604 Youre frend that doth truly honor you Henry Wotton.

therfore resolve to borrowe him of you for the
tyme that I shalbe abroade, and I must
needs say that besides youre testimonies
of him he hath brought me very good characters in his face which is the first thing
that I doe beleeve in any man. I
will now say no more because you promise
me so soone the enjoying of you agayne.
Only lett me beseeche you before youre comming
from thense to remember my humble and harty
service to youre good Ladie and my most
affectionat wishes to those sweete plants
that speake about youre boord.

From my chamber this 5 of June
1604

Youre frend that
doth truly honor you

Henry Wotton.

27

Ben Jonson
1573?–1637

Autograph presentation inscription, signed, to John Wilson, in a copy of "The Workes of Benjamin Jonson" (London: Stansby, 1616). PML 16254.

In 1637, the year of Jonson's death, Sir John Suckling published *A Sessions of the Poets*, which recalls in imaginary fashion the poetical gatherings of the "Tribe of Ben" at "the *Sun*, the *Dog*," and "the triple *Tunne*":

> The first that broke silence was good old *Ben*,
> Prepar'd before with Canary wine,
> And he told them plainly he deserv'd the Bayes,
> For his were calld Works, where others were but Plaies.

Shown here is an inscribed copy of the book that provoked this stanza, *The Workes of Benjamin Jonson*, a title that reflects the seriousness with which Jonson took himself and his joint professions of poet, critic and playwright. It was Jonson's claim to defend the good name of poetry as a vocation at a time (like almost all times for poetry) when "[she] hath proved but a meane *Mistresse*, to such as have wholly addicted themselves to her; or given their names up to her family." Pugnacious and immensely learned, Jonson offered an example in his verse and a standard in his criticism that set itself squarely against the tastes of the multitude who "commend Writers, as they doe Fencers; or Wrastlers; who if they come in robustiously, & put for it, with a deale of violence, are received for the *braver-fellowes* . . . ." It is uncertain to which of several contemporary John Wilsons this volume was inscribed; the most likely candidates are a rather shadowy John Wilson who was a player and singer in Shakespeare's company and the John Wilson who was headmaster of Westminster School (where Jonson was educated) from 1610 to 1622.

---

*To his most worthy, & learned Freind M*r*. John Wilson. Ben: Jonsons guift & testimony of his Love.*

THEATRVM
GVL
LOCVM TENEANT S
THE
WORKES
OF
Beniamin Jonson
—neque, me ut miretur turba laboro:
Contentus paucis lectoribus.
Imprinted at London by Will Stansby
PLAVSTRVM
VISORIVM
An° D. 1616.

To his most worthy, & learned Friend
Mr: John Wilson.

Ben: Jonsons guift & testimony of his Love.

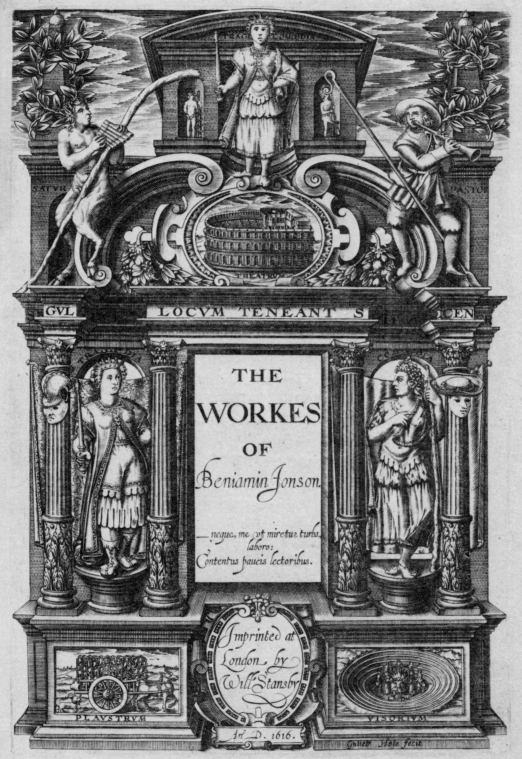

Joseph Hall
1574–1656

Autograph letter signed, dated 21 December 1649, to James Calthrop.
1 p. 287 x 181 mm.

When he was a young man of twenty-three, Joseph Hall claimed in his *Virgidemiarum* (1597) to be the first poet to introduce into the English language satires written on a classical model: "I first adventure: follow me who list,/ And be the second English satyrist." The strength of his satires and "his adaptations of antient to modern manners" (Warton) ally him to the eighteenth century, an age of satire above all others. In his *History of English Poetry* Thomas Warton reasserted Hall's priority in formal English satire, and Thomas Gray, in a letter of 1752, described *Virgidemiarum* as "full of spirit & poetry; as much of the first as Dr Donne, & far more of the latter." Like Donne, Hall was also a noted divine. After 1603, when he last published verse, his philosophical writings, epistles and meditations earned him renown as the "English Seneca" for his neo-Stoicism and the Senecan purity of his prose style. Following his elevation to the see of Norwich in 1641, Hall, with other bishops, encountered the displeasure of a largely Puritan Parliament. He enjoyed only a brief tenure as bishop: an act of sequestration stripped him of his property, and the populace of his town sacked the cathedral and drove him out of his "quondam palace at Norwich." He retired to nearby Higham where he depended greatly on the kindness of friends, one of whom he thanks in this letter.

Much honored S^r. I confesse I am to seek in what termes I may expresse my thanks to you for this yor bountifull token to an unknowne hand; Only let me say this, that I am more beholden to you, then to all Norfolk besides: My great desire is to see the face of so worthy a frend whom once, if I be not deceived, I saw in my quondam palace at Norwich; may it please you when yor occa̅o̅ns draw you to these parts, to renue this favour upon a man so much obliged to you; that I may personally present my thanks to you In the meane time I send you this poore litle pocketing of mine, though namelesse; wishing for some oportunity of a more acceptable testimony of my great, and deserved respects to you; w^t the harty profession whereof I take leave; and am Yo^r unfaynedly devoted and thankfull frend Jos: Hall. B.N. Higham Dec. 21° (1649.)

1773 March 17
F.

Much honored Sr. I confesse I am to seek
in what termes I may expresse my thanks
to you for this yor bountifull token to
an unknowne hand; Only let me say, this,
that I am more beholden to you, then to
all Norfolk besides: My great desire is
to see the face of so worthy a frend
whom once, if I be not deceived, I saw
in my quondam pallace at Norwich; may
it please you when yor occasions draw you to
these parts, to renue this favour upon
a man so much obliged to you; that I
may personally present my thanks to you
In the meane time I send you this poore
little pocketing of mine, though namelesse;
wishing for some oportunity of a more
acceptable testimony of my great, and deserved respects to you; wth the harty profession whereof I take leave; and am

Yor unfaynedly devoted
and thankfull frend

Jos. Hall B. N.

Higham
Dec. 21º (1649.)

29

JOHN DONNE
1571–1631

Autograph letter signed, undated but written in 1610, to Sir Thomas Egerton, Baron Ellesmere. 1 p. 289 x 194 mm. Anonymous loan.

By the date of this letter, 1610, Donne had spent nearly fifteen years vainly seeking a secular appointment. His most promising opportunity, in the employ of Sir Thomas Egerton, the man to whom this letter was written, had been blighted by his own folly. At York House, he had met Ann More, daughter of Sir George More, who was being raised by Lady Egerton. In spite of the differences between Donne's financial position and that of Ann's family, they fell in love and were secretly married in 1601. When their marriage was finally avowed, Donne was discharged from the service of Egerton, who went on to become Lord Chancellor, and could certainly have assured the employment of an intelligent, literate man like Donne. This letter was sent with a copy of his *Pseudo-Martyr* (1610) to his former employer. His first extensive published work, *Pseudo-Martyr* attacks those Catholics who remained recusants and refused "to take the Oath of Allegeance." Since Donne's family was Catholic, he had, as he remarks in the Preface, "a longer worke to doe then many other men; for I was first to blot out, certaine impressions of the Romane religion. . . ." The letter of presentation pinned to the back of this volume has an added interest, for it alludes to the problem of Donne's marriage. "All good that ys in ytt [*Pseudo-Martyr*], yor L^{p} may be pleasd to accept as yo^{rs}; and for the Errors, I cannot despayr of yor Pardon, since you have longe since pardond greater faults in mee."

Aside from Donne letters in the British Library, the Bodleian Library and the Huntington Library, there is also a group at the Folger Library in Washington, D.C., that includes four letters to Egerton and four to Sir George More.

As Ryvers, though in there Course they are content to serve publique uses, yett there end ys, to returne into the Sea, from whence they issued. So, though I should have much Comfort, that thys Booke might give contentment to others, yet my Direct end in ytt was, to make yt a testimony of my gratitude towards yor L^{p}. and an acknowledgement, that those poor sparks of Understandinge or Judgement wch are in mee were derived and kindled from yo^{u}, and owe themselves to yo^{u}. All good that ys in ytt, yor L^{p} may be pleasd to accept as yo^{rs}; and for the Errors, I cannot despayr of yor Pardon, since yo^{u} have longe since pardond greater faults in mee. Yo^{r} L^{ps} humble and faythfull Servant J: Donne

All Ryuers, though in there Course they are content
to serue publique uses, yett there end ys to returne
into the Sea, from whence they issued. So, though I
should haue much Comfort, that thys Booke might
giue contentment to others, yet my Direct end in ytt
was, to make yt a testimony of my gratitude towards
yor Lp. and an acknowledgement, that those poor
sparks of Vnderstandinge or Judgement wch are in mee,
were derived and kindled from yow and owe themselues
to yow. All good that ys in ytt, yor Lp may be pleased
to accept as yors; and for the Errors, I cannot despayr
of yor Pardon, since yow haue longe since pardond greater faults in mee.

Yor Lps

humble and fayth-
full Seruant

J. Donne.

EDWARD HERBERT, FIRST BARON HERBERT OF CHERBURY 1583–1648

Autograph letter signed, dated 8 May 1626, to Charles I. 2 pp. 287 x 197 mm. Anonymous loan.

In May 1619 the distinguished diplomatic team of Edward Herbert and Thomas Carew sailed for France and the embassy in Paris. Herbert proved to be a capable ambassador; he obtained great favor in the French court and suggested the marriage that was later fulfilled (after an embarrassment with the Infanta of Spain) between Charles I and Henrietta Maria. In 1624, however, he offended James I and was obliged to return to England where he found himself encumbered by debt and in possession only of the King's promises to assist him. In this letter to Charles I Herbert takes the delicate step of reminding the new sovereign (Charles succeeded to the throne in 1625) of his father's pledges: "Neyther have I anything to comfort mee, but your Majesties many gracious promises, both in your blessed fathers time, and sithence . . . ." His requests for financial assistance and "beinge made a Baron of Englande" were both honored: the former when he and his brother George Herbert, the poet, received the manor of Ribbesford in Worcestershire, the latter when he was made first Baron Herbert of Cherbury in 1629. Like his brother, Herbert also wrote verses, though of much less distinction; he is best remembered as a philosopher. Before he returned to England he had printed in Paris his treatise *De Veritate*, one of the first metaphysical works by an Englishman and a source of pride to its author: "I not only dispersed it among the prime Scholars of Europe, but was sent to not only from the nearest but furthest parts of Christendome, to desire the sight of my Book, for which they promised any thing I shou'd desire by way of return . . . ."

The largest collection of Herbert's manuscripts is in the British Library.

May it please your most excellent Majestie: Havinge given my most faithfull attendance to your Majesties father of blessed Memorie, from the beginnings of his raigne, to the later ende and in all that time havinge neyther demanded suite nor had any; your Majestie will easily knowe how small advantage, I made of his Service. Yet, I must confesse, I was chosen Ambassador, when I least thought of it, But as I livd in a more chargeable fashion then any before mee, and notwithstandinge saved his Majestie a 1000^{l} yearly, wch others spent him, and havinge withall done all marchants busines freely, wch never any other did in my place, I spent not only all the means I had from his Majestie, together with my owne annuall rents, but somethinge above; So that still your Majestie may be pleasd to consider mee, as a looser; But If the losse had beene only to my purse, I could better have indured it, but it was (though without my fault) in my Name and Estimation too, for when, after the reconcilinge of the distracted affections of this, and that other people where I served, I hoped in this later treaty of Marriage to bee admitted to the same Honor, wch was granted to Sr Thomas Edmunde in the former . . .

May it please your most excellent Majestie; 7 1..

Havinge given my most faithfull attendance to your Majesties Father, of blessed memorie, from the beginninge of his raigne to the later end, and in all that time havinge neyther demanded suite nor had any; your Majestie will easily knowe how small advantage I made of his Service. Yet I must confesse I was chosen Ambassadour, when I least thought of it, But as I lived in a more chargeable fashion then any before mee, and notwithstandinge saved his Majestie a 1000li yearly, wch others spent him, and havinge withall done all marchants busines freely, wch never any other did in my place, I spent not only all the means I had from his Majestie, together with my owne annuall rents, but somethinge above; So that still your Majestie may be pleased to consider mee, as a loser; But if the losse had beene only to my purse, I could better have indured it, but it was (though without my fault) in my Name and Estimation too, for when, after the reconcilinge of the distracted affections of this, and that other people where I served, I hoped in this later treaty of Marriage to be admitted to the same Honor, wch was granted to Sr Thomas Edmonds in the former, I was not only excluded, but repeald with the most publique disgrace, that ever Minister in my place did suffer; neyther have I anythinge to comfort mee but your Majesties many gracious promises, both in your blessed fathers time, and sithence, the effect of wch I cannot doubt of, not only in regard of my many services and sufferings, but that noman, in the memory of man, ever returned from the charge I had in that Countrey, that had not some place of Honor and preferment given him; In the meane while I shall crave leave to present these my most humble suites; 1. That whereas his late Majestie made mee a Baron in Irelande, as in the way of beinge made a Baron of Englande (wch my L. Duke of Buckingham, I assure myselfe, well remembers) your Majestie would be graciously pleased to make good that promise; 2. Whereas all his late Majesties Ambassadors in France have at their returne beene sworne of the Privy Counsaile your good Majestie may be graciously pleased not to thinke mee lesse worthy that Honor; 3. Whereas I am so farre from beinge payd that wch was promised by my privy seals, that I am not a saver, yet by about 3000li, your good Majestie some way or other would recompense mee;

31

William Drummond
1585–1649

Autograph signature in his copy of Juan Huarte's "Examen de Ingenios para las Sciencias..." (Leyden, 1591). PML 3952.

In his essay "Of Libraries," Drummond remarked, "Libraries are as Forests, in which not only tall Cedars and Oaks are to be found, but Bushes too and dwarfish Shrubs." In his own way he was a consequential shrub among literary oaks. Drummond had made a figure for himself in London in the early seventeenth century, but after 1610 he lived quietly at Hawthornden, his family estate near Edinburgh. There he read, wrote poetry and history, supervised his lands, and corresponded with old friends, among them the poet Michael Drayton. To later centuries Drummond is, of course, best known as the compiler of the anecdotes that became *Heads of a Conversation betwixt Ben Johnson and William Drummond* (first published in Edinburgh in 1711). Drummond entertained the great man in late 1618 and early 1619, after Jonson had walked to Edinburgh from London, followed (in what abject pose one wonders) by the Water-poet, John Taylor. As a guest the playwright was apparently congenial, though his host later wrote that he "was a great Lover and Praiser of himself, a Contemner and Scorner of others, given rather to lose a Friend than a Jest . . . ."

Among Drummond's many activities, he also collected books; a large part of his library is preserved at Edinburgh University. This work by Juan Huarte was translated into English (from an Italian version) in 1591 by Richard and Thomas Carew with the title *The Examination of mens Wits, in which, by discovering the varietie of natures, is shewed for what profession each one is apt, and how far he shall profit therein.*

Gui. Drummond

EXAMEN DE INGENIOS PARA LAS SCIENCIAS.

Donde se muestra la differencia de habilidades que ay enlos hombres, y el genere de letras que a cada vno responde en particular.

Es obra donde el que leyere con attencion hallara la manera de su ingenio, y sabra escoger la sciencia en que mas ha de aprouechar: y si por ventura la vuiere ya professado, entendera si atinó a la que pedia su habilidad natural.

Compuesta por el Doctor Juan Huarte, natural de sant Iuan del pie del Puerto.

EN LEYDA

Con Licencia, por Iuan Pats.

M. D. XCI.

Robert White
fl. 1617

Contemporary manuscript copy of "Cupids Banishment. A Maske Presented To Her Majesty By younge Gentlewomen of the Ladies Hall In Deptford at Greenwich the 4th of May 1617," on vellum. 44 pp. 200 x 160 mm. MA 1296.

The dramatic entertainment known as the masque reached a state of perfection during the reign of James I and Queen Anne, primarily because James and Anne had at their disposal the services of Inigo Jones, who designed the sets and costumes, and Ben Jonson, the court poet, who composed the lyrics and speeches. In the ornate form it attained during the early reign of the Stuarts, the masque may be said to represent the ennoblement of the theatre, for an important characteristic of the Stuart masque was its incorporation of the (often royal) audience in at least one of its dances. *Cupids Banishment* was written by Robert White, who seems otherwise unknown to fame, and the manuscript shown here, which he presented to Lucy, Countess of Bedford, is in the hand of a copyist. In the performance before Queen Anne at Deptford on 4 May 1617, White played the role of "Occasion"; Richard Browne (who was twelve in 1617) played "Diana." (Browne later became the father-in-law of John Evelyn, who, like Browne, at one time owned this manuscript.) Among the other performers was Charles Coleman, who played "Hymen" and became a distinguished instrumentalist, singer, composer and a member of the King's Musick before his death in 1664.

Cupids Banishment was printed for the first and probably the only time in a compilation by John Nichols entitled *The Progresses, Processions and Magnificent Festivities, of King James the First* (1828). Shown here is a delightful composition, the music and lyrics of a song for Bacchus.

Bacchus at thy call, they here come marching roundly/ yt will not flinch at all, but take theyr liquor soundly:/ thay'le doe thayr parts thay'le drinke whole quarts,/ a pinte with them is but a swallow./ thay'le ne're give o're, till the welkin roare,/ the house runne round and the skye looke yellow.

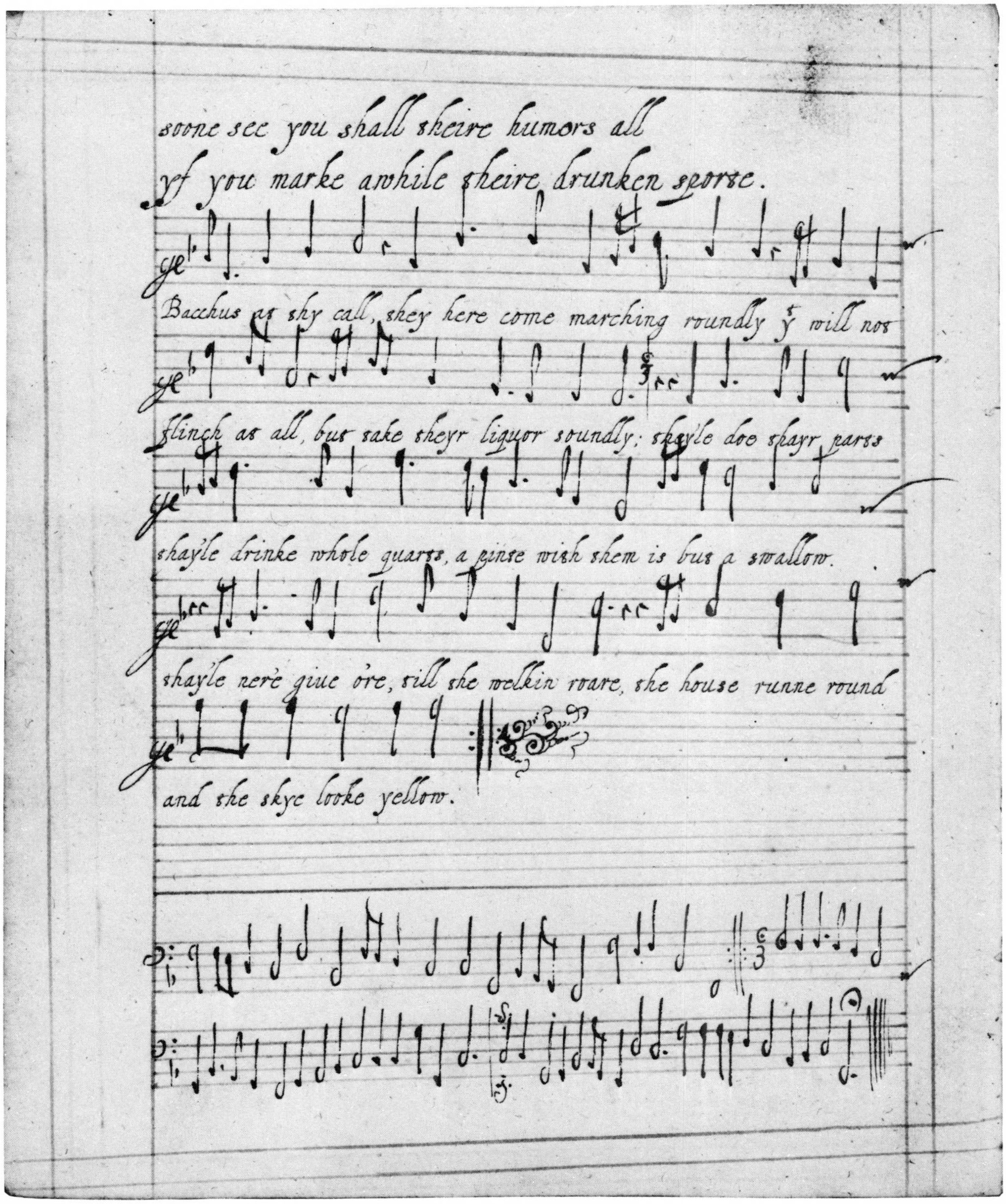
soone see you shall theire humors all
yf you marke awhile theire drunken sporte.
Bacchus at thy call, they here come marching roundly ye will not
flinch at all, but take theyr liquor soundly; theyle doe theyr parts
theyle drinke whole quarts, a pinte with them is but a swallow.
theyle nere giue ore, till the welkin roare, the house runne round
and the skye looke yellow.

33

HOLGATE COMMONPLACE BOOK

Manuscript commonplace book written probably by a member of the Holgate family, Saffron Walden, Essex, between 1603 and 1645, with later additions. 333 pp. 194 x 144 mm. MA 1057.

During the sixteenth and seventeenth centuries, it was usual for poetry to circulate in manuscript form and then be copied down in commonplace books by interested readers. The collections that have survived have often provided reliable texts of poetry otherwise lost to us, as well as important variants of printed poems. The Holgate commonplace book is a personal anthology of early seventeenth-century verse and character essays, and it includes an index of its contents. Scattered among works by lesser poets like Richard Corbet and William Strode are poems by John Donne, Ben Jonson, Thomas Carew, Francis Beaumont, Sir Henry Wotton and a single example, shown here, by Shakespeare, a variant text of Sonnet 106 copied probably from manuscript and not from print. At the back of the volume are several "characters" copied from John Earle's *Micro-cosmographie* (1628); these include "A younge raw Preacher," "A meere dull Physitian," and "A ploddinge Student": "Hee is a great discomforter of young students by tellinge them what travell it hath cost him, & how oft his braine turned at Phylosophy, & makes others feare studyinge as a cause of duncerie." Interspersed throughout the middle pages of this volume are copies of epitaphs and Restoration poetry in a different and later hand. The few editors of seventeenth-century verse who have worked with the Holgate manuscript have accorded it high authority, though many of its poems remain unidentified.

On his Mistris Beauty   When in the Annalls of all wastinge Time/ I see description of the fairest wights/ And beauty makeinge beautifull old mine [rime],/ In praise of Ladyes dead and lovely Knights/ then in the Blazon of sweet beauties best/ of face, of hands, of lip, of eye, or brow/ I see their antique pen would have exprest/ Ev'n such ą beauty as you master now/ Soe all their praises were but prophecies/ of those our dayes, all you prefiguringe/ And for they saw but with divininge eyes/ they had not skill enough thy worth to singe/ for wee which now behould these present dayes/ have eyes to wonder, but no tongues to praise:

And on each side, two faire Limbes for defence
(As keepers fitt for beauties excellence)
Stand and from thence, two slender twiggs take life,
Mutually mouinge with out any strife.
And now the founder of this goodly frame
(Least to vs Mortalls his state should seeme Lame
In his unsearched wisdome) thought it meete,
to perfect all with two most prettie feete.
But what haue I forgott; eares had shee none?
Yes sure, But they were wantinge to my mone,
Haue I not reason I should them forgett
that neare knew mee, therfore neare in their debte,
Yet cause in shew there is a way to enter
Into rich Joyes, Ile on their praises venter.
These little Dores, in fashion like two shells
of Mother of Pearle, shininge plainely tells,
that though Meander-like the passage is,
the guest shall finde an easie way to bliss,
And that same power which him thither drewe,
shall bringe him out againe, with out a clewe.
But oh Deare Saint, lett mee but enter yett
and locke mee euer in the Cabinett
Of thy sweete memorie wher let mee dwell,
Ile thinke my prison Heauen, and freedome Hell: ffinis

On his Mistris Beauty

When in the Annalls of all wastinge Time
I see description of the fairest wights
And beauty makeinge beautifull old rime,
In praise of Ladyes dead and louely Knights
then in the Blazon of sweet beauties best
of face of hand, of lip, of eye, or brow
I see their antique pen would haue exprest
Euen such a beauty as you master now
Soe all their praises were but prophecies
of those our dayes all you prefiguringe
And for they saw but with diuininge eyes
they had not skill enough thy worth to singe
for wee which now behould these present dayes
haue eyes to wonder, but no tongues to praise:

Francis Lenton
fl. 1625–1650

Autograph manuscript of "The Muses Oblation on Hymens Altar," dated April 1647. 9 ff. 204 x 159 mm. MA 3381.

The "Joyfull Muse" of Francis Lenton was not so joyful that she survived with any celebrity into the twentieth century. The immodest prolixity of this title page indicates why. Lenton was a minor poet whose claim to distinction is the doubtful title *poeta reginæ,* the Queen's poet. Like most such poets, his primary task was to fulfill the need for occasional poems. This slim manuscript volume was produced for the wedding of the Earl of Northampton and Lady Isabella Sackville, which took place on 5 July 1647. One hopes that the wedded couple did not set great store by these epithalamial verses, for Lenton seems to have been even more of a hack than was usual among minor occasional poets: two other *Muses Oblations* by him survive in manuscript, one dated 1641, one 1649. The titles of some of his other works give a sufficient indication of his literary predilections: *The Young Gallants Whirligigg* (1629); *Characterismi, or Lenton's Leaves* (1631); *The Innes of Court Anagrammatist* (1634); and *Great Britain's Beauties* (1638).

The Muses Oblation/ on Hymens Altar/ expressed/ In Epithalamigne, or Nuptiall Odes, Songs And Devices, on the Happy Espousalls, of the highly discended, Heroick and Right Honourable James, Lord Compton, Earle of Northampton; And the Right Vertuous, and Beauteous Lady Isabella Sackville. Sole virgin daughtre to the Right Honourable Richard Earle of Dorsett deceased &c Quid datur a Divis Felici optatiûs Hora? Englishd/ What can the Godds on Reall Lovers showre,/ more wishd, and wellcome, then theyr Wedding howre?/ Composed, and sung in Hono:r of their Unition & Celebration of the day;/ By the Joyfull Muse of Fra: Lenton, Gent: Poeta Reginæ./ Aprill 1647/

In The Muses Oblation on Hymens Altar

expressed

In Epithalamique or Nuptiall Odes Songs
And Devices on the Happy Espousalls of
the highly discended, Heroick and Right
Honourable James, Lord Compton, Earle
of Northampton, And the Right
vertuous and Beauteous Lady
Isabella Sackville sole virgin daughter
to the Right Honourable Richard
Earle of Dorsett deceased &c

Quid datur a divis Felici optatius Hora?

Englished

What can the Godds on Reall Lovers showre,
more wished and wellcome then theyr Wedding howre.

Composed and sung in Honor of their
Unition & Celebration of the day:

By the Joyfull Muse of
Fra: Lenton Gent:
Poeta Reginæ
Aprill 1647

John Chalkhill
1595?–1642

Autograph letter signed, dated March 1638, to Katherine Packerre, or Packer. 3 pp. 309 x 205 mm. MA 3342. Purchased as the gift of the Fellows in honor of Charles Ryskamp on the occasion of his tenth anniversary as Director.

In London, 1683, there appeared a small volume entitled *Thealma and Clearchus. A Pastoral History in smooth and easie Verse*, with a preface by Izaak Walton. The title page declared that its author was one John Chalkhill, "An Acquaintant and Friend of Edmund Spencer." For many years, scholars denied Chalkhill an identity separate from Walton, who, after all, had printed in *The Compleat Angler* almost all the known verse by Chalkhill and was the only author associated with the name. In 1958, however, a small group of manuscripts by Chalkhill, known to be his by the signature on the present letter, was discovered among the papers of a Derbyshire family. These manuscripts revealed little about Chalkhill's life—he was related to Walton by marriage and he attended Trinity College, Cambridge—but the literary recommendation implied by friendship with Spenser was rejected: extrapolating from the date of his admission to Cambridge, one discovers that Chalkhill would have been born just four or five years prior to Spenser's death. Chalkhill's verse possesses an average amount of grace in the Jacobean manner. His best work is the poem sung by Coridon in *The Compleat Angler*:

> Oh the sweet contentment
> The country man doth find!
>   high trolollie loliloe
>   high trolollie lee.
> That quiet contemplation
> possesseth all my mind:
> Then care away,
> and wend along with me.

In this letter to his cousin, Katherine Packerre, he discusses the Christian applications of illness (Katherine was sick) and includes a poem to cheer her up. All the Chalkhill manuscripts known to survive are now in the Morgan Library.

I cannot thinke Nun Nan will stay longe after/ Nunnes must lie hard; and marriage bed, is softer/ As for my wife if ere she prove a Nun/ or dye a Virgin, all my hopes are donne/ My mother Bess she couppled longe agone/ and now hath gott a father for her sonne/ But what am I y^n^ better: I am sure/ I loose by what I gett: and must endure/ My losses and my crosses: ~~and~~ tis in vayne/ to hope for such a time of hope, againe/ Poure frier John may now goe shake his eares/ And drinke his muses helth in brymè teares/ Like to a Hermite sequestred from men/ ile study woes to dictate to my pen/ for all have left me, but my cares and feares/ least some unwellcome newes should reach my eares . . .

I cannot thinke Nan, Nan will stay long after
Nunnes must lie hard; and marriage bed, is softer
As for my wife if ere she proue a Nun
or die a virgin, all my hopes are donne
My mother Bess she cropp'd long agoe
and now hath gott a father for her sonn
But what am I ye better: I am sure
I loose by what I gett: and must endure
My losses and my crosses: and in vayne
to hope for such a time of hope, againe
Poore seely John may now goe shake his eares
And drinke his masters health in beyond beeres
Like to a Hermite sequestred from men
to study how to dictate to my pen
for all haue left me, but my cares and feares
that sende unwellcome newes those reaching darts
Or, words I make my bed: no help for that
Urgent state alowes me not a Matt
Wett Jeanes out and now I thinke our fleas
makes me rubb oftner then is for my ease
But there hanges a tale: I pry thee Cuss
Chide Matt for me, or giue the girle a buss
I know she loues thee: though she scold at home
Husbands must suffer: but me thinkes I see
thou growest a weary of my prattlinge Muse
I can not blame thee; I my selfe accuse
my selfe of follie yet twas my intent
to cheare not harme thee with my merriment
I ask thy pardon if I doe amisse
if not thou shalt not want such stuffe as this
if thou canst read his hand that will ouer be

Thy truly louinge freind and Cosson
John Chalkhill or Sr Hobson.
ask my Lady etc.

dated the very same
day my wife went to
London beinge worst
ere day of March my Allminack
or I cannot agree ytt
1638

I haue writt to my wife because
I saw noe other

36

Robert Herrick
1591–1674

Autograph letter signed, undated but written ca. 1615–6, to his uncle, Sir William Hearick. 1 p. 196 x 192 mm. MA 3382. Purchased as the gift of Miss Julia P. Wightman in honor of Charles Ryskamp.

Only fifteen letters by Herrick survive (one in this country) and each is a plea for money, written from Cambridge and addressed to his guardian and somewhat hesitant patron, Sir William Hearick. One does not naturally associate Herrick with the unpleasant tones of a dunning correspondence. Between 1629, when he left the literary circle led by his friend, "the rare Arch-poet" Ben Jonson, and 1647, when he was ejected from his living for his royalist views, he inhabited the relatively self-sufficient and pastoral world of the Devonshire countryside at Dean Prior. There he wrote the greater part of the lyrics that fill *Hesperides*, the volume of poetry he published in 1648 after his return to London. In *Hesperides* Herrick united a classical sensibility with his occasional love of retirement and the themes of country life, as well as the topics of "*Youth*, of *Love*" and "cleanly-*Wantonnesse*." Herrick is best known for the lyric which begins "Gather ye Rose-buds while ye may" and "Corinna's *going a Maying*," but his muse reaches fullest voice in "*The Hock-cart*, or *Harvest home*," an expression of plenitude worlds away from the poverty of St. John's College, Cambridge:

> Come Sons of Summer, by whose toile,
> We are the Lords of Wine and Oile:
> By whose tough labours, and rough hands,
> We rip up first, then reap our lands.
> Crown'd with the eares of corne, now come,
> And, to the Pipe, sing Harvest home.

Herrick's other surviving letters are all in the County Archives at Leicester.

Cambridg St Johns S^r—the first place testifies my deutie. the second only reiterats the former letter, of which (as I may iustly wonder) I heard no ~~ne~~ answeare, nether concerning the payment or receat of the letter, (It is best knowne to your self) Upon which ignorance I have sent this oratour, entreating you to paye to mr Adrian marius bookseller of the black fryers the some of 10^{li} from whome so soone as it is payd I shall reaceave a dew acknowledgment: I shall not need to amplyfy my sense for this warrants sufficiencie. I expect your countenance and your furtherance to my well beeing who hath power to command my service to eternitie: Heaven be your guide to direct you to ꝑfection which is the end of mans endevour: I expect an answeare from mr Adrian concerning the recipt:. Robin Hearick obliged to your virtue eternally:

Cambridg St Johns

Sr the first place testifies my dutie
the second only reiterats the former
letter of which (as I may iustly wonder)
I heard no answare, neither concerning
the payment or receat of the letter.
(It is best knowne to your selfe) upon which
ignorance I have sent this oratour, entreating
you to paye to mr Adrian marius bookseller
of the black fryers the some of 10 li
from whome so soone as it is payd I shall
receave a dew acknowledgment. I shall
not need to amplyfy my sense for this
warrants sufficiencie. I expect your countenance
and your furtherance to my well being,
who hath power to command my service
to eternitie: Heaven be your guide
to direct you to perfection which is the end of
mans endevour:

I expect an answare from
mr Adrian concerning the
receipt:

Robin Hearick
oblidged to your
virtue eternally:
///

37

Izaak Walton
1593–1683

Autograph inscription signed, dated Farnham Castle, 19 December 1678, to Mrs. Dorothy Wallop, in a copy of "The Universal Angler" (London: Richard Marriott, 1676), on recto of engraved part title. PML 6572.

Amidst the civil chaos and tough prose of the mid-seventeenth century, Izaak Walton's *The Compleat Angler or the Contemplative Man's Recreation* (1653) is a pastoral interlude. From his practical experience in ponds and streams, Walton fashioned a volume that seems to belong more to the literary landscape of the English renaissance than to the literal topography of Interregnum England. As Piscator, the fisherman, Walton purveys in dialogue form a strange store of knowledge, never straying far, however, from his two loves of angling and poetry. For Walton, fishing is not a solitary sport; fishermen belong to a separate order of mankind, characterized by their "*quietnesse*, and *vertue*." "I would you were a brother of the Angle," Piscator says to Coridon, "for a companion that is cheerful and free from swearing and scurrilous discourse, is worth gold. I love such mirth as does not make friends ashamed to look upon one another next morning. . . ." Walton wrote this inscription to Mrs. Dorothy Wallop from Farnham Castle, the seat of the Bishop of Winchester, George Morley, with whom he had lived since 1662. Morley was the "Friend whom I reverence, and ought to obey" under whose roof Walton wrote his *Life of Mr. Richard Hooker* and *Life of Mr. George Herbert*.

For Mrs Wallop. I think I did some years past, send yo^{u} a booke of Angling: This is printed since and I think better; And, because nothing that I can pretend a tytell too, can be too good for yo^{u}: pray accept of this also, from me that am really, Madam yo^{ur} most affectionate Friend; And, most humble servant Izaak Walton. farnham castell Decem. 19°. 1678.

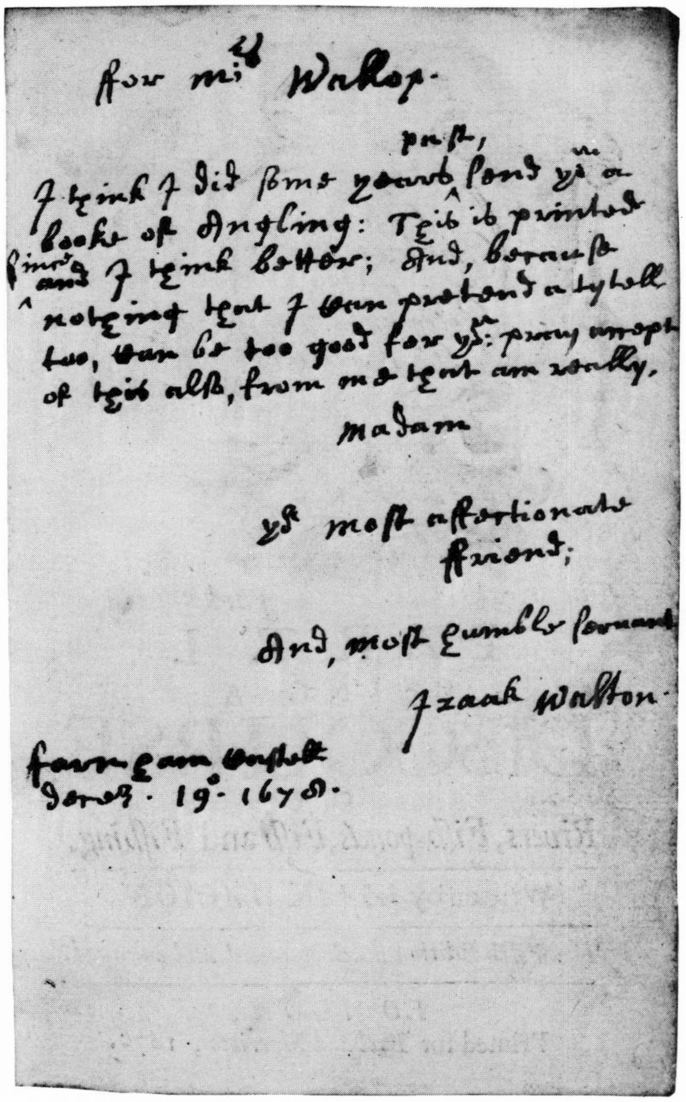

For Mrs Wallop.

I think I did some years past, send yu a booke of Angling: This is printed since and I think better; And, because nothing that I can pretend a tytell to, can be too good for yu: pray accept of this also, from me that am really,

Madam

yr most affectionate friend;

And, most humble servant

Izaak Walton.

Farnham Castle Decr. 19. 1678.

Sir Thomas Browne
1605–1682

Autograph letter signed, dated Norwich, 27 October 1658, to William Dugdale. 3 pp. 303 x 192 mm. From the Collection of Mr. Roger W. Barrett.

In 1658, the year he wrote this letter to William Dugdale on the subject of burial mounds, Thomas Browne published his *Hydriotaphia, Urne-Buriall.* There he explained a small part of his interest in the graves of antiquity: "to keep men out of their Urnes," he wrote, "and discourse of humane fragments in them, is not impertinent unto our profession." For more than twenty years Browne had been the local doctor in Norwich, and he continued his practice until his death in 1682. A skilled antiquarian and naturalist, he first acquired fame in 1642 when *Religio Medici*, a very personal and broadminded account of his beliefs, was published in an unauthorized edition. Browne's interests were wide-ranging, but always returned to a humane and ethical application of his learning, and the charm and flexibility of his personality are fully preserved in his superb prose style. Dugdale and Browne exchanged several letters in 1658 and 1659, primarily on antiquarian topics. Though they shared a love of scholarship, the results of their labors could hardly have been more different. Dugdale recorded funereal data, but Browne makes "the dead to live"; for a calm wonder at the yet undiscovered seems to permeate his antiquarian writings: "That great Antiquity *America* lay buried for thousands of years; and a large part of the earth is still in the Urne unto us."

Manuscripts and letters by Sir Thomas Browne are principally in the British Library and in the Bodleian Library.

[Starting on second page, line 4:] And for such an attempt there will not want encouragement; since a like mount was opened in the dayes of Henrie the eighth upon Barrham downe, in Kent, under the care of Mr Thomas Digges, and the charges of Sr Christopher Hales, as is recorded by Thomas Twinus a learned man of that countrie./ [from margin] de rebus Albionicis/ Sub incredibili terræ acervo urna cinere ossiumque magnorum fragmentis plena, cum galeis clypeis æreis et ferreis, rubigine fere consumptis inusitatæ magnitudinis eruta est. Sed nulla inscriptio, nomen nullum, testimonium tempus aut fortunam exponebat. And not long since (as Camden delivereth) in two of the mounts of Barklowe hills in Essex, being leavied, there were found three broughes containing broken bones.

Some men considering the place might be apt to suspect that these hills of your observation in the lowe and fenny parts, might be raised to secure the people and cattell in great inundations: very commodious in such exigencies. But I rather accept them in the intensions before expressed, and especially as sepulchrall monuments: which seemes to [deletion] mee a noble and safe way to conserve the ashes or bones of the ~~deceased~~ dead, and beyond the securitie of tombs or mechanicall preservations./ Sr Your very Respectfull freind and Servant Thomas Browne. Norwich. Octob 27 1658

of the Gyrvij or fenne inhabitants; for that there were princes and mightie men among them, you cannot doubt from severall records, or while you reade of Tombert prince of the south Gyrvij, whose wife Audrie married the King of Northumberland, and whose name is yet famous in these and other parts.

How ever probable it is that this part of England hath beene the seat of many notable exployts; as evidently recorded from actions since the Normans; from some account of Danes, and Saxons; and probably of the Romans, in their conquests of the Britans, and their owne civil dissentions; this being a fast, and retiring place in all ages. Nor wholely improbable that the dust of Boadicea the famous Queene of the Iceni may lye about these parts. For ~~in~~ ~~her~~ in her speech before the Battayle, shee encouraged the

Dion in Nerone: ~~Romans~~ Britans that if the day went against them, they would retire into the fennes, where the enemie could neither take nor finde them; and that they should be able to swimme over those rivers, and waters which the Romans could hardly passe wth boates. And therefore after her overthrowe by the Romans, shee may be well concei= ved to have retraited into these parts; where not long survivinge the Britans honorably interred her; although

πολυτελως ἐθαψαν not after this hilly or submontaneous sepulture.

But of these hills there can be noe cleare and assured decision, without ocular exploration, by cutting through one of them, either directly or crosswise; for so with lesser charge discouerie might be made of what is under them, and the intension of their erection.

For if they were raised for remarkable and eminent boundaries, then at their foundations may be found the lasting substances of half burnt bones of beasts, of potsheards, tiles, brickes,

de conditionibus agrorum. Lime, or coales, according to the description of Siculus Flaccus, and the event in that picked hill digged up in hope of treasure, neare Lilborne in Northamptonshire; where nothing

Cambden. was found but coales.

If urnes ~~beset~~ contayning ashes be found, they were erected by Romans before the period of urne-buriall, or that the custome of burying the dead expired. If by Romans after that terme, Inscriptions, swords sheilds and Armes may ~~possibly~~ probably distinguish them./

If by Saxons or Danes, discouerie may be ~~made~~ probable from the fashion of their armes, the bones of horses, armour, and other distinguishing substances, buried with them.

And for such an attempt there will not want encouragement; since a like mount was opened in the dayes of Henrie the eighth upon Barham downe, in Kent, under the care of Mr Thomas Digges, and the charges of Sr Christopher Hales,

De rebus Albionicis. as is recorded by Thomas Twinus a learned man of that countrie. Sub incredibili terra acervo urna cinere ossiumque fragmentis magnorum ~~plena~~; cum galea clypeis aereis et ferreis, rubigine fere consumptis insolitae magnitudinis eruta est. sed nulla inscriptio, nomen nullum, testimonium tempus aut fortunam exponebat. And not long since (as Camden deliv= ereth) in two of the mounts of Barklowe hills in Essex, being leavied, there were found three troughes conteyning broken bones.

Some men considering the place might be apt to suspect that these hills of your observation in the lowe and fenny parts, might be raised to secure the people and cattell in great inundations: very commodious in such exigencies. But I rather accept them in the intensions before expressed, and especially as sepulchrall monuments: which seemes to ~~be~~ mee a noble and safe way to con= serve the ashes or bones of the ~~deceased~~ dead, and beyond the securities of tombs or mechanicall preservations./

Sr

Your very respectfull friend and servant

Thomas Browne

Norwich. Octob 27 1658

39

Sir William Dugdale
1605–1686

Autograph letter signed, dated 19 April 1652, to William Boothe. 1 p. 272 x 160 mm. MA 1346 (92).

The antiquarian spirit draws upon many emotional sources—the love of local topography, family heritage, a lifetime's habitation—but it is quickened by fear of radical change. This may be the reason that no century has produced a greater body of antiquarian literature than the seventeenth, which was torn apart by religious dissension, the beheading of Charles I, and the English civil war. The appearance of the first part of William Dugdale and Roger Dodsworth's *Monasticon Anglicanum*, a history of English monasteries, during Cromwell's protectorate is a remarkable sign of the connection between social upheaval and the conservative goal of the antiquary: "to preserve the memory of what is of soe great ornament to our countrye." Dugdale, who combined his antiquarian zeal with several heraldic offices (when such offices were required), lived for nearly sixty years at Blythe Hall near Coleshill in Warwickshire. During that time he turned to many historical projects, but the best of them was a history of his own county, *The Antiquities of Warwickshire* (1656). Dugdale rendered his greatest service to the royalty of England by proclaiming Charles II at Coleshill in May 1660, marking a restoration of order and continuity. In this letter to William Boothe, Dugdale inquires about a problem in determining the validity of a local title, and he offers to divert Boothe "for two or three houres in observing ye track of an old Romane way, wch cutts over the countrey from Derby by Whichnoure-bridge. . . ."

Worthy Sr The good affection wch you beare to Antiquityes, and faire approbation of my labours in that ꝑticular worke relating to this county, emboldens me to trouble you now wth these lines, Whereby I intreate you, if your interest wth Sr Thomas Holt be such as that you thinke he will rellish the motion well, to get me a resolution to these inclosed Queres

I finde (amongst my notes from Records) that Sr William Bagot who was a very potent man in R.2 time has gott an intrest in Aston and Dudston, but I doubt much whithere it were by a good title or not; soe that Margerie the widow to Walter Holt was constrayned, the better to protect her right, to passe it out of her selfe unto John of Gaunt Duke of Lancaster; And that, afterwards, the same Sr William Bagot and William Holt (who was one of ye sonnes of Walter) came to an Agreem^{t} by referring that difference to ye Arbitration of Edward Duke of Yorke and Richard Beauchamp Earle of Warwick. This William was ye Kings servant in some speciall [illegible deletion] place for in 1°.H.4 the king calls him dilectus armiger noster. . . .

Worthy Sr

The good affection wch you beare to Antiquityes, and faire approbation of my labours in that particular worke relating to this county, emboldens me to trouble you now wth these lines, whereby I intreate you, if your interest wth Sr Thomas Holt be such as that you thinke he will rellish the motion well, to get me a resolution to those inclosed Queres.

I finde (amongst my notes from Records) that Sr Willm Bagot who was a very potent man in R. 2 time had gott an interest in Aston and Dudston, but I doubt much whether it were by a good title or not; soe that Margerie the widow to Walter Holt was constrayned, the better to protect her right, to passe it out of her selfe unto John of Gaunt Duke of Lancaster; And that, afterwards, the same Sr Willm Bagot and Willm Holt (who was one of ye sonnes of Walter) came to an Agreemt by referring that difference to ye Arbitration of Edward Duke of Yorke and Richard Beauchamp Earle of Warwicke. This Willm was ye Kings servant in some speciall place for in 1o. H. 4 the King calls him dilectus armiger noster.

The vulgar opinion (as I have often observed) is, that Sr Thomas Holt's gentility is but of a late edition; in wch errour I have rectified many; and shall be able to discover, from uncontroulable authorityes, that his ancestoures, for divers descents, have had eminent imployments in their times.

I am now going for London, where, if you be ye next Terme, I will wayte on you, and acquaint you how farr I have allready proceeded in my worke. I have a good minde after I returne, wch perhaps may be about 3 months hence, to take ye veiw of Bermingham in perspective (as I have done Kenilworth castle and Warwicke wch I thinke I showed you) and of Sr Thomas Holts house, soe as ye Church of Aston may be brought wthin the same, wch, wth ye trees and some ordinary houses, would sett it of very finely.

I perceive by the ruine of all the late Kings great houses what we may iustly feare in relation to private persons; and therefore am desirous to preserve the memory of what is of soe great ornament to our countrye. I have much more to say, wch, till I have the happinesse to see you, shall be respighted; for if you be not in London I will, some day, accompany Mr Dilke my neighbour to you, and desire your patience for two or three houres in observing ye tract of an old Romane way, wch cutts over the countrey from Derby by Whichnoure-bridge and soe, leaving Lichfeild on the right hand, passes by Little Aston over Sutton parke, and ye Colefeild, and coming over Tame, not farr from Aston Church, runnes up to Dudston, and, being for the most part thwarted by inclosures, goeth at length to Alcester in this county, wch was the seate of a Romane colony. I rest.

Your very humble servant

19o Apr: 1652

Willm Dugdale

40

EDMUND WALLER
1606–1687

Autograph letter signed, undated but written ca. 1657, to William Cavendish, third Earl of Devonshire. 3 pp. 200 x 152 mm.

For the poets of Dryden's and Pope's generations, Waller was the laureate of amorous verse and a master of "sweetness" and the Roman virtue, *rotunditas versorum*. Within a very short time, his particular talent had become a critical catchword and soon a cliché. Little of Waller is still read; only his song "Goe lovely Rose" and a handful of other poems have retained their currency. This letter, written to the Earl of Devonshire, records his frustration with the Committee of Trade, of which he had been a member since 1655. That he was allowed to reenter the political world during the Interregnum is a sign of his interest with the protector, Oliver Cromwell. In 1643 Waller had been implicated in a plot, which still bears his name, to seize the defenses of London on behalf of Charles I, then at war with Parliament. The plot was discovered, Waller imprisoned and—after naming his co-conspirators and paying a fine of 10,000 pounds (which he was well able to afford)—banished from England. He left the country in 1644; his first volume of poetry was published the following year, with this note: "Thus [these poems] go abroad unsophisticated, and like the present condition of the Author himselfe they are expos'd to the wide world, to travell, and try their fortunes. . . ." Pardoned by the House of Commons in 1651, Waller returned to England and his home at Beaconsfield in Buckinghamshire.

[all I have left to] hope for is, that either y^{r} Lo^{p} will put of this voyage untill another yeare, or that your return will be so speedy that I may yett see you in the country before the rigor of winter drive us all to London. Mr Martin tells me he will write all the newes & truly by discours with him I found he knewe more than I doe, all mens expectations being bent upon the approaching parlm^{t}: as that wch must either settle the state or leave us in despayr of ever seeing ~~us~~ it settled: (My Lord) I beseech you lett me have the assurance of being retained in y^{r} memory & favour in y^{r} absence by receaving the honour of some com̄ands from you wch shall be carefully obeid by (My Lord) Y^{r} Lo^{ps} most obedient servant E: Waller

hope for is, that either yr
Lord will put of this voyage
untill another yeare, or that
your return will be so speedy,
that I may yett see you in
the country before the rigor
of winter drives vs all to
London: Mr Martin tells
me he will write all the newes
& truly by discourse with him
I found he knewe more then
I doe, all mens expectation
being bent upon the ap-
proaching parlt. as that
wch must either settle the
state or leave vs in despaye
of ever seeing it settled:
My Lord I beseech you lett
me have the assurance of being
retained in yr memory & favor
in yr absence by receaving the hono

of your commands for you wch shall be
carefully obeid by My Lady
yr Lops most obedient servant E: Waller

John Milton
1608–1674

Manuscript of "Paradise Lost," Book I, in the hand of an amanuensis, dictated by Milton, probably ca. 1665. 33 pp. 200 x 150 mm. MA 307.

Without question, this is the most important British literary manuscript in the Morgan Library, for it is the sole remnant of Milton's manuscript of *Paradise Lost*, dictated by him to an amanuensis, corrected under his supervision and used as copy by his printer, Samuel Simmons. It bears the imprimatur—which authorized the printing of the poem—of Thomas Tomkyns, a chaplain to Gilbert Sheldon, Archbishop of Canterbury. Throughout the years of his blindness, Milton employed several scribes, drawn from among the numbers of his students, family and friends. Although the name of the person who prepared this copy is unknown, the hand of Edward Phillipps, Milton's nephew, has been identified in some of the corrections made on his uncle's behalf. A draft of *Paradise Lost* was almost certainly completed by the summer of 1665 when the plague drove Milton out of London and he gave a friend the opportunity to read it in manuscript. Two years later, after London had begun to recover from the Great Fire, it was printed in ten books, and in 1674 it was published in a revised edition of twelve books.

In Book I, Milton reveals the "dismal scituation wast & wilde" into which God cast Satan and his angelic army. Satan and Bëëlzebub recruit the pride of the downfallen horde and, having resolved on war with the Almighty, they gather for a military council. Satan resolves to reign in Hell, and, in the second of the great epic similes in *Paradise Lost*, his shield is compared to the moon and "His legions" to "Autumnall leaves that strow the brooks/ In Vallombrosa."

[the broad circumference]/ Hung on his shoulders like the moon whose orb/ Through optick glasse the Tuscan Artist views/ At evening from the top of Fesole,/ Or in Valdarno, to descry new lands,/ Rivers or Mountaines in her spotty globe./ His speare, to equall which the tallest pine/ Hewn on Norwegian hills, to be the mast/ Of some great Ammirall, were but a wand,/ He walkt with, to support uneasy steps/ Over the burning Marle, not like those steps/ On Heavens azure; and the torrid clime/ Smote on him sore besides, vaulted with fire;/ Na'thlesse hee so endur'd, till on the beach/ Of that inflamed sea, hee stood and calld/ His legions, Angell form's, ~~that~~ who lay intrans'~~t~~'t/ Thick as Autumnall leaves that strow the brooks/ In Vallombrosa, where th'Etrurian shades/ High overarcht imbowre: or scatterd sedge/ Afloat when with fierce winds Orion arm'd/ Hath vext the red-sea coast, whose waves orethrew/ Busiris and his Memphian chivalry/ While with perfidious hatred they persu'd/ The sojourners of Goshen, who beheld/ From the safe shore thir floating carcasses/ [And broken chariot wheeles.]

Hung on his shoulders like the moon whose orb
Through optick glasse the Tuscan Artist views
At evening from the top of Fesole,
Or in Valdarno, to descry new lands,
Rivers or Mountaines in her spotty globe.
His speare, to equall which the tallest pine
Hewn on Norwegian hills, to be the mast
Of some great Ammirall, were but a wand,
He walkt with, to support uneasy steps
Over the burning Marle, not like those steps
On Heavens azure; and the torrid clime
Smote on him sore besides, vaulted with fire;
Nathlesse hee so endur'd, till on the beach
Of that inflamed sea, hee stood and call'd
His legions, Angell form's, ~~that~~ who lay intrans't
Thick as Autumnall leaves that strow the brooks
In Vallombrosa, where th' Etrurian shades
High overarcht imbowre: or scattered sedge
Afloat when with fierce winds Orion arm'd
Hath vext the red-sea coast, whose waves orethrew
Busiris and his Memphian chivalry
While with perfidious hatred they pursu'd
The sojourners of Goshen, who beheld
From the safe shore their floating carcasses

Sir John Suckling
1609–1642

Autograph letter signed, undated but written ca. April–May 1640, to Viscount Conway. 1 p. 318 x 201 mm. From the Collection of Mrs. Donald F. Hyde.

A friend of Carew, Lovelace and Davenant, and a royal favorite, Sir John Suckling represents all that was brilliant, witty and foolhardy about the Court of Charles I. His reputation as a poet depends only on a small group of poems, published posthumously in *Fragmenta Aurea* (1646), and several plays; but he managed to invest his works with the same aura of high romance as he did his life. Staging his play *Aglaura* "At the Private House in *Black Fryars*" in 1637, he distinguished himself by fantastic expenditures for costumes; the same was true when he brought a troop of horse to Scotland in defense of the King in 1639: his men came clad in "white doubletts and scarlett breeches," a gesture that provoked some sarcasm. In this letter to Lord Conway, General of the Horse, Suckling excuses his temporary absence from a muster of troops called for May in preparation for the Second Bishops' War. His unfortunate performance in both Bishops' Wars did not daunt his ardor on behalf of the royal cause. He contended that for the King to "lie still now, would, at the best, shew but a calmnesse of mind, not a magnanimity. . . ." Suckling's zeal betrayed his common sense: he became involved in the "army plot"—an attempt to seize the army on Charles's behalf and free Strafford from the Tower—then fled the country, and is believed to have committed suicide in Paris in 1642.

My Lord. By the Letter I receavd from you, I find how much y^r. L^{dip} imitates the great and highest Agent, who is never so buisied wth governing heaven and the nobler parts of the world, as that hee neglects the Lower and Lesse Considerable. I shall expect (my Lord) y^r Commands for our march to Durham, and must beseech y^r Lordship to believe, that I had not staid for those Summons, but had been as Earlie in paing my respects, as anie, had not Sicknesse taken me betwixt the Stirrop and the Saddle. I hope it will have the g[ood] Manners, to Leave me, when you shall have occasion to use mee. if it should not, my Will (my Lord) shall Side wth my mind, and in spite of all Opposition, show, that, you have not an humbler Servant anie where, then Jo: Suckling

My Lord.

By the Letter I receaued from you, I find how much yr Lp imitates that great and highest Agent, who is neuer so bussied wth gouerning heauen and the nobler parts of the world, as that hee neglects the Lower and Lesse Considerable. I shall expect (my Lord) yr Commands for our march to Durham, and must beseech yr Lordship to beleeue, that I had not staid for those Summons, but had been as Earlie in paying my respects, as anie, had not sicknesse taken me betwixt the Stirrop and the Saddle. I hope it will haue the manners, to Leaue me, when you shall haue occasion to vse mee. If it should not, my Will (my Lord) shall side wth my minde, and in spite of all Opposition shew, that you haue not a humbler seruant anie where then,

Jo: Suckling

Edward Hyde, first Earl of Clarendon 1609–1674

Autograph notes entitled "Papers of the Army," unsigned and undated. 2 pp. 338 x 231 mm.

Beginning his *History of the Rebellion and Civil Wars in England* (published posthumously from 1702 to 1704), Clarendon looked over the prospect he intended to describe and called it "this mass of confusion now before us." Confusion seems to have been the element in which Clarendon thrived, for having grown accustomed to the turmoil of civil war and exile, he painfully discovered with the rest of the nation "How strangely active are the arts of Peace" when Charles II was restored to the throne. The rewards of power, which the arts of war had consolidated, fell quickly around Clarendon after 1660; second only to Charles, he was the most powerful man in the kingdom. His role in the Restoration had been primarily a conservative one—to preserve the traditions of common law and constitutional monarchy—and he used his power soberly, yet the isolation of his position at court left him open to an unwarranted but entirely natural amount of suspicion and envy. Eventually, even Charles began to seek his removal from office. In 1667, after having served as Lord Chancellor since the Restoration, Clarendon was forced to relinquish the seals of office and was impeached by Parliament. On 27 August 1667, John Evelyn visited him and "found him in his bed Chamber very Sad: The Parliament had accused him, & he had enemies at Court, especially the boufoones & Ladys of Pleasure. . . ." Two months later, Clarendon left England for an embittered exile in France, where he died.

One of the sole benefits of his banishment was the time needed to organize and write his *History of the Rebellion*, a copious and often meandering account of the troubles of the mid-seventeenth century. Begun "by the express command of King Charles the First," the *History* combines elements from Clarendon's autobiography and a much earlier narrative of events during the civil war. The manuscript shown here contains notes taken probably from army records. Nearly all of Clarendon's private papers are in the Bodleian Library, including the manuscript of *The History of the Rebellion*, which, like this manuscript, is in a hand best described as "small, cramped, and indistinct."

I could not now falsify my selfe, but by absentinge my selfe at this tyme, rather then by my presence to give any shadow or countenance of the authority of Parliam.^t to such apparent violations therof, nether can the omission of a circumstance, or some formality in the adiournement of the house (when though torne and misled it cannot meete and sitt in any sorte as a Parliam.^t) to any preiudice to the future meetinges and proceedinges therof, when it may meete and sitt agayne as a free Parliam.^t pp. 108. Speakers declaration . . .

Passages of the Army.

I could not now satisfy my selfe, but by absenting my selfe at this tyme, rather then by my presence to give any shadow or countenance of the authority of Parliament to such apparent violations thereof, rather then the omission of a circumstance, or some formality in the adiournment of the house (when through force and violence it cannot meete and sitt in any forme as a Parliament) for any prejudice to the future meetings and proceedings thereof, when it may meete and sitt againe as a free Parliament. pa. 108. Speakers declaration

— Of the Proposalls —— Though all circumstances necessary to be determined in an actuall settlement, be not so fully & perfectly expressed, as upon the treaty intended, they might speedily have bene, yet all men may see and understand in these, the effects & bottome of our desires, &c. in the establishing of his Maty & others to their rights pa. 111.

— Of the Militia of London —— That in a season this trust should be taken out of the hands, and putt into the hands of others &. That this should be ~~forced~~ pressed, and in a manner forced upon the parliament with such importunity from the Common Councell, &c. That they would not be satisfied &c. these things ministred great cause of suspicion pa. 122.

We have thought fitt in the name of the Army to declare, that all such members of either house of Parliament as are already with the Army for the security of their persons, & for the ends aforesayd, are forced to absent themselves from Westm. that wee shall hold and esteeme them as persons in whome the publique trust of the kingdome is still remaining, though they cannot for the present sitt as a Parliament with freedome and safety at Westm. & by whose advice & councells, wee desire to governe our selves &c. Declare against that late new choyce of a Speaker by some gentlemen at Westm. &. there is no free or legall Parliament sitting &c. the votes of the few Lords & gentlemen at Westm. ought not to be submitted to. &c. 127.

It being our chiefe aime to settle peace with truth and righteousnesse throughout the kingdome, that none may be oppressed in his iust freedome & liberties, much lesse the parliament it selfe, which things being duly settled, wee shall be as ready also to assert unto the king his iust rights and authority. pa. 128.

The house of Commons have not only not concurred with the Lords, in any of these things, but rather seeme to have cast them aside &c. the safety & immunity of the Speakers, & those so faithfull members that were driven away by violence, & the immunity of the Army in advancing to London, (which hath bene acknowledged with publique thanksgiving to god for it,) is slighted & exposed to question pa. 140. 141.

If any of those members, who during the absence of the Speakers & the rest of the members of both houses did sitt & vote in the pretended houses then remaining at Westm. or shall hereafter intrude themselves to sitt in Parliament before &c. wee cannot any longer suffer the same, but shall do that right to the Speakers & members of both houses &c as to take some speedy & effectuall course &c.

Thomas Killigrew
1612–1683

Autograph letter signed, dated 12 November 1649, to Sir Robert Long.
7 pp. 301 x 210 mm.

The court of Charles II nourished two kinds of rakes: the sharp, keen-edged variety, represented by the Earl of Rochester, and the sturdier, bluff old Cavalier, represented by Thomas Killigrew. When the two collided, as they did one evening when Rochester struck Killigrew in the presence of the King, Charles was apt to side with the former. Nonetheless, he had rewarded Killigrew well for his services to the Stuart line. Having followed Henrietta Maria to France in 1644, Killigrew served the young Prince Charles when he escaped to France several years later, first as the purveyor of his allowance and then as a diplomat after his young master was crowned King Charles II in January 1649. Killigrew was long suspected of riotous living while representing the King in Venice and Turin, but the diplomatic papers which have survived, including this letter to Sir Robert Long, a member of Charles's Privy Council, have disproved this allegation. The ship that carried Charles II back to England in 1660 also carried Killigrew; and upon their return to London, Charles granted him a royal patent to build and manage the theatre that eventually became Drury Lane. In 1662 he succeeded Sir Henry Herbert as Master of the Revels. Killigrew also wrote several plays that are now best remembered for their indecency. The most interesting of these is one called *Thomaso the Wanderer* (ten acts in all) written about 1654 and never acted, though Aphra Behn staged a version of it entitled *The Rover*. As its title implies, the play is rather fantastic autobiography, the adventures of a cavalier abroad in the service of his King.

[Starting with line 7:] Pray Sur propoes to his Magey the conferming theis men, in thar kindnes to him, which may be dun with his letters to each of them, & will not be lost time to keip suh [such] a resserfe of frintes aginst we haef ues of them. If you shall thinke fit to conssell his Mag. to this pray doe me the honure to let me send the Packet to them, in which letters, if you please to take notis of me, as one that gaef the good caracter of this plaes and persones, twill advanes my intrest, and consequentley, his Mag- Servis. in enney suh [such] propossissians as you shall thinke fit to command me to propoes in this cort, till his Magey be abell to mentane, an agent heare which if the desine of Willa Franca goes one, will be verey nessessarey. ...

and of am confident, thay ar reddy to serve his Maje
in the same nature, if it ware proposed, but i hart
noe commission but to thanke them for what was
past. yet i dare say when ouer shipes ar heare
if thare shud fall out a nessessity for a good
sum could not be denied for his maj. ocasions.

For Letters to them

Pray sur propos to his Maj. the conserning the
men, in thar kindness to him, which may be dun
with his letters to each of them, will not be lost
time to keip such a ressente of frinds aginst
we hart uss of them. At you shall thinke
fit to consult his Maj. to this pray doe me
the honour to let me send the packet to
them, in which letters, if you please to take
notis of me, as one that gave the good carackter
of this place and persons, will advance my
interest, and consequently, his maj. servis.
in every such propositions as you shall thinke
fit to command me to propos in this court, till his
Majty. be abell to mentane, an agent heare

An Agent nesessary at Turin

which if the desine of Villa Franca goes one
will be very nessessary.

A Letter to Sr H. Hyde for a sum of mony to be lent him.

Sur i hart in my jurnny, mead aquantance with
Sur Harry Hied, and if you please to wright to
him in your next, he will most willingly
out of his sallery, furnish me with such a sum
as you shall thinke fit to alow towards my subsistance;
i shud not desire such ordinary way to life, but
that i am yet absolutely unfurnished of every,
and at Turin, a bill of 60 pistolls from Liones
is refused, and it not lost becaus Mr. Foster procured
it, yet, for the pressent i am to sinke such
another blow will make mis Resident his Magesty
~~[illegible]~~ fort lost

Sur you knew, my lo frinds, ar youre umbell sarvants,
and therfor i wright them noe particulars of my
bisnes, but refer them to what you thinke fit to
aquant them with, i meane Mr. Tho. Elliot and
deare Progers, sur though i hart little bisnes yet
i hart great enemys which in my absence gives
me great feares but my confidence is in my frinds
representing of my intensions, to his Magestys
hey goodnes, and Justis; i shall ever bild upon,
and beg youre favour and pardon for this tedious letter
and ill hand. as sone as i cum to Venis ill
to the writting further and then in a fare
hand tell you i am most faithfully

Youre umbell sarvant.
Thomas Killigrew

Sur I hart thought better of it and sins i can
doe his Majy noe better servis at this time i hart resolved
to spare him the unnessesion of a letter in my ill
hand and unbly beg my duty may pressented by youre
selfe. Tho: Killigrew

Sur sins i wright this letter i have had sum discours with Madam
and her ministers conserning the marchant whom i recommend
to you in this letter Mr. Dudley and i finde him so ill there
opinion as will not be fit for this imployment not for
want of honesty caparsity but as a person that has
disgusted this court yet will be very usefull to his
Maj. in privat.

The Secritary has not sent me his Majty letter
as apromist me but the next post you shall have it
this is going and i am loth to loss the ocassion
to tell you i am your most obedient servant
i shall hart letters from Madame Royal at the duke
to Flanders in favor of my selfe and bisnes in that court
and they may be usefull for they are [illegible] a suddain

maniage betwix the Prince Duke's sun and the
Second dauter of Savoy. ones agin i am youre
i hart given the Queen an acount of my bisnes in
this place Madame required me to doe it and i
hart sent her Maj. a coppy of theis propossitions
and the answer to them inclosed in a letter to
my Lord Armin By Chappell. her Maj has given very good
caracters of our Master and his Brother
and his ministers and has bin very kind to me
pray sur when a way to cut let his Majty
take notis of it to him.

yours. T.K.

45

Richard Crashaw
1612?–1649

Manuscript, partly autograph, of "A Hymn to the name and honour of the renowned S. Teresia" and "An Apologie," undated but written ca. 1638. 12 pp. 223 x 170 mm. MA 1385.

Crashaw's life is an emblem of the religious polarities at play in the seventeenth century. He was born in London, son of William Crashaw, a poet and forceful anti-Catholic controversialist, and he died in Loreto where he held a position at the Cathedral of the Santa Casa, the site of an important shrine of the Virgin Mary. Between these extremes, he took a degree at Cambridge, preached with great success at Little St. Mary's there, and became an intimate of the Anglican community established by Nicholas Ferrar at Little Gidding. Aware that Parliamentary forces would not tolerate his High Anglican convictions, Crashaw, like many others, traveled first to Leyden and then to Paris, where he became a close friend of the poet Cowley and was materially assisted by Cowley's employer, Queen Henrietta Maria. She provided him with a letter of introduction to the Pope, remarking that Crashaw "by the good example of his life has greatly edified all who have conversed with him." Even before his conversion to Catholicism, he felt a special devotion to St. Teresa, whose vision of a flaming heart seemed to symbolize the passionate intensity of his own religious desire, a quality amply reflected in his ecstatic verse. Shown here is the only complete manuscript of his most famous poem, "A Hymn to the name and honour of the renowned S. Teresia," the title page of which is believed to be in his autograph. This poem first appeared in Crashaw's *Steps to the Temple, Sacred Poems, With other Delights of the Muses* (London, 1646). It is bound into a copy of *Las Obras De La S. Madre Teresa* (1630).

The only other autograph known to be in Crashaw's hand is a brief dedication in Latin in the British Library (Add. MS. 40176).

A HYMN to the name and honour of the renowned S. TERESIA Foundres of the Reformation of the Order of barefoote Carmelites; A Woman for Angelicall height of Contemplation, for Masculine courage of Performance, more then a woman. Who yet a Child outranne Maturity, & durst plott a Martyrdome; but was reserved by God to dy the living death of the life of his love. of whose great impressions as her noble heart had most high experiment, so hath she in her life most heroically exprest them, in her Spirituall posterity most fruitfully propagated them, and in these her heavnly Writings most sublimely, most sweetly taught them to ye world.

A HYMN

to the name and honour of
the renowned

S. TERESIA

Foundres of the Reformation of the Order of
barefoote Carmelites;

A Woman
for Angelicall height of Contemplation,
for Masculine courage of Performance,
more then a woman.

Who yet a Child
outranne Maturity,
& durst plott a Martyrdome;
but was reserved by God
to dy the liuing death of the life of his loue.
of whose great impressions
as her noble heart had most high experiment,
so hath she in her life most heroically exprest them,
in her Spirituall posterity most fruitfully propagated them,
and in these her heaunly Writings
most sublimely, most sweetly
taught them to ye world.

Love thou art absolute sole Lord
Of life & death. To prove the word
Wee'l need to goe to none of ye all
Those

46

Jeremy Taylor
1613–1667

Autograph letter signed, dated Portmore [Ireland], 10 February 1659, to John Evelyn. 1 p. 239 x 175 mm. MA 3383. Purchased as the gift of Mrs. W. Randolph Burgess.

The friendship between the diarist John Evelyn and Dr. Jeremy Taylor grew out of sympathetic religious and political opinions (both were Anglican and Royalist) and out of a common interest in science and antiquity. Evelyn thought of Taylor not only as "my Ghostly Father" but also as a "greate *Virtuoso*." Thanks to his abilities as a writer of sermons and the support of William Laud, Archbishop of Canterbury, Taylor rapidly ascended the ranks of the Anglican hierarchy until the English civil war interrupted his progress, as it did the progress of most divines. During an interval spent at Golden Grove in Wales, he wrote the two books that have preserved his memory throughout the following centuries: *The Rule and Exercises of Holy Living* (1650) and *The Rule and Exercises of Holy Dying* (1651). Together they form a complete manual of devotion. The long tradition of teaching man the Christian art of dying well reached its culmination in the latter volume. "I shall entertain you in a Charnel house," Taylor wrote in *Holy Dying*, "and carry your meditations awhile into the chambers of death, where you shall finde the rooms dressed up with melancholy arts, and fit to converse with your most retired thoughts. . . ." Advising Evelyn on his intended magnum opus, *Elysium Britannicum*, and consoling him for the illness of his son, Taylor wrote the letter shown here in both his capacities, as virtuoso and spiritual counselor.

Portmore, Febr: 10. 16$^{59}/_{60}$ Honourd & Deare S^r I receivd yours of Decemb^r 2. in very good time; but although it came to me before Christmas, yet it pleas'd God, about that time to lay his gentle hand upon me; for I had beene in the worst of our winter weather sent for to Dublin by our late Anabaptist Commissioners; & found the evil of it so great, that in my going I began to be ill; but in my returne had my ill redoubled & fixt; but it hath pleas'd God to restore my health; I hope ad Majorem Dei gloriam: and now that I can easily write, I returne you my very hearty thankes for your most obliging letter; & particularly for the enclosed. S^r, the apology you were pleas'd to send me I read both privately & heard it read publikely with no little pleasure, & satisfaction. The materials are worthy, & the dresse is cleane, & orderly & beauteous: & I wish that all men in the Nation were oblig'd to reade it twice; it is impossible but it must doe much benefit to those guilty persons to whom it is not impossible to repent, your character hath a great part of a worthy reward, that it is translated into a language in which it is likely to be read by very many beaux esprits. But that which I promise to my selfe as an excellent entertainement is your Elysium Britannicum: . . .

Portmore. Febr: 10. 16 59/60

Honourd & Deare Sr

I receiv'd yours of Decembr: 2. in very good time; but although it came to me before Christmas, yet it pleas'd God, about that time to lay his gentle hand upon me; for I had bene in the worst of our winter weather sent for to Dublin by our late Anabaptist Commissioners; & found the evil of it so great, that in my going I began to be ill; but in my returne had my ill redoubled & fixt; but it hath pleas'd God to restore my health; I hope ad Majorem Dei gloriam: and now that I can easily write, I returne you my very hearty thankes for your most obliging letter; & particularly for the enclosed. Sr, the apology you were pleas'd to send me I read both privately & heard it read publikely with no little pleasure, & satisfaction. The materials are worthy, & the dresse is cleane, & orderly & beauteous: & I wish that all men in the Nation were oblig'd to reade it twice; it is impossible but it must doe much benefit to those guilty persons to whom it is not impossible to repent, your character hath a great part of a worthy reward, that it is translated into a language in which it is likely to be read by very many beaux esprits. But that which I promise to my selfe as an excellent entertainement is your Elysium Britannicum: But Sr, being you intend it to the purposes of piety as well as pleasure; why doe you not rather call it, Paradisus then Elysium; since the word is us'd by the Hellenist Jewes to signify any place of spiritual & immaterial pleasures, & excludes not the material & secular. Sr, I know you are such a curieux & withal so diligent & inquisitive that not many things of the delicacy of learning relating to your subject can escape you; & therefore it would be great imprudence in me to offer my little mite to your already digested heaps. I hope ere long to have the honour to waite on you, & to see some parts & steps of your progression; & then if I see I can bring any thing to your building, though but haire & stickes, I shal not be wanting in expressing my readinesse to serve & to honour you, & to promote such a worke, then which, I thinke in the world you could not have chosen a more apt &, a more ingenious.

Sr, I doe really beare a share in your feares & your sorrowes, for your Deare boy. I doe & shal pray to God for him; but I know not what to say in such things; if God intends by these clouds to convey him & you to brighter graces & more illustrious glories respectively; I dare not with too much passion speake against the so great good of a person that is so Deare to me, & a child that is so Deare to you. But I hope that God will doe what is best: and I humbly beg of him to choose what is that best for you both. As soone as the weather & season of the spring gives leave, I intend by Gods permission to returne to England; & when I come to London, with the first to waite on you; for whom I have so great regards, & from whom I have receiv'd so many testimonies of a worthy friendship, & in whom I know so much worthinesse is deposited. Sr

I am most faithfully & Cordially

Your very affectionate & obliged servant Jer: Taylor.

47

Richard Baxter
1615–1691

Autograph manuscript, signed, of "A Preface opening the true state of the controversie . . . about the Churches Successive or Continued Visibility, & shewing where our Church was before Luther . . . ," dated 5 April 1664. 6 pp. 310 x 198 mm. MA 3384. Purchased as the gift of Mr. Haliburton Fales, 2nd, and Dr. Samuel W. Lambert, Jr.

Baxter's fifth point in the preface to his *Saints Everlasting Rest* (1649) is this: "Beware of extreams in the controverted points of Religion. When you avoid one Error, take heed you run not into another; specially if you be in heat of disputation or passion." The error of extremity prevailed in England throughout Baxter's life, and it is a tribute to his character and his principles that he was able to pass through the seventeenth-century maze of conscience without the imputation of false conformity and without blurring the clarity of his faith. Baxter contended that the "controverted points of Religion" are precisely those which have the least to do with the ethical teachings of the church and the essential truths of Christianity. Before his auditors at Kidderminster, before Cromwell and the Army, before Judge Jeffreys, he maintained the belief he voices in the manuscript shown here: "We protest before all the world that we owne no *Religion* but *Christianity*. . . ." This manuscript represents one of many times that Baxter was drawn into the heat of disputation, in this case by a Catholic who used the pseudonym W. Johnson (his real name seems to have been Terret). Johnson argued that while the Catholic church can demonstrate a direct lineal descent from St. Peter, the Protestant church has been "successively visible" only since Luther. Baxter refuted this argument by pointing out the divisions within the Catholic church itself and concluded, "Mr *Johnsons* Reply [to Baxter's first pamphlet on the subject] is merely a puddling in the waters of Church history . . . ." Apparently, this *Preface* was not published, presumably because Baxter learned of Johnson's death immediately after he received a copy of Johnson's *Reply*. This manuscript was written in Acton, Middlesex, where Baxter had retired after the passing of the Act of Uniformity in 1662.

Today, Baxter is remembered for *Reliquiæ Baxterianæ*, an autobiographical compilation, and his *Saints Everlasting Rest*, a masterpiece of religious prose which, as Baxter remarked, "dropt from my pen" and was intended to be "my own funeral Sermon."

A Preface opening the true state of the controversie between the Papists & the Protestants, about the Churches Successive or Continued Visibility, & shewing where our Church was before Luther ~~& giving the Reasons why we canot become Papists,~~ with a few words to Mr W. Johnsons Reply, & the Catholick Gentlemans provocation.

Having received this Book from the Reverend & Pious Author, to peruse, & im̃ediatly after received the tidings of his death, I saw there was no expectation of y^{t} review & last hand wch he intended; & I was very loth to be bold in any alterations of another mans work; And therfore ye clearer stating *of ye controversie, being the chiefe thing y^{t} I ꝑceived wanting, I shall here premise it as exactly as I can . . . .*

A Preface opening the true state of the controversie between the Papists
& the Protestants, about the Churches Succession or continued visibility, &
shewing where our Church was before Luther & giving the reasons why
we cannot become Papists, with a few words to m^r W. Johnsons Reply, & the
Catholick Gentlemans provocation. ||

Having received this Booke from the Reverend & Pious Author, to peruse, & immediatly
after received the tidings of his death, I saw there was no expectation of y^t revised
& last hand wch he intended, & I was very loth to be bold in any alterations of another
mans works; and therefore ye clearer stating of ye controversie, being the chiefe thing
y^t I deemed wanting, I shall here premise it as exactly as I can. ||
1° As to ye Name; 1° ye word Church is somtimes taken for ye whole, politically considered, y^t is ye Universall Kingdome of Christ, comprehending ye King & all ye subjects in Heaven & Earth. 2° somtimes
it is taken for ye whole Body in Heaven & Earth, as distinct from ye Head. 3° somtimes
it is taken for all y^t Part of ye Body wch is on Earth at once, with its relation to its Head
in Heaven. 4° somtimes it is taken for particular Congregations or Churches politically
considered, as including Officers & people. 5° Somtimes it is taken for ye same officers alone
as being ye nobler guiding part. 6° somtimes it is taken for a Community, or ye people
alone without their officers. And Here 7° somtimes it is taken only for reall serious beleevers. 8° somtimes
it is taken for all Professors of true beliefe, containing ye hypocrites with ye sincere. ||
2° As to ye Things, In ye Church there is considerable 1° The matter considered with its Disposition
Christ & Men. 2° The Disposition of ye Matter, & y^t is, 1° Before God, True Christianity. 2° Before
men, Professed Christianity. Or Thus either 1° in heart, or 2° in word only, in Covenant with Christ. ||
3° The Forme of ye whole Church, & y^t is, Monarchia absoluta, ex pleno Dominio, jure Redem-
ptionis, supposito jure Creationis: Christs absolute Monarchy, with plenary propriety, by Right
of Redemption, the Right of Creation being presupposed. It is a transcendent kind of Mo-
narchy, such as no meer Creature is capable of. This is ye Political forme. ||
4° The Integrall parts (ye Constituent being before mentioned, viz Christ ye Pars imperans, &
Christians ye Pars subdita): & these are 1° The minutest parts, y^t is, all individuall Christians or members; 2° The inferior politick or combined parts, & those are ye particular
Churches. The constituent parts, of w^ch [illegible] particular, are 1° the Pastors. 2° the flocks. ||
5° The Administration: wch is 1° Soveraigne by Christ. 1° In his Legislation. His 2° Judgment
[illegible] His execution of Judgm^t. 1° In rewards. 2° Punishm^t. 3° His Protection of his subjects.
2° The Administration of his officers over their severall flocks: wch are 1° Preaching the Gospel
2° Baptizing. 3° Prayer & praise. 4° Celebrating ye Sacram^t of Christs Body & blood. 5° Guiding ye flock. ||
6° The Adjuncts: As 1° Internall adjuncts. As ye purity of doctrine, worship, Sacram^ts, Discipline,
& members. 2° The Objective adjuncts, as Christ, Scripture, Heaven, & our soules, the matter of
eternall worship, objectively considered. 3° The Signes of ye Church. 4° The Circumstances: as
1° The Countryes in wch particular Churches are. 2° The Ages in wch they live. 3° Their prosperity. 4° Their Riches; ye favour of Princes; their humane honours & titles. 4° The publike
openness of their profession & worship. 5° Their persecutions & sufferings, & recesses. ||
The word [Visible] signifying y^t wch may be seene (not Visum y^t wch is seen) needeth no
distinguishing, save only as to ye persons whose sight ye Church as visible relateth to. ||
Now in w^t sense we Affirme or Deny ye Church to have bin still Visible, I shall tell you
in these propositions following. ||
Aff. Prop. 1° Christ the Churches Head & Monarch was visible to mortall men on earth. ||
2° Christ is now visible to ye better part of ye Church wch is glorified in Heaven. ||
3° Christ is, by unexpressible wayes of apparition, visible still to men on Earth when
he pleaseth to show himselfe: as he appeared after his Ascension to Stephen & Paul & John. ||
4° Mankind who is ye matter of y^t part of ye Church wch is on earth, is visible here. ||
5° Angels & blessed soules in Heaven, ye rest of ye matter, are there visible to each other.
6° The profession of ye Christian faith by Christians (wch is all o^r Religion) hath bin audible
& in writings & actions of worship visible, to those y^t were within sight & hearing
of them in all ages of ye Church till now. ||
7° There have bin particular Churches or Congregations for holy worship, in all ages
visible to those y^t were within sight of y^m. W^ch are to ye Church universall
as Corporations are to the Kingdome. ||
8° There have bin Pastors of these particular Churches in all ages, visible to those
that had the opportunity of seeing them, & in a remote sense to ye rest. ||

Abraham Cowley
1618–1667

Autograph letter signed, dated Paris, 1 January 1650, to Sir Robert Long. 3 pp. 307 x 193 mm.

Abraham Cowley was a poet of youthful genius: his first volume of verse, *Poetical Blossomes*, appeared when he was fifteen years old. He fulfilled the promise of these early years—not without some delay, however, for he, like all his generation, was overtaken by the English civil war, "that violent Publick storm which would suffer nothing to stand where it did, but rooted up every Plant, even from the Princely Cedars to me, the Hyssop." At Oxford he fell in with several members of the Royalist party and entered the service of Charles I. "He cypher'd and decypher'd with his own hand," wrote his biographer Thomas Sprat, "the greatest part of all the Letters that passed between their Majesties, and managed a vast Intelligence in many other parts . . . ." This letter to a fellow servant of the Queen is part of that "vast Intelligence"; here he provides information about the turbulent events in Paris during the Frondeur rebellion against Mazarin, principal regent during the minority of Louis XIV. Political intrigue was not wholly to Cowley's taste; much of his poetry is contemplative in nature (though *The Mistresse* [1647], comprised of "Love-Verses," was his most popular work). Throughout his life he expressed a desire "like to Covetousness" for "a small house and large Garden":

> Here let me careless and unthoughtful lying,
> Here the soft winds above me flying,
> With all their Wanton Boughs dispute,
> And the more tuneful Birds to both replying
> Nor be my self too Mute.

Other letters from Cowley to Long may be found in the Historical Society of Pennsylvania and among the Carte MSS in the Bodleian Library, Oxford. Nearly all of Cowley's private correspondence (especially that with his friend Thomas Sprat) has disappeared.

Sir, I am not ashamed to retract the advise I gave you y^t^ things in this place were soe near to a perfect settlement, since I followed the opinion of the gamesters, who upon some good fortune are often deceived in thinking the set their own before the last dealing. The Frondeurs whom they thought gasping, have already recovered strength enough to give them many new troubles, and the busines concerning the exclusion of the Prince of Conde, his Brother, and the Primier Presid^t^ as well as the Duke de Beauford the Coadiutour, and de Bruxelles, is still undecided, and draws soe into length, y^t^ it is thought the designe is to let the whole matter vanish by degrees away; In the mean time it is by the diligence of the Frondeurs infused into the people y^t^ the whole busines [is] an artifice contrived by y^e^ Pr. of Conde, and acted by some of his freinds, to ruine the Duke of Beauford and others, upon whom they thought to cast the envy of the fact . . . .

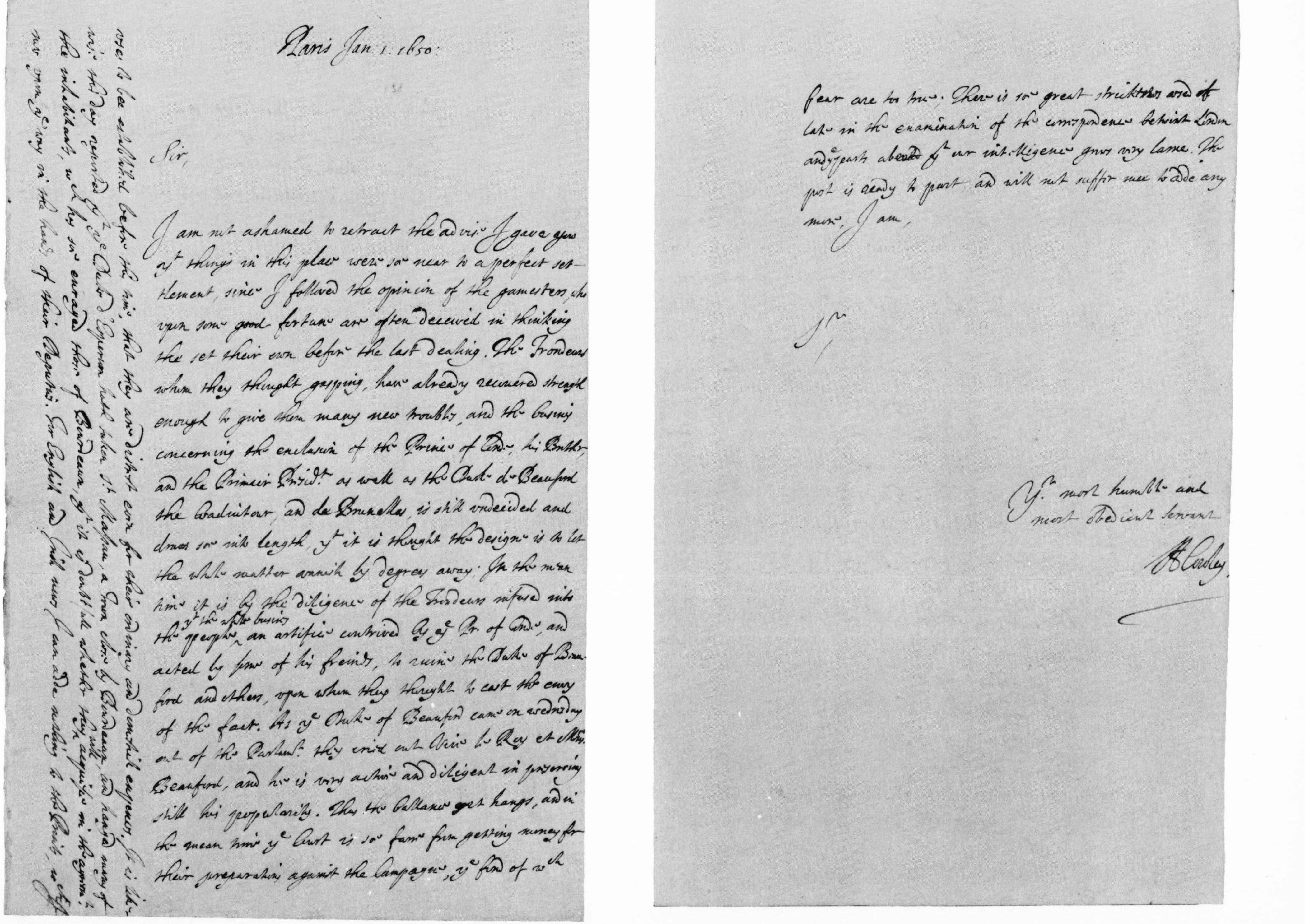

Paris Jan: 1: 1650:

Sir,

I am not ashamed to retract the advice I gave you yt things in this place were soe near to a perfect settlement, since I followed the opinion of the gamesters, who upon some good fortune are often deceived in thinking the set their own before the last dealing. The Frondeurs whom they thought gasping, have already recovered strength enough to give them many new troubles, and the business concerning the enclosure of the Prince of Condé, his Brother, and the Primier Presidt as well as the Duke de Beaufort the Coadjutour, and de Broussels, is still undecided and draws soe into length, yt it is thought the designe is to let the whole matter vanish by degrees away; In the mean time it is by the diligence of the Frondeurs infused into the people yt the whole business an artifice contrived by ye Pr. of Condé, and acted by some of his freinds, to ruine the Duke of Beaufort and others, upon whom they thought to cast the envy of the fact. As ye Duke of Beaufort came on wednesday out of the Parliamt they cried out Vive le Roy et Monr Beaufort, and hee is very active and diligent in preserving still his popularity. Thus the ballance yet hangs, and in the mean time ye Court is soe farre from getting money for their preparations against the campagne, ye fund of wch vses to bee established before the time, that they are distrest even for their ordinary and domestick expenses. It is likewise this day reported yt ye Duke d'Espernon hath taken St Massan, a town close by Bourdeaux, and hanged many of the inhabitants, wch has soe enraged those of Bourdeaux, yt it is doubtfull whether they will acquiesce in the agreemt now going ye way in the hands of their Deputies. For English and Irish news I can adde nothing to the Prints, wch I fear are too true; There is soe great strictness used of late in the examination of the correspondence betwixt London and these parts abroad yt our intelligence grows very lame. The post is ready to part and will not suffer mee to adde any more, I am,

Sr

Yr most humble and
most obedient servant

A Cowley.

49

John Evelyn
1620–1706

Autograph letter signed with initials, dated 4 October 1680, to Thomas Tenison. 1 p. 226 x 160 mm. MA 3385. Purchased as the gift of Miss Julia P. Wightman.

In this letter to Thomas Tenison, who was appointed rector of St. Martin-in-the-Fields four days after it was written, Evelyn remarks that he finds it "absolutely necessary, to make a more accurate Discussion & Search into all the passages of my whole Life, to this large period." Very few men or women have recorded the secular and religious passages of their lives more fully than Evelyn. His *Diary* begins with his birth—"I was borne about 20 minuts past two in the morning"—and ends twenty-four days before his death. Scarcely a single event of importance occurring between 1641 and 1706 goes uncommented upon by him; and his perspective is always interesting, for he moved among the highest intellectual, political and religious circles of England. In December 1661, for example, the "Philosophic Assembly" which he had helped to found voted "that I should receive their Publique Thanks for the honorable mention I made of them by the name of *Royal Society.*" This event Evelyn considered "Too greate an honour for a trifle." His association with the Royal Society spurred some of his own writings. In 1662 he published *Sculptura: or the History, and Art of Chalcography and Engraving in Copper* (a copy of which, inscribed by Evelyn to Sir Thomas Browne, is in the Morgan Library), based on his communications to the Royal Society. Though his books, covering subjects from town planning to forestry, convey the diversity of his interests, they cannot compare with his *Diary*, which reflects the man himself, a person of integrity, some conceit (though as Pepys remarked, well-founded conceit) and true piety.

The manuscript of the *Diary* is still in the possession of the Evelyn family; other important Evelyn manuscripts may be found at Christ Church, Oxford.

4th 0^{br}—80 My Revd Lord, Being now (thrô the infinite Clemency of a gratious God) ariv'd to the Sixtieth-*yeare of my age; I have (upon very Serious Consideration) thought it absolutely necessary, to make a more accurate Discussion & Search into all the passages of my whole Life, to this large period; And that what I have but hitherto don perhaps (yea, doubtlesse) too partialy, and upon Solemn Occasions Chiefe-ly, with greate infirmities; I might now do Universaly, and so, as I would desire to have my last Audits & Accompts stated, when God shall calle me to die; and have then onely [illegible deletion] that Work (which is also a very greate one) to finish: I cannot expect my time should now be long in this World: By the Course of Nature (thô blessed be God I have enjoyd wonderfull health of body) I must, and do now looke when my Change shall come, and I would not be Surpriz'd (as I perceive daily, most men are) with either Weakenesse, paine or stupidity, which renders them exceed-ingly indispos'd for the finishing of any-thing of this nature, and altogether, for beginning of it with any certaine Comfort. . . .*

14
4: 9br — 80

My Revd Lord,

Being now (thro the infinite Clemency of a gracious God) arriv'd to the Sixtieth-yeare of my age; I have (upon very serious Consideration) thought it absolutely necessary, to make a more accurate Discussion & search into all the passages of my whole Life, to this large period; And that what I have but hitherto don perhaps (yea, doubtlesse) too partialy, and upon solemn Occasions Chiefely, with greate infirmities; I might now do Universaly, and so, as I would desire to have my last Audite & Accompts stated, when God shall call me to die; and have then onely ~~[illegible]~~ that Work (which is also a very greate one) to finish: I cannot expect my time should now be long in this World: By the Course of Nature (tho blessed be God I have enjoyd wonderfull health of body) I must, and do now looke when my Change shall come, and I would not be surpriz'd (as I perceive daily most men are) with either weaknesse, paine or stupidity, which renders them exceedingly indispos'd for the finishing of any-thing of this nature, and altogether, for beginning of it with any certaine Comfort. To put this then to adventure, I have not the Courage; and do there=fore endeavoure so to prepare, that I may have nothing then to do, but resigne my-selfe wholy to the mercifull Jesus. I have now ben in this Exercise some time; but find greate necessitie of your prayers, which I beg you will send-up for me in particular; that God will especialy soften my heart, pardon my greate sins, Accept, & sanctifie my purposes of so living, as I may die his Ser=vant, and behold his Glorious presence with joy: And if it were not too bold an interruption, I would also humbly desire to know, about what houre tomorrow in the Evening, or Saturday, I might waite upon you with least inconveniency, for I know you are full of businesse; but You are also full of Charity; and it would be no small Consolation to me at this time, to receive more particularly the Seale of Remission from yr Ministry & discerning Spirit, and (I am perswaded) extraordinary power with God, full of holy Compassion as you are. I humbly implore your Lps prayers & Blessing, & remaine

Yr Lps

most dutifull Servant

E:

ANDREW MARVELL
1621–1678

Autograph letter signed, dated Westminster, 29 May 1660, to the "Commissioners of the Militia for the town & Country of Kingston upon Hull." 1 p. 302 x 204 mm.

This letter marks the turning of an age, for it was written on the day of Charles II's entry into London "after a sad, & long Exile, and Calamitous Suffering both of the King & Church: being 17 yeeres." The diarist John Evelyn described the scene as one of "unexpressable joy: The wayes straw'd with flowers, the bells ringing, the streetes hung with Tapissry, fountaines running with wine." Whether Marvell shared entirely in this feeling is doubtful, for he had flourished under Cromwell and his son during the Commonwealth. He had assisted John Milton in the Latin secretaryship and been elected to Parliament as a member for Hull. The reign of Charles II was to prove difficult, calling forth from Marvell the numerous pamphlets and political satires for which he was famous among his contemporaries. During his lifetime he published few poems. With the exception of his verses to Cromwell, which were canceled in almost all copies, the poetry on which his modern reputation rests was published posthumously in *Miscellaneous Poems* (1681). "To his Coy Mistress," "The Nymph complaining for the death of her Faun," "The Garden" and "Upon Appleton House, to my Lord Fairfax" are all products of an earlier period of his life, composed in the 1650s. Of his later days, he might have observed as he did in his poem "To his Noble Friend Mr. Richard Lovelace, upon his Poems":

> Our times are much degenerate from those
> Which your sweet Muse which your fair Fortune chose,
> And as complexions alter with the Climes,
> Our wits have drawne th'infection of our times.

Gentlemen We have received yours of the 25 & would not misse answering you this same Post though it be the day of the kings arrivall. The Counsell of Joabe was broke up & acted no more before the receit of yours. So that nothing at all could be done thereupon concerning Mr Bloom & Mr Hall. And truly Gentlemen, if we may presume to advise you, seeing it falls out so, be pleased to interpose yet while it is time your discretions for the composing of a businesse wch it will be difficult for us to handle so dextrously but that Some reflexion may fall here upon your own judgements and upon the Town. But we shall decline nothing nor thinke any thing better then that which you shall resolve on & if you please after some few days to write about it to his Majesties Privy counsell & for the approbation of Mr Maior to be one of your number we will serve you therein. Only we must beg of you that in whatsoever you shall use us you will acquaint us also with matter of fact distinctly & perfectly For Else your businesse can not be well done. We remain Gentlemen Your most affectiona[te] friends to serve you John Ramsden Andrew Marvell Westminster May 29. 1660.

Gentlemen

We haue received yours of the 25th & would not misse answering you the same Post though it be the day of the Kings arrivall. The Councell of State was broke up & acted no more before the receit of yours. So that nothing at all could be done thereupon concerning Mr Bloom & Mr Hall. And truly Gentlemen, if we may presume to advise you, seeing it falls out so, be pleased to interpose yet while it is time your discretions for the composing of a businesse wch it will be difficult for us to handle so dextrously but that some reflexion may fall here upon your own judgements and upon the Town. But we shall decline nothing nor thinke any thing better then that which you shall resolue on & if you please after some few days to write about it to his Majesties Privy Counsell & for the approbation of Mr Maior to be one of your number we will serve you therein. Onely we must beg of you that in whatsoeuer you shall use us you will acquaint us also with matter of fact distinctly & perfectly. For else your businesse can not be well done. We remain

Gentlemen

Your most affectionat friends to serve you

John Ramsden

Andrew Marvell

Westminster May 29.
1660.

51

George Villiers, second Duke of Buckingham 1628–1687

Manuscript will signed, dated 4 September 1674. 2 pp. 405 x 318 mm.
MA 3386. Purchased as the gift of Mr. David Pleydell-Bouverie.

Buckingham, son of the murdered royal favorite, came into the world with all the adornments of position but few of the blessings of character. His life was punctuated with reversals of fortune, some of which were the fault of his pride and vanity, some the natural result of the English civil war. His political vicissitudes aside, Buckingham wrote one play—with collaborative assistance by several authors—entitled *The Rehearsal* (1671), which supplied the Restoration and eighteenth-century stage with a convenient satiric vocabulary. The play's basic structure is reflexive: Bayes, an author modeled on Sir William D'Avenant and Dryden, conducts a rehearsal of his most recent play. His ludicrous responses to the sensible questions of the actors and the evident stupidity of the play within the play provide an ironic commentary on the absurdity of contemporary drama. As the epilogue has it,

> The play is at an end, but where's the plot?
> That circumstance the poet Bayes forgot.
> And we can boast, tho' 'tis a plotting age,
> No place is freer from it than the stage.

The Rehearsal was a great success, and the names of Bayes and Drawcansir (the hero of Bayes's play) became dramatic commonplaces. Buckingham's will contains several bequests to literary figures: among them, an annuity of one hundred pounds to the playwright William Wycherley and another of the same sum to Thomas Sprat, Buckingham's chaplain and the author of *The History of the Royal Society* (1667).

Pounds per Annū. Unto Francis Doles my Servant at Burleigh one Annuity or yearly payment of One hundred Pounds And unto William Wicherley one annuity or yearly Sume of One hundred Pounds per Annū. The same Annuityes to be paid at Christmas and Midsomer by equall portions . . .

Pounds per Annu. Unto ffrancis Dolee my Servant at Burleigh one Annuity or yearly payment of One hundred Pounds And unto William Wicherley one annuity or yearly Sume of One hundred pounds per Annu. The same Annuityes to be paid at Christmas and Midsomer by equall porcons Item I give unto the Pages that shall be Living with mee and my wife at the tyme of my decease two hundred Pounds apeece And to my Cozens Izabella Bladen and Jamieta Challoner One hundred pounds apeece And to all my Servants Living with mee at the tyme of my decease to whom I have not given Annuityes or Legacyes Two yeares Salary ffee or wages over above and besides the Salary ffee or wages which shall be then due and oweing to every such Servant Item I Give unto my Loveing friends and Trustees the said Edward Seymour Sr Charles Herbord Sr Robert Clayton Ranald Grahme and John Wildman the Sume of Two hundred Pounds apeece To my freind Sarah Trott sister to the Lady Clayton Two hundred pounds To Butler Esqr Two hundred Pounds and to Doctor Birkett One hundred Pounds. To John Morris Esqr One hundred Pounds. The Residue of my personall Estate I Give my Executors herein afternamed for and towards Satisfying and defraying my funerall Charges and Expences wch I would not have exceede Tenn thousand pounds and to recompence them all such damages and expences as they shall Susteine expend or be put unto in about or concerning ye Trust hereby by mee in them reposed And the more speedy payment of the debts by mee oweing at the tyme of my decease And I hereby make and ordaine my said Loveing friends the said Edward Seymour Sr Charles Herbord Sr Robert Clayton Ranald Grahme and John Wildman Executors of this my Last Will and Testament and revoke all former wills by mee made In Witnes whereof I have sett my hand and seale to this my Last Will and Testament conteined in this and the precedent Sheete this fowerth day of September 1674

Buckingham

Sealed signed published and declared by the said Duke as his Last Will and Testament after the interlineing these words vizt (wch I would not have exceede Tenn thousand pounds) in the presence of

Rob: Clayton John Morris

Rb: Leman Wm Belke

Anth: Keck

JOHN BUNYAN
1628–1688

Manuscript warrant for the second arrest of John Bunyan, dated Bedford, 4 March 1674/5, written in a clerical hand and signed by various justices with their seals. 1 p. 302 x 193 mm. MA 39.

With the restoration of Charles II and the Anglican religion in 1660, preachers of John Bunyan's faith fell under harsh probation. Rather than submit to the strictures of an alien church, Bunyan continued his Puritan teachings and was arrested in 1660 and imprisoned in the county jail at Bedford for twelve years. By 1674 (1675 new style) he had enjoyed three years of relative freedom under a Declaration of Indulgence which restricted the persecution of Nonconformists and their preachers. In March of that year, however, a change in the political administration of England led to a revocation of this unpopular declaration. When news of the reversal reached Bedford on March 4, the local magistrates were ready with this warrant for Bunyan's arrest, which accuses him in the following words: "one John Bunnyon of yo[r] said Towne Tynker hath divers times within one month last past in contempt of his Maj[ties] good Lawes preached or teached at a Conventicle meeting or assembly. . . ." During his subsequent imprisonment for six months, Bunyan is believed to have completed *The Pilgrim's Progress*, the most popular and moving allegory of Christian tribulation and reward ever to have been written. For over two centuries, *The Pilgrim's Progress*, alongside the Bible, formed the core of any English or American home library; only in the third century of its history has its popularity begun to diminish.

The only known and unquestioned handwriting of John Bunyan is in documents in the Library and Museum of the Trustees of Bunyan Meeting, Bedford.

Whereas informaton and complaint is made unto us that (nothwithstanding the Kings Maj[ties] late Act of most gracious gen[er]all and free pardon to all his Subjects for past misdemeanours that by his said clemencie and indulgent grace and favour They might bee mooved and induced for the time to come more carefully to observe his Higheness lawes and Statutes and to continue in theire loyall and due obedience to his Maj[tie]) yett one John Bunnyon of yo[r] said Towne Tynker hath divers times within one Month last past in contempt of his Maj[ties] good Lawes preached or teached at a Conventicle meeting or assembly under colour or pretence of exercise of Religion in other manner then according to the Liturgie or practise of the Church of England . . .

To the Constables of Bedford and to
every of them

Whereas information and complaint is made unto
us that (notwithstanding the Kings Maj:ties
late Act of most gratious generall and free
pardon to all his Subjects for past misdemeano:
that by his said clemencie and indulgent grace
and favo: They might bee mooved and induced
for the time to come more carefully to observe
his Highnes lawes and Statutes and to
continue in theire loyall and due obedience to
his Maj:tie) yett one John Bunnyon of yo:
said Towne Tynker hath divers times
within one Month last past in contempt of
his Maj:ties good Lawes preached or teached
at a Conventicle meeting or assembly under
colo: or pretence of exercise of Religion in other
manner then according to the Liturgie or
practise of the Church of England These
are therefore in his Maj:ties name to comand
you forthwith to apprehend and bring the
Body of the said John Bunnion before
us or any of us or other his Maj:ties Justice
of peace within the said County to answer the
premisses and further to doe and receave
as to Lawe and Justice shall appertaine and
hereof you are not to faile Given under
our handes and Seales this ffowerth day of
March in the Seaven and twentieth yeare of
the Raigne of our most gratious Soveraigne
Lord King Charles the Second A:o q Dni
juxta &c 1674 Will: ffoster

Napier
W. Beecher
G. Blundell
Hum. Monoux
Will Franklin
John Ventris
Will Gery
St. Chernocke
Wm Daniels
W. Foster
T. Browne
Gaius Squire

53

Sir William Temple
1624–1699

Autograph letter signed, dated The Hague, 4 October 1669, to Sir Robert Southwell. 1 p. 305 x 202 mm.

Temple made his greatest impression on English literature during his years of retirement at Sheen and Moor Park, a time when his personal secretary was Jonathan Swift and his interests had more to do with poetry and the defense of ancient learning than with the complexities of international politics. This letter to Temple's fellow diplomat, Sir Robert Southwell, belongs to the period of his most frenzied political activity. The year before, 1668, he had succeeded in negotiating the Triple Alliance between England, Holland and Sweden, an event that brought him the acclaim of his countrymen. Unfortunately, his success also brought about a change in his condition, "all my lucky stars having left mee since the King [Charles II] was pleased to spoyle a good Resident by making an Ill Ambassader." At The Hague, Temple was foiled by the secret understanding between Charles and Louis XIV; the result was his dismissal from the post (requested by Louis) and his return to Sheen in Surrey. The next time he traveled to The Hague, in 1674, it was to render the conspicuous service of arranging the marriage of the future sovereigns of England, William of Orange and Princess Mary, daughter of the Duke of York.

Hague Oct^{br}, 4 S.N. 69 Sr I should sooner have acknoledged the favor you pleased to doe me by Mr Lloyd, but that I thought it fit to make my returnes by the same hande that brought it mee, especially having made mee beleeve his journey backe would bee something more sudden then it has proovd by some delays in Mr Taylers businesse, who would certainly have gaind by yr recomendation, if it had been more in my power to advance the dispatch of his affaire. But wherein I can assist him hee shall bee sure of it that by acquitting my self well of yr first commission I may deserve more & greater from You. In the mean time I have been much obliged by the favor of yr memory, & the civilitys of yr letter, & rejoyce very heartyly with you upon all the successes of yr imployments, & yr happy returne home, wch the circumstances of so much reputation as you have brought with you, & so pleasant a dwelling as you have chosen, as well as My Lady Southwels company must needs make very agreeable to you, and possess you of all you can expect from the quiett you professe so much to affect. I wish you all you desire in the injoyment of it, or whatever else you propose to yrself, & hope you will retaine good thoughts of us who are left at Sea, whatever voyage wee make, since the successe of that in spite of all steerage will depende upon windes and tides, wch wee are not masters of. . . .

Hague Octbr 1
St N. 69

3

I should sooner have acknowledged the favor you pleased to doe mee by Mr Floyd, but that I thought it fitt to make my returnes by the same hande that brought it mee, especially having made mee believe his journey backe would bee something more sudden then it has proved by some delayes in Mr Taylors businesse, who would certainly have gained by yr recomendation if it had been more in my power to advance the dispatch of his affaires. But wherein I can assist him hee shall bee sure of it that by acquitting my self well of yr first commission I may deserve a more greater from you. In the mean time I have been much obliged by the favor of yr memory, & the civility of yr letter, & rejoyce very heartily wth you upon all the successes of yr imployments, & yr happy returne home, wth the circumstances of so much reputation as you have brought with you, so pleasant a dwelling as you have chosen, aswell as My Lady Southwells company must needs make very agreeable to you, and possess you of all you can expect from the quiett you professe so much to affect. I wish you all you desire in the injoyment of it, or whatsoever else you propose to yrself, & hope you will retaine good thoughts of us who are left at Sea, whatever voyage wee make, since the successe of that in spight of all steerage will depend upon windes and tides, wch wee are not masters of. I see you have not been long at home by yr complementing mee upon my successes the waste of wch you will heare after I lost to my charge, all my lucky starr having left mee since the King was pleased to spoyle a good Resident by making an ill Ambassador, since wch time all I have been able to doe has been onely to keepe things from unravelling wch I had the good lucke to knitt before, but the best on't is as I never challenged any part of the credit of any hitts I have had so I am very sure to have deserved no part of the blame of what I have mist. You will not finde all men at Court not upon the exchange of my minde, but I should bee glad to live well in the good opinion of my friends, & to deserve yrs by all occasions I can gaine of expressing my self alwaies

Sr Yr most humble servant
W Temple

I am my Lady Southwells most humble servant as my Wife is to you both.

John Dryden
1631–1700

Autograph letter signed, dated 12 December [1693], to William Walsh. 2 pp. 224 x 178 mm. MA 130.

During the early 1680s the political situation in England deteriorated rapidly as the religious vagaries of Charles II and James II became evident. Always a poet of great political sensitivity and loyalty, Dryden had turned his genius to satire during this decade, publishing some of the finest poems he would ever write. These works did little, however, to assist him financially; therefore in 1690, after a lapse of seven years, Dryden, a Catholic convert, again began to write for the stage, largely to replace his income as Poet Laureate and Historiographer Royal, lost when the Protestant William of Orange assumed the vacant throne in 1688. By the end of 1693, the date of this letter, it had become clear to Dryden that the stage would not repair his fortunes. He had recently written two of his best plays, *Don Sebastian* and *Amphitryon*, but neither these nor his final play, *Love Triumphant*, were as successful as his early productions. On the stage, if not in print, Dryden was superseded by a younger generation to whom he was notably kind and encouraging; indeed, his relations with younger friends like Congreve, Southerne, Oldham and the poet Walsh, to whom he writes here, form one of the most attractive elements of his brilliant career. These men learned from him in turn the art of graceful poetical patronage: Walsh and Congreve sponsored the next great poet of the realm, Alexander Pope (who called Walsh "the Muse's Judge and Friend"). Dryden's prefatory verses to Congreve's *The Double Dealer* (1694) are perhaps the supreme expression of this quality in Dryden. They mark the natural progression of generations and the turning of an era:

Well then; the promis'd hour is come at last;
The present Age of Wit obscures the past.

Almost none of Dryden's poetry survives in autograph manuscripts; the only example is the manuscript of his "Heroique Stanza's" among the Lansdowne manuscripts in the British Library.

[Starting halfway down first page:] Your Critique, by your description of its bulk, will be to large for a preface to my Play, which is now studying; but cannot be acted till after Christmasse is over. I call it Love Triumphant, or Nature will prevaile: Unless instead of the second Title you like this other Neither Side to blame: which is very proper, to the two chief Characters of the Heroe & Heroine: who notwithstanding the Extravange of their passion, are neither of them faulty, either in duty, or in Honour. Your Judgment of it, if you please. When you do me the favour to send your Booke, I will take care to correct the press; & to have it printed well. It will be more for your Honour, too, to print it alone & take off the suspition of your being too much my friend, I meane too partiall to me, if it comes in company of my Play. I have rememberd you to all your friends; and in particular to Congreve, who sends you his play, as a present from him selfe, by this conveyance; & much desires the honour of being better known to you. His Double Dealer is much censurd by the greater part of the Town: & is defended onely by the best Judges, who, you know, are commonly the fewest. . . .

Deare Mr Walsh

I have read over your letter many times: & you know that what we repeat very often, tis with pleasure. The Method which you have taken, is wonderfully good; & not only all present Poets, but all who are to come in England, will thanke you for freeing them from the too servile imitation of the Ancients. If hereafter the Audience, will come to tast the confinement of the French (which I believe the English never will) then it will be easy for their Poets, to follow the strictness of the Mechanique rules, in the three Unities. In the meane time I am affrayd, for my sake, you discover not your opinion, concerning my Irregular way, of Tragicomedies, in my doppia favola. I beseech you let no consideration of mine hinder you from making a perfect Critique. I will never defend that practice: for I know it distracts the Hearers. But I know, withall, that it has hitherto pleasd them, for the sake of variety: & for the particular tast, which they have to low Comedy. Mascardi, in some of his Miscellany Treatises, has a Chapter concerning this, & exemplifys in the Satyr & Corisca of the Paster Fido: As I remember those two persons though not of a piece with the rest, yet serve in the conclusion, to the discovery & beauty of the Design. Your Critique, by your description of its bulk will be to large for a preface to my Play, which is now studying; but cannot be acted till after Christmasse is over. I call it Love Triumphant, or Nature will prevaile: Unless instead of the second Title you like this other Neither side to blame: which is very proper, to the two chief Characters of the Heroe & Heroine: who notwithstanding the Extravagancy of their passion, are neither of them faulty, either in duty, or in Honour. Your Judgment of it, if you please: when you do me the favour to send your Book: I will take care to correct the presse, & to have it printed well. It will be more for your Honour too, to print it alone, & take off the suspition of your being too much my friend, I meane too partiall to me, if it comes in company of my Play. I have remembred you to all your friends, and in particular to Congreve; who sends you his play, as a present from him selfe, by this conveyance; & much desires the honour of being better known to you. His Double Dealer is much censured by the greater part of the Town: & is defended onely by the best Judges, who you know, are commonly the fewest. yet it gets ground daily, & has already been acted Eight times. The women thinke he has exposd their Bitchery too much; & the Gentlemen, are offended with him; for the discovery of their follyes: & the way of their Intrigues, under the notion of Friendship to their Ladyes Husbands.

My verses, which you will find before it, were written before the play was acted. but I neither altered them nor do I alter my opinion of the play. For other news, you will heare from all hands; that the House of Lords grow very warm: & have a mind to try the Lord Admiralls. Those of the sea having been acquitted by the Commons, yet they have orderd Rook, Killigrew, Shovell, & the Turkish Merchants, to appear before them: And on the other side, the King has taken away the commissions of the Marine Admiralls. You know Russell will be the Man. The whig party, who brought in the King thinke Killigrew & my Brother Jacobites; & My Lord Caermarthen with all the High Church men to be betrayers of the Government. In my conscience they wrong them. The Commons, are inspecting their own House for the private pensions: which Squire pretends to discover, & will name above an Hundred men: it will all come to nothing I believe; by the over voting of the other side in both Houses: when they are tird, they will give the six Millions; & next Michaelmass we shall have a new Parliament: but for the Trienniall Bill, now sent down from the Lords, I conceive it will be thrown out by the Commons: because of the Rider, which explains the word Holding, not to signify to hold. We heare of about ten of our Eastindia ships, & two small men of war, are taken by Du Bart, & carryed into France: they were laden with corn & other provisions. Last, for my selfe: I have undertaken to translate all Virgil: & as an Essay, have already paraphrasd, the third Georgique, as an Example. it will be publishd in Tonsons next Miscellanyes, in Hillary terme. I propose to do it by subscription: having an hundred & two Brass Cutts, with the Coats of Armes of the Subscriber to each Cutt: Every subscriber to pay five guineys: half in hand: besides another inferiour subscription of two guineys, for the rest whose names are onely written in a Catalogue, printed with the Book. I am Dear Sr

Your most faithfull Servant John Dryden

Dec: 12th. I have just received your verses to Mr Wycherley: but cannot stay to read them before I put up this letter, tis so late at night.

John Dryden

Autograph letter signed, dated 7 November [1699], to Mrs. Elizabeth Steward. 2 pp. 186 x 150 mm. MA 130.

Only about sixty autograph letters by John Dryden survive; of those, the largest single group (seventeen) is in the Morgan Library. Among these letters are several from Dryden to his young kinswoman, Mrs. Elizabeth Steward, to whom he was willing to defend the most controversial action of his life, his conversion to Roman Catholicism. Dryden's change of heart unfortunately coincided with the accession to the throne of James II, a known Catholic. Not surprisingly, he was severely criticized for tending his political interests more than his conscience. This letter to Elizabeth Steward is a remarkable defense of his decision and an accurate estimate of his service to English literature; it is also a plea for toleration. Dryden on his part promises to forbear satire on the government of William III if, as he writes, "they will consider me as a Man, who have done my best to improve the Language, & Especially the Poetry . . ." and do not attempt to coerce his religious opinions.

During the final decade of his life, Dryden turned to translation. In 1697 his translation of Virgil (mentioned in the previous letter) appeared. Published by subscription, it helped ease Dryden's financial burden; and it represented by proxy a project that Dryden had long cherished but never completed: the writing of an original epic poem. The verses alluded to in this letter, "to the Duchess of Ormond, & my worthy Cousin Driden," appeared in a volume entitled *Fables, Ancient and Modern* (1700), a collection of superb poetic narratives translated from Chaucer, Boccaccio, Homer and Ovid. Dryden's renown as a translator was assured by this work, though its composition was a happy accident: "I have built a house, where I intended but a lodge; yet, with better success than a certain nobleman, who, beginning with a dog-kennel, never lived to finish the palace he had contrived."

Madam Even your Expostulations are pleasing to me: for though they shew you angry; yet they are not without many expressions of your kindness: & therefore I am proud to be so chidden. Yet I cannot so farr abandon my own defence, as to confess any idleness or forgetfulness on my part. What has hindred me from writing to you, was neither ill health nor a worse thing ingratitude, but a flood of little businesses, which yet are necessary to my Subsistance, & of which I hop'd to have given you a good account before this time; but the Court rather speaks kindly of me, than does any thing for me, though they promise largely: & perhaps they think I will advance as they go backward: in which they will be much deceivd: for I can never go an Inch beyond my Conscience & my Honour. If they will consider me as a Man, who have done my best to improve the Language, & Especially the Poetry, & will be content with my acquiescence under the present Government, & forbearing Satire on it, that I can promise, because I can perform it: but I can neither take the Oaths, nor forsake my Religion, because I know not what Church to go to if I leave the Catholique;...

Madam

Even your Expostulations are pleasing to me: for though they shew you angry; yet they are not without many expressions of your kindness: & therefore I am proud to be so chidden. Yet I cannot so farr abandon my own defence, as to confess any idleness or forgetfulness on my part. What has hindred me from writing to you, was neither ill health, nor a worse thing ingratitude; but a flood of little businesses, which yet are necessary to my subsistance, & of which I hop'd to have given you a good account before this time; but the Court rather speaks kindly of me, than does any thing for me, though they promise largely: & perhaps they think I will advance, as they go backward: in which they will be much deceiv'd: for I can never go an Inch beyond my Conscience & my Honour. If they will consider me as a Man who have done my best to improve the Language, & Especially the Poetry, & will be content with my acquiescence under the present Government, & forbearing Satire on it, that I can promise, because I can perform it: but I can neither take the Oaths, nor forsake my Religion, because I know not what Church to go to, if I leave the Catholique; they are all so divided amongst themselves in matters of faith, necessary to Salvation: & yet all assuming the name of Protestants. May God be pleased to open your Eyes, as he has opend mine: Truth is but one; & they who have once heard of it, can plead no Excuse, if they do not embrace it. But these are things too serious, for a trifling Letter. — If you desire to hear any thing more of my Affairs, the Earl of Dorsett, & your Cousin Montague, have both seen the two Poems, to the Duchess of Ormond, & my worthy Cousin Driden: And are of opinion that I

John Dryden

Autograph letter signed, dated 11 April 1700, to Mrs. Elizabeth Steward. 2 pp. 186 x 149 mm. MA 130.

This is Dryden's last surviving letter; he died on the first of May 1700. In his illness he did not cease to write, nor did he withdraw from controversy. In 1698 Jeremy Collier had published an attack on the immorality of the English stage, naming Dryden among others as one of the chief offenders. In the "Preface" to *Fables, Ancient and Modern*—his greatest prose work—Dryden acknowledged in part the justice of Collier's remarks, but doubted the propriety of his argument: "[Collier] comes to battle like a dictator from the plough. I will not say, 'the zeal of God's house has eaten him up;' but I am sure it has devoured some part of his good manners and civility."

The ease of lifelong practice and his sense of human passage strongly mark Dryden's final works. The famous lyric from "A Secular Masque," performed in late April 1700 and referred to in this letter as "A New Masque," might serve as a motto for Dryden's career, so full is it of simultaneous disillusionment and hope, implicit satire and praise:

All, all of a piece throughout;
Thy chase had a beast in view;—
Thy wars brought nothing about;—
Thy lovers were all untrue.
'Tis well an old age is out,
And time to begin a new.

The latter end of last week, I had the honour of a visite from my Cousine your Mother, & my Cousine Dorothy, with which I was much comforted: within this Moneth there will be played for my profit, an old play of Fletchers calld the pilgrim corrected by my good friend Mr Vanbrook; to which I have added A New Masque, & am to write a New prologue & Epilogue. Southerns tragedy, calld the Revolt of Capoua, will be playd At Bettertons House within this fortnight. I am out with that Company, & therefore if I can help it, will not read it before tis Acted; though the Authour much desires I shou'd. do not think I will refuse a present from fair hands; for I am resolvd to save my Bacon. I beg your pardon, for this slovenly letter; but I have not health to transcribe it. My Service to my Cousin your Brother who I heare is happy in your Company, which He is not, who most desires it, & who is, Madam, Your most Oblig'd, Obedient Servant John Dryden. Thursday, April the 11th ~~16~~700.

The latter end of last week, I had the honour of a visite from
my Cousin your Mother, & my Cousin Dorothy, with which I
was much comforted: within this Moneth there will be playd
for my profit, an old play of Fletchers, calld the pilgrim, corrected, by my good friend Mr Vanbrook; to which I have
added A New Masque, & am to write a New prologue & Epilogue.
Southerns tragedy, calld the Revolt of Capoua, will be playd
At Bettertons House within this fortnight. I am out with
that Company, & therefore, if I can help it, will not read it
before tis Acted; though the Authour much desires I shou'd.
do not think I will refuse a present from fair hands, for I
am resolvd to save my Bacon. I beg your pardon for this
slovenly letter; but I have not health to transcribe it. My
service to my Cousin your Brother, who I heare is happy in
your Company, which He is not, who most desires it, & who
is, Madam,

Your most oblig'd, Obedient
Servant

John Dryden.

Thursday, April the 11th
1700.

Anthony à Wood
1632–1695

Autograph letter signed, dated Oxford, 22 July 1687, to William Lloyd, Bishop of St. Asaph. 1 p. 301 x 199 mm.

England has always been rich in naturalists and antiquaries, and they are familiar figures in its literature: one thinks of genial country parsons lost to the larger world amidst sample jars and cases, virtuoso's cabinets, and inscriptions from parish registers and gravestones. Anthony à Wood, one of England's (certainly Oxford's) greatest antiquaries, does not live up to this pleasant fiction. Inspired by the appearance of William Dugdale's great folio *The Antiquities of Warwickshire* in 1656, he elected to perform a similar labor for Oxford. For over thirty-five years, Wood lived in a garret across the street from his college, Merton, avidly collecting and verifying documents for his various works, chief among which was *Athenæ Oxonienses. An exact history of all the Writers and Bishops who have had their education in the most ancient and famous University of Oxford*... (1691–2). Aside from this work, which has been a standard biographical source since its publication, Wood's years of study also brought about a crabbed temper and a disproportionate sense of his own importance in the world of learning, thus pointing a rather Johnsonian moral about the perils of isolated scholarship. This letter illustrates Wood at his work, requesting a catalogue of Deans and Archdeacons from the Bishop of St. Asaph, and appealing to collegiate sentiment as his strongest argument: "consid[er]ing yt it is for a public work & for the honor of our com̃on mother, ther's no man of a generous spirit but will be ready to give his assisting hand towards it."

May it please yr Ld̃ship To und̃stand yt there is ready for the press an Historie of Oxford writers & Bp̃s, to w^h will be added a part called Fasti, wherin will be set down the naẽs of all noted ꝑsons yt have either takẽn degrees in this said Universitie, or have had them confer'd on them as honorary. Among them, will be put all such yt have enjoyed Dignities in the Church, as Deanes, Archdeacons, Chantres, Chancellours &c. Now S^r so it is, yt I having little or no knowledge concerning the Dignitaries of ye church of S. Asaph, it is my humble desire yt yu would be pleased to take so much paines, or get some other prudent ꝑson to do it, as to draw up for me a Catalogue of yr Deanes, & Archdeacons—If yr Reg̃rs be imꝑfect, I shall be contented if the said catalogues doe com̃ence with the yeare of our Lord 1500 (15. Hen. 7.) so yt they be well timed, I meane yt ye day & yeare wn each ꝑson was collated or installed, & whether they came in by death or resignation—...

To Dr. Wm. Lloyd then Bp. of St. Asaph, afterwd. of Worcr.

50

May it please yr Ldship

To understand yt there is ready for the press an Historie of Oxford writers & Bps, to wch will be added a part called Fasti, wherein will be set downe the names of all noted psons yt have either taken degrees in the said Universitie, or have had them conferr'd on them as honorary. Among them, will be put all such yt have enjoyed Dignities in the Church as Deanes, Archdeacons, Chantors, Chancellors &c. Now Sr so it is, yt I having little or no knowledge concerning the dignitaries of yr church of S. Asaph, it is my humble desire yt yo would be pleased to take so much paines, or get some other prudent pson to do it, as to draw up for me a Catalogue of yr Deanes, & Archdeacons — If yr Registers be imperfect, I shall be contented if the said catalogues doe commence with the yeare of our Lord 1500 (15. Hen. 7.) so yt they be well timed, I meane yt ye day & yeare wn such pson was collated or installed, & whether they came in by death or resignation —

In like manner (pardon my boldness) yo may be pleased to let me have the like catalogue of ye Deanes of Bangor, for yr Ldship being a curious searcher into antiquities, there's no doubt but yt you have such a thing laying by yo, wherein I hope to find the time of death & place of buriall of Dr Griffith Williams Bp of Ossory, who, tho a Cambridge man, yet he was originally of Oxon —

There is no doubt but yr Lordship will be ready to say, yt this will be a great trouble to yo; but then considering yt it is for a public work & for the honor of our comon mother, there's no man of a generous spirit but will be ready to give his assisting hand towards it — So craving yr Lordships pardon, I desire to remaine

yr most humble servant
Anthony Wood.

From my lodging
neare Merton coll
in Oxford

22. Jul. 87

58

John Locke
1632–1704

Manuscript, probably autograph, of "An Essay concerning Humane Understanding," Books I and II, dated 1685. 383 pp. 165 x 110 mm. MA 998.

In December 1692, Locke wrote to his friend William Molyneux, "I should be loath to differ from any thinking man, being fully persuaded there are very few things of pure speculation, wherin two thinking men who impartially seek truth can differ if they give themselves the leisure to examin their hypotheses . . . ." It was in the full confidence of this sentiment that Locke composed his *Essay concerning Humane Understanding* (1690), a treatise devoted to examining the limits of human comprehension. Typically, the need for this work arose from a practical problem. Sometime in 1671 Locke and several of his friends had gathered for philosophical discussion and had quickly become embroiled in "Difficulties." Locke's response to the dilemma before them is one of the luminous points in seventeenth-century philosophy: "it came into my Thoughts, that we took a wrong course; and that before we set our selves upon Enquiries of that Nature, it was necessary to examine our own Abilities, and see what Objects our Understandings were, or were not fitted to deal with." Though Locke's claims for his book were modest enough—he considered himself "an Under-Labourer in clearing the Ground a little"—the *Essay* proved to be a fountainhead of British philosophy and a work which, as Molyneux wrote to Locke, one could read and reread "and always make New discoverys therin of something Profound."

Locke's *Essay* was written during a span of nearly twenty years. Two drafts were completed in 1671 (one is in the Lovelace Collection in the Bodleian Library, Oxford, another is in private possession) and a third, the manuscript shown here, was written in 1685. This manuscript of the *Essay* contains only Books I and II and is in a hand that very closely resembles Locke's; the corrections are certainly in his hand. This draft was prepared for Edward Clarke, to whom Locke wrote a long series of letters about educating his son; these letters eventually formed the core of *Some Thoughts Concerning Education* (1693). By far the most important collection of manuscripts by Locke is that formerly in the possession of the Earl of Lovelace, now in the Bodleian Library, Oxford.

An Essay concerning Humane Understanding Lib: 1. Cap. 1
Since it is ye understanding y^{t} sets man above ye rest of sensible beings & gives him all ye advantage & dominion wch he hath over y^{m} it is certainly a Subject even for its noblenesse worth o^{ur} labour to enquire into The understanding like ye Eye whilst it makes us see & perceive all other things takes noe notice of it self & it requires art & paine to set it at a due distance & make it its own object. But w^{h}ever be ye difficultys y^{t} lye in the way of this enquiry w^{h}ever it be y^{t} keepes us soe much in ye darke to o^{ur}selves sure I am y^{t} all ye light we can let in upon o^{ur} own mindes all ye acquaintance we can make wth o^{ur} own understandings will not only be very pleasant but bring us great advantage both in directing o^{ur} thoughts in ye search of other things & shaping their enquiry where it is fit makeing us content to sitt downe in a quiet ignorance of those things wch upon Examination we shall finde to be beyond ye reach of o^{ur} capacitys . . .

An Essay concerning Humane Understanding

Lib. 1. Cap. 1

Since it is the understanding that sets man above the rest of sensible beings and gives him all the advantage and dominion which he hath over them, it is certainly a subject even for its noblenesse worth our labour to enquire into. The understanding like the eye whilst it makes us see and perceive all other things takes noe notice of it selfe, and it requires art and pains to set it at a distance and make it its own object. But whatever be the difficultys that lye in the way of this enquiry, whatever it be that keeps us soe much in the darke to our selves, sure I am that all the light we can let in upon our own minds, all the acquaintance we can make with our own understandings will not only be very pleasant but bring us great advantage both in directing our thoughts in the search of other things and stopping their enquiry where it is fit, making us content to sitt downe in a quiet ignorance of those things which upon examination we shall finde to be beyond the reach of our capacitys, and not out of an affectation of universall knowledg raise Questions and perplex our selves and others with disputes about things to which our understandings are not suited and of which we cannot frame in our minds any cleare or distinct percep-

59

Samuel Pepys
1633–1703

Autograph notes in shorthand, dated 29 August 1695, of an interview concerning the birth of the Prince of Wales. 3 pp. 298 x 186 mm. MA 3387. Purchased as the gift of Mr. Henry S. Morgan.

The casual literature of England has suffered no greater loss than that occasioned by the failing eyesight of Samuel Pepys. On the thirty-first of May 1669, only halfway through his life and before he had reached his greatest success as a naval administrator, Pepys's diary records the frivolity of the previous evening—"Thence to the World's-end, a drinking-house by the park; and there merry, and so home late"—then adds: "And thus ends all that I doubt I shall ever be able to do with my own eyes in the keeping of my journall, I being not able to do it any longer . . . and, therefore, resolve from this time forward, to have it kept by my people in longhand, and must therefore be contented to set down no more than is fit for them and all the world to know." Only the journals of Boswell reveal their author more intimately, and Pepys is so much more worth knowing. An avid theatergoer, musician, trusted administrator and amateur scientist (he served for a brief time as President of the Royal Society), Pepys was also a domestic sinner with a remarkably vivid personality, reflected in every detail in his diary. At his death in 1703, Evelyn, a friend of forty years, entered in his own diary his lamentations for Pepys, "universaly beloved, Hospitable, Generous, Learned in many things, skill'd in Musick, a very greate Cherisher of Learned men, of whom he had the Conversation." The manuscript shown here is Pepys's shorthand record of an interview about the birth of the Old Pretender in 1688. Pepys's shorthand diary and numerous other manuscripts are in the Pepys Library, Magdalene College, Cambridge.

Thursday, August. 29. 1695. Notes—from my conference this day with Mrs. D. upon my revisiting her with the book she had trusted me with about the Pr. of W.'s birth.

Abt. Ashton—At G Man and Sr. The O.'s repeated desires she sent to desire leave of princess ~~A. of D.~~ of Orange to come to her in private. She appointed the next morning 10 o clock. And she had opportunity, and both pulling off their gloves, she kissed it, and while on her knees told her errand and for whom. It was only for a repreive, for she was bid not to name a pardon by his friends. She said they would never be quiet till somebody was made an example. She then pulled her up by the hand, and Mrs. D. went on with the same. And she said that that was next to a pardon. And D. saying that he was condemned without anything proved against him that was against the law, and observed that he was an old servant of her father's, and a good one, and a man that had many accounts to clear, and only desired a reprieve, and that she would not make him the first example of her severity.

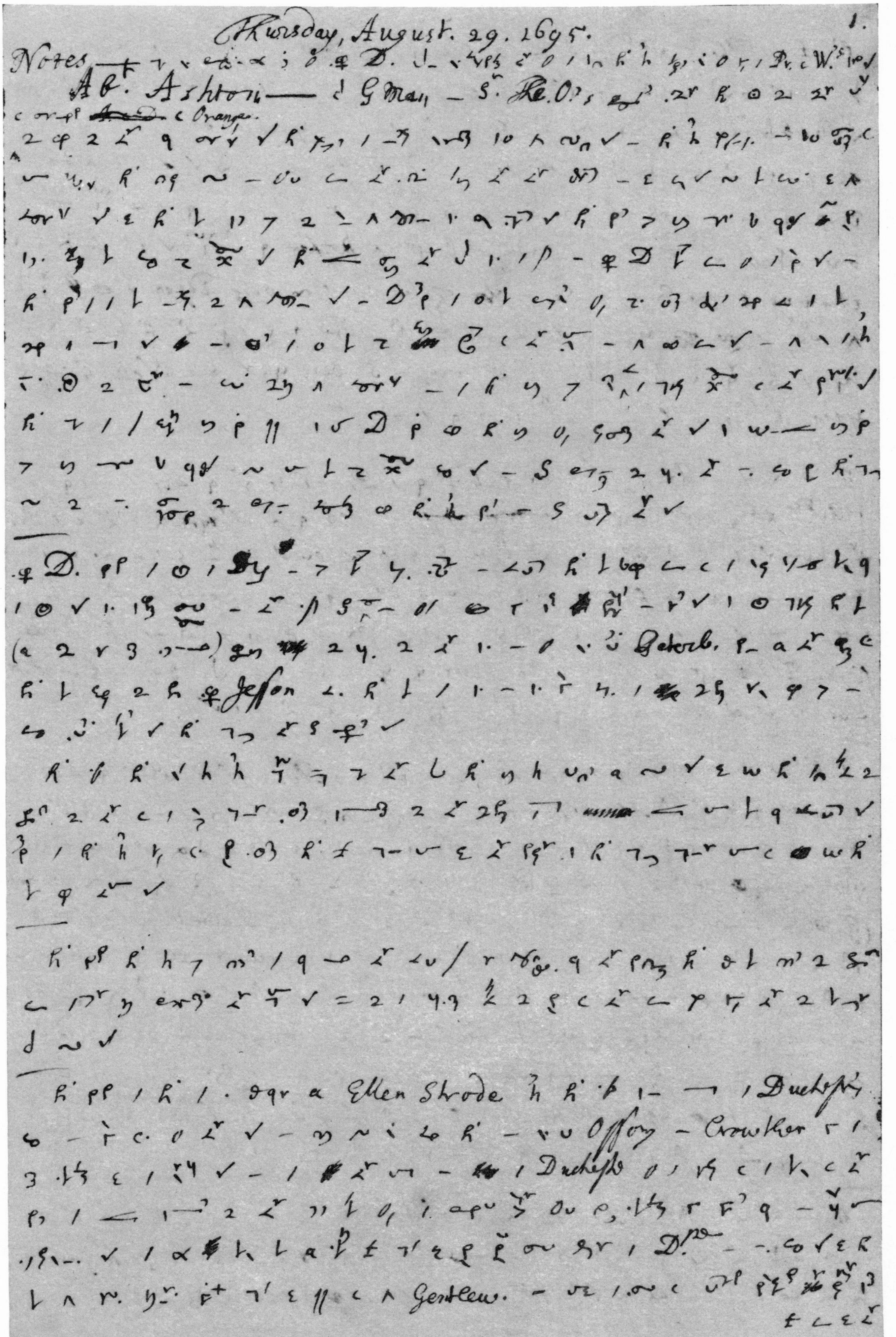
Thursday, August. 29. 1695.
1.
Notes
Ab. Ashton
Orange
Jesson
Ellen Strode
Duchess
Ossory
Crowther
Duchesse
Gentlew.

Sir Isaac Newton
1642–1727

Autograph notebook, dated by Edward Secker 2 October 1659. 94 ff. 124 x 73 mm. MA 318.

The scientific and mathematical achievements of Sir Isaac Newton have naturally cast a certain august haze around his memory. This little notebook, abandoned by him about the age of seventeen, portrays the youthful Newton as few other documents do; and though some of it is eminently serious—several pages are covered with astronomical observations and mathematical calculations—a large part of it is frivolous. Newton took notes on pronunciation, drawing, remedies for sore eyes and corns. There are also other notes of a more dubious nature: a method "To turne waters into wine," "To make pearles of Chalk," and his amusingly laconic method "To make pigeons, partriges ducks & other birds drunk": "Set black wine for them to drink where they come." He also made extensive notes on the preparation of colors for painting, one of which is transcribed below.

This notebook also contains what is believed to be Newton's earliest autograph letter; however, it has the formal wording and appearance of a copybook exercise.

How to write a gold colour. Take a new laid egg, make a hole at one end & let out ye substance y^n take ye yolk without ye white, & four times soe much quicksilver in quantitie as of ye former grind y^m well together & put y^m into ye shell Stop ye hole therof wth chalk & ye white of an egg y^n lay it under a hen y^t sitt wth 6 more for ye space of 3 wekes, ye break it up & write wth it.

Of Drawing.

A bras colour.
This is made of Masticot, & umber.

A marble or ash colour.
This is black & white.

A russit colour
A little white & a good quantety of red.

A browne blew
Take 2 two parts of Inde baudias, & a third of cerushe

A crane colour.
It is of black lead ground wth gum water.

To write gold wth ye pen or pensill.
Take a shell of gold, & put a little gum water into it, & work wth it.

How to write a gold colour.
Take a new laid egg, make a hole at one end & let out ye substance yn take ye yolk without ye white, & four times soe much quicksilver in quantitie as of ye former grind ym well together & put ym into ye shell stop ye hole thereof wth chalk & ye white of an egg yn lay it under a hen yt sitt wth 6 more for ye space of 3 weekes, yn break it up & write wth it.

Flesh colour.
Take white lead grind it wth oyle, lake, & vermilion so you may make it pale or high colloured at yor pleasure.

A White colour.
White lead ground wth nut oyle.

Charcole black & seacole black
Grind charcole very small wth water, let it dry yn grind it wth oyle. thus make seacole black.

Daniel Defoe
1660–1731

Autograph letter signed with initials, dated 11 October 1704, to Samuel Elisha. 1 p. 270 x 205 mm. MA 788.

By 1704, Daniel Defoe's political fortunes and affinities had nominally reversed themselves. Always a moderate in regard to radical Dissenters and reactionary High Churchmen (known as High Flyers), Defoe was charged with seditious libel in 1703 for publishing his brilliant satirical pamphlet *The Shortest-Way with the Dissenters*, which ironically advocated that "whoever was found at a conventicle should be banished the nation, and the preacher be hanged." Dissenters and Anglicans alike misunderstood the ironic call to "pull up this heretical weed of sedition that has so long disturbed the peace of our Church, and poisoned the good corn." Defoe was fined, pilloried and imprisoned. But Robert Harley, one of the secretaries of state, recognized the political value of Defoe's pen, and arranged for his release from prison in November 1703. Defoe, an opponent of party tyranny in any form, and Harley, a moderate Tory, soon found common ground in their advocacy of rational solutions to extreme situations; within months Defoe had become Harley's close adviser and political correspondent and together they overcame the High Flyers, who had been responsible for Defoe's imprisonment.

Because of the official nature of his correspondence, over two hundred autograph letters by Defoe exist, mainly in the Public Record Office in London and in the collection of the Duke of Portland. In this letter, probably to Samuel Elisha, a lawyer in Shrewsbury, Defoe alludes to three concurrent literary productions: his recently published *Hymn to Victory*; the ongoing periodical entitled the *Review* (1704–13), his main contribution as a government spokesman; and his most ambitious poem, not to be published for another two years, *Jure Divino*. In *Jure Divino*, Defoe asserted his independence of party lines by celebrating the Whigs as political and military leaders; significantly, he dedicated the poem to Reason.

S^r^ I have yor kind Letter and had Answerd it sooner but I have been out of Town for above 3 Weeks

What Treatm^t^ I have had since I have been Abroad you will See in ye Review where I have been Oblig'd to Vindicate my Self by an Advertisement, and had Not ye Malice of people reported me fled from justice, wch made me think it Necessary to Come up and Sho' myself, I dont kno' but I might ha given you a short Visit.

I am Glad to hear you had ye Hymns and Thank your Acceptance of the single One but I must own myself Sorry m^r^ Rogers is leaving you

I thank you for yor kind proposall but tho' I have a Family Large Enough Would not have my useless Accquaintence Burthensome to my Friends Especially you of whom I have been Capable to meritt Very Little.

I rejoyce that I shall see you in Town and wish you a good journey up—I beg ye favour of you to remind m^r^ Rogers of Jure Divino wch Now Draws near putting forward. I am S^r^ yor Oblig'd Humble Servt DF Octob.^r^: 11 1704

Sr

I have yor kind Letter and had Answer'd it Sooner but I have been Out of Town for above 3 Weeks.

What Treatmt I have had Since I have been Abroad you will See in ye Review where I have been Oblig'd to Vindicate my Self by an Advertisement, and had Not ye Malice of people Reported me Fled from justice, wch made me think it Necessary to Come up and Sho' my Self, I dont kno' but I might ha given you a Short Visit.

I am Glad to hear you had ye Hymns and Thank your Acceptance of the Single One but I must own my Self Sorry mr Rogers is leaving you

I Thank you for yor kind proposall but tho' I have a Family Large Enough I Would not have my useless Acquaintance Burthensome to my Friends Especially you of whom I have been Capable to merit Very Little.

I Rejoyce that I shall See you in Town and wish you a good journey up — I beg ye favour of you to Remind mr Rogers of Jure Divino which Now Draws near putting forward

I am

Sr

Yor Oblig'd Humble Servt

DF

Octob. 11. 1704

Richard Bentley
1662–1742

Autograph receipt signed, dated 23 May 1732, to Jacob Tonson. 1 p. 187 x 115 mm. MA 2901. Purchased as the gift of Mr. Leonard Schlosser.

King's Librarian and Master of Trinity College, Cambridge, Bentley distinguished himself by brilliant scholarship and by a single, colossal failure to recognize the limitations of his scholarly methods. He was unjustly pilloried by contemporary writers. For proving correctly that the *Epistles to Phalaris*, a central text in the defense of the Ancients against the Moderns, were spurious, Pope portrayed him as "slashing Bentley with his desp'rate Hook," and Swift characterized him as one who "had a humor to pick the worms out of the schoolmen, and swallow them fresh and fasting." In attacking Bentley, Grub Street achieved near unanimity of opinion, probably the only time this happened during this tumultuous period. Yet Bentley's contemporary reputation in the press does not reflect his intimacy with Newton, Locke, Evelyn and Wren, nor does it acknowledge the revolutionary nature of his textual criticism or his discovery of the Greek *digamma*, an accomplishment similar in importance to Thomas Tyrwhitt's recovery later in the century of the true principles of Chaucer's meter.

Bentley's great error, the one that earned him a place in *The Dunciad* as the scholar who "humbled Milton's strains," was the publication in 1732 of an edition of Milton's *Paradise Lost* emended according to a critical technique that had proved highly successful in the analysis of classical texts. On the assumption that Milton's manuscript had been guided through the press by an unscrupulous and ignorant editor, Bentley suggested extensive corrections, in effect rewriting the poem. An examination of the manuscript of Book I of *Paradise Lost* used as printer's copy left no doubt that Bentley was in error. By a pleasing coincidence, the Morgan Library houses that manuscript; the letter by Jacob Tonson, the elder, that refuted Bentley's claims; and Bentley's receipt for payment for his edition of *Paradise Lost*, shown here.

May ye 23^d^ 1732 Receivd of Mr Jacob Tonson one hundred Guin[eas] & Twelve Copies of my Edition of Milton's Paradise lost, which is in full for the first Impression of it publishd Christmas last; I say receivd by Me Ri: Bentley 105-0-0

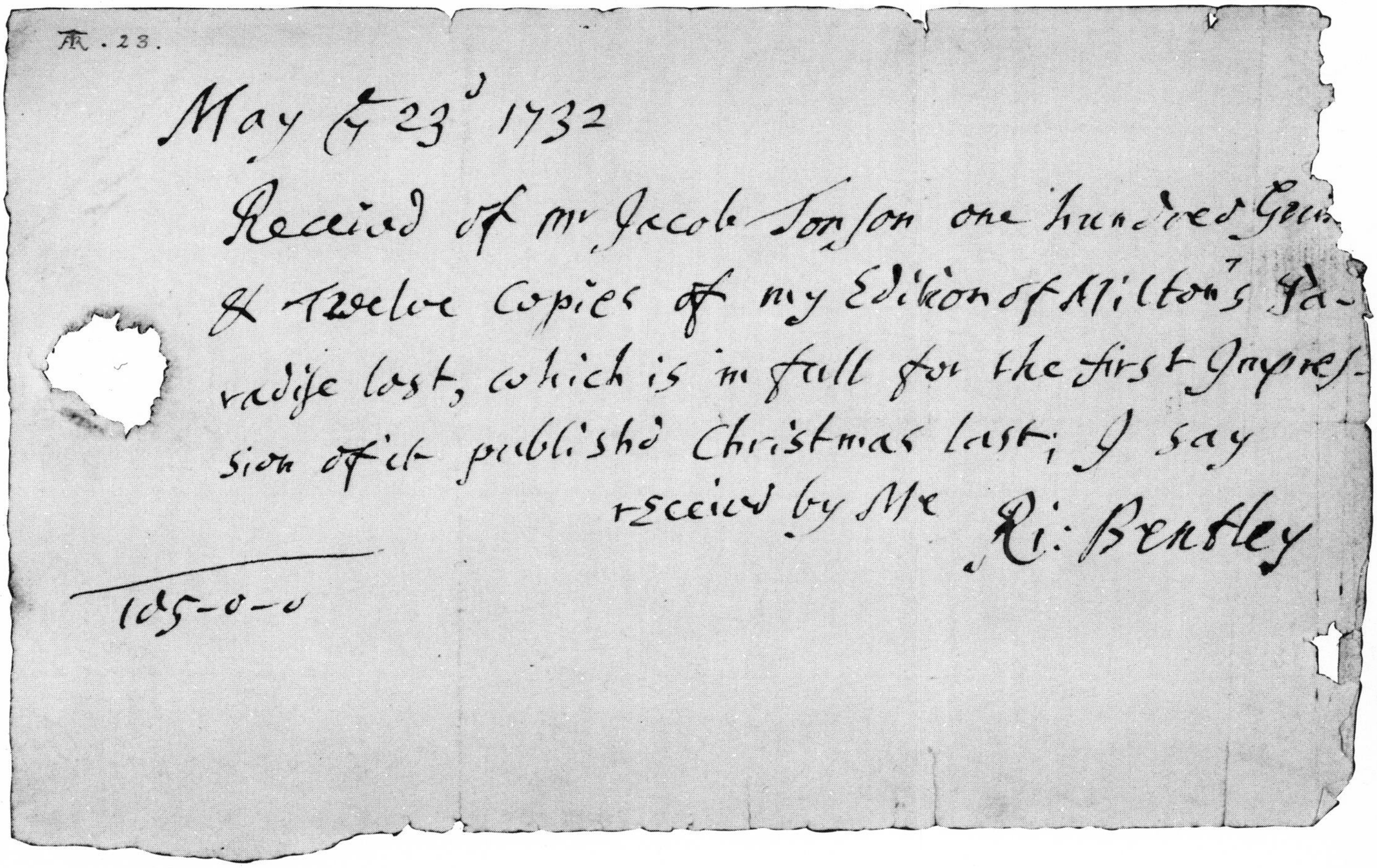

Æ. 23.

May ye 23d 1732

Received of Mr Jacob Tonson one hundred Guin
& Twelve Copies of my Edition of Milton's Paradise lost, which is in full for the first Impression of it publish'd Christmas last; I say
received by Me Ri: Bentley

105-0-0

63

Matthew Prior
1664–1721

Autograph letter signed, dated Westminster, 9 September 1708, to Sir Thomas Hanmer. 3 pp. 201 x 156 mm. MA 754.

Towards the end of his life Matthew Prior busied himself with several projects in prose, among them *Heads for a Treatise upon Learning*. "I remember nothing further in life," he recalled there, "than that I made Verses . . . But I had two Accidents in Youth which hindred me from being quite possest with the Muses: I was bred in a Colledge [St. John's, Cambridge] where prose was more in fashion than Verse, and as soon as I had taken my First Degree was sent the Kings Secretary to the Hague . . . ." Prior became a trusted diplomat and, like so many able Tories, was impeached by the Whig government that came in with the accession of George I. His sustenance lay in party appointments, and when these were stripped from him, Swift, Gay, Pope and Arbuthnot arranged for the publication of his poems by subscription, a device that considerably eased his last days. Though poetry was only the "Amusement" of his life, he acquired a substantial and well-deserved reputation for his lyric verse, among the finest written in his period. Poets of the later eighteenth century considered him a model of poetic grace and simplicity, though he occasionally wrote (but with less success) in a more serious genre than the lyric. In 1718 he published his *Solomon on the Vanity of the World*, a poem which he had the modesty to see was not all it could have been:

Indeed poor SOLOMON in Rhime
Was much too grave to be Sublime.

Gravity was not Prior's customary fault; generally, he erred in the other direction. This letter, written to Sir Thomas Hanmer, records the good humor and self-sacrificing wit that characterized the poet among his friends.

[Starting with line 5:] I will not dispair however of seeing You before Holyrood day, if I am there then you know 'tis soon enough: by the next return of the Carryer my friend Mr Drift and I will pack up the very little of this Sommer's product worth sending to you. I begg my humblest Services and duty may be given to my Lady Dutchesse, and to my Lady Sans queue, *all my good wishes, thô in an other Stile.*

Pray don't forgett Yo^r. Yarmouth reflexions; I do not perceive that my fortune does any way design to Lessen my liberty, and I am sure I cannot employ that liberty better then in following that Man thrô the World whom I really love as well as Most in it. Adieu, my dear Sr Thomas, beleive Me thô the most uselesse the most ob^t. of Your Serv^ts: Mat: Prior. Bobb Friend and I have drank to your health, ad Hilaritatem; Steward, Philips and my friend M^r. Shelton, ad Ebrietatem but that the reformers need not know.

come to Euston, tho' I paced all the way down,
but that I am tyed by the legg here by a
businefs, tho' so frivolous to any but myself that I am ashamed to mention it.
I will not dispair however of seeing you
before Holyrood day, if I am there then
you know 'tis soon enough: by the
next return of the Carryer my
friend m.r Drift and I will pack up
the very little of this Sommer's pro-
-duct worth sending to you.
I begg my humblest Service and duty
may be given to my Lady Dutchess, and
to my Lady Sans queüe, all my good
wishes, tho' in an other Stile.
Pray don't forgett Yo.r Yarmouth reflex-
-ions: I do not perceive that my for-
-tune does any way design to lessen
my liberty, and I am sure I cannot
employ that liberty better then in
following that Man thro' the World whom
I really love as well as Most in it.
Adieu, my dear S.r Thomas; beleive
Me tho the most useless the most ob.t
of Your Serv.ts:

Mat: Prior.

Bobb Friend and I have drank to your
health, ad Hilaritatem; Steward, Philip
and my friend m.r Shelton, ad Ebrietatem
but that the reformers need not know.

Sir John Vanbrugh
1664–1726

Autograph memorandum, unsigned and undated, concerning the salaries of actors. 1 p. 185 x 145 mm.

Vanbrugh's contribution to the cultural landscape of early eighteenth-century England was enormous. In 1705 he built the Queen's Theatre in the Haymarket and staged there his own popular plays, first produced elsewhere: *The Relapse* (1696; the source of Lord Foppington, one of Cibber's greatest roles) and *The Provok'd Wife* (1697). Using the Queen's Theatre as his base, he was also instrumental in introducing Italian opera, a dramatic genre that soon became all the rage in England, despite Addison's protests that "its only Design is to gratify the Senses, and keep up an indolent Attention in the Audience." A single career of such success would have sufficed for most men. But Vanbrugh also built Castle Howard for the Earl of Carlisle, designed the gardens at Stowe and, amid much controversy, erected Blenheim Palace, the nation's grudging tribute to the Duke of Marlborough. This was all too much for Swift, who satirized Vanbrugh's architectural ambitions in two poems—"The History of Vanbrug's House" and "Vanbrug's House Built from the burnt Ruins of Whitehall"—the manuscripts of which are now in the Morgan Library. Swift traces Vanbrugh's architectural training to its foundation, that is, watching the construction of a house of cards and a mud wall:

> From such deep Rudiments as these
> Van is become by due Degrees
> For Building fam'd, and justly reckond
> At Court, Vitruvius the Second.

The manuscript shown here is a memorandum written by Vanbrugh, probably in early 1708 when he resumed control of the Queen's Theatre, after having leased it to Owen Swiney for several years. (In May 1708 Vanbrugh sold out his interest in the Queen's Theatre to Swiney, "only reserving my Rent.") The building and operation of the Queen's Theatre had encumbered Vanbrugh financially; this memorandum is a proposal to reduce daily operating expenses by having his musical stars "coine into Shares instead of Salarys." Valentini, Katherine Tofts and Mlle Margarita (Francesca Margarita de l'Epine) were famous singers; Charles Dieupart, Niccolo Haym and John Christopher Pepusch were composers and musicians.

If Seig.r Valentini, Mrs Tofts, Mlle Margarita Mr Dieupart, Mr Hayms & Mr Papusch coine into Shares instead of Salarys; The daily Charge (Cloaths &c excepted wch must be furnish'd by Subscription) may be reduc'd to £70 p day

The Receipts this Season have amounted to £125 p day, one day with an Other But shou'd the Receipts next Year [illegible; run?] to but £115 the Proffits wou'd then be £45. p day. Two thirds of wch going to the Performing Shares, ~~wou'd~~ Viz: £30. each Share wou'd be worth £450—dividing their £30 p day in four parts One to Vall: One to Mrs Tofts One to Marg. : & One divided in 3 between the Men

109

If Seig.r Valentini, Mrs Tofts, Mde Margarita
Mr Dieupart, Mr Haym & Mr Papusch
come into Shares instead of Salarys; The
daily Charge (Cloaths &c excepted wch must
be furnished by Subscription) may be reduced
to £70. pr day

The Receipts this Season have amounted
to £125 pr day, one day with an Other

But should the Receipts next Year rise
to but £115 the Proffits would then be
£45. pr day. Two thirds of wch going to
the Performing Sharers, ~~[illegible]~~ vizt: £30.
each Share would be worth £450—
dividing their £30 pr day in four parts
One to Vall:
One to Mrs Tofts
One to Marg.
& One divided in 3 between the Men—

Jonathan Swift
1667–1745

Autograph manuscript of "Apollo to the Dean," undated but written ca. 1720. 3 pp. 319 x 203 mm. MA 1207.

While Swift was a young man employed by William Temple he met Esther Johnson, still a child, a member of the Temple household, who became the Stella of his later years. Some time after Temple's death in 1699, Swift, who had received several clerical appointments in Ireland, encouraged Mrs. Johnson and her friend Rebecca Dingley to settle near him, the better to conserve their small fund of money. For almost thirty-five years Stella and Swift were the closest of friends, for she was, as he said, "a person of my own rearing and instructing, from childhood, who excelled in every good quality that can possibly accomplish a human creature." She was also the inspiration for much prose and poetry by Swift. While he negotiated with Harley, St. John and the Tories in London in 1710 and 1711, he also found time to write a minutely detailed account of his activities (the *Journal to Stella*), which he then posted to his favorite ladies in Ireland. In the poem shown here Swift relates (in the guise of Apollo) an incident involving Stella and Dr. Patrick Delany, a colleague of Swift. The two had apparently written a poem on the window glass of the Deanery house. Apollo accuses Delany of stealing some verses he had "lock'd in my Box at *Parnassus*." Finding them guilty of the crime, he condemns Delany to a splenetic existence:

> And lastly for *Stella*, just out of her Prime,
> I am too much reveng'd already by Time;
> In return to her Scorn, I send her Diseases,
> And will now be her Friend whenever she pleases;
> And the Gifts I bestow'd her, will find her a Lover,
> Tho' she lives 'till she's Grey as a Badger all over.

Also in the Morgan Library are Swift's manuscripts of "Baucis and Philemon," "Stella at Wood-Park" and several other poems. The manuscript of his *Journal to Stella* is in the British Library.

Apollo to the Dean/ Right Trusty (and so forth) we let you to know,/ We are very ill us'd by You Mortals below./ For, first, I have often by Chimists been told/ (Though I know nothing on't) it is I that make Gold,/ Which when you have got, you so carefully hide it,/ That Since I was born, I hardly have spy'd it./ Then, it must be allow'd that whenever I shine/ I forward the Grass, and I ripen the Vine;/ To me the good Fellows apply for Relief/ Without whom they could get neither Claret nor Bief;/ Yet their Wine and their Vittels, those Curmudgeon Lubbards/ Lock up from my Sight in ~~Pantryes~~ Cellars and Cubbords:/ That I have an ill Eye they wickedly think,/ And taint all their Meat, and sow'r all their Drink./ But thirdly, and lastly, it must be allow'd/ I alone can inspire the Poeticall Crowd;/ This is gratefully own'd by each Boy in the Colledge,/ Whom if I inspire, it is not to my Knoledge;/ This ev'ry Pretender in Rime will admit,/ Without troubling his Head about Judgment or Wit:/ These Gentlemen use me with Kindness and Freedom,/ And as for their Works, when I please I may read'um;/ They ly open on Purpose on Counters and Stalls,/ And the Titles I view when I shine on the Walls. . . .

Apollo to the Dean

251

Right Trusty (and so forth) we let you to know,
We are very ill us'd by You Mortals below.
For, first, I have often by Chimists been told.
(Though I know nothing on't) it is I that make Gold,
Which when you have got, you so carefully hide it.
That since I was born, I hardly have spy'd it.
Then, it must be allow'd that whenever I shine
I forward the Grass, and I ripen the Vine;
To me the good Fellows apply for Relief
Without whom they could get neither Claret nor Bief;
Yet their Wine and their Vittels, those Curmudgeon Lubbards
Lock up from my Sight in Cellars and Cubbords:
That I have an ill Eye they wickedly think,
And taint all their Meat, and sow'r all their Drink.
But thirdly, and lastly, it must be allow'd
I alone can inspire the Poeticall Crowd;
This is gratefully own'd by each Boy in the Colledge.
Whom if I inspire, it is not to my Knoledge;
This ev'ry Pretender in Rime will admit,
Without troubling his Head about Judgment or Wit:
These Gentlemen use me with Kindness and Freedom,
And as for their Works, when I please I may read 'um;
They ly open on Purpose on Counters and Stalls,
And the Titles I view when I shine on the Walls.
But a Comrade of Yours, that Traitor Delany
Whom I for your Sake have us'd better than any,
And of my meer Motion, and speciall good Grace,
Intended in time to succeed in Your Place;
On Tuesday the tenth, seditiously came
With a certain false Traitress, one Stella by name,
To the Deanery House, and on the North Glass
Where for fear of the Cold, I never can pass,
Then and there, vi et armis, with a certain Utensill
Of value five shillings, in English a Pencill,
Did maliciously, falsly, and traitrously write,
While Stella aforesaid stood by with the Light:

92-a

JONATHAN SWIFT

Letter, copied in the hand of John Gay and signed "Richard Sympson," dated London, 8 August 1726, to Benjamin Motte. 1 p. 319 x 196 mm. MA 563.

In September 1725 Swift informed Pope that his "Travells" were finished and "intended for the press . . . when a Printer shall be found brave enough to venture his Eares." His recent experience with the publication of the *Drapier's Letters* (1723–4) had taught him the value of a pseudonym, and he intended to adopt one for the volume now popularly called *Gulliver's Travels.* "The chief end I propose to my self in all my labors," Swift wrote in the same letter to Pope, "is to vex the world rather than divert it, and if I could compass that designe without hurting my own person or Fortune I would be the most Indefatigable writer you have ever seen." Accordingly, when Swift sailed for England the following March, he brought with him a transcript of *Travels into Several Remote Nations of the World* and arranged for its publication under the false name of Lemuel Gulliver. Even the negotiations with the bookseller Benjamin Motte were carried on pseudonymously. This letter, signed "Richard Sympson" and copied by John Gay, is the cover letter sent with the transcript of *Travels* to Motte. Swift negotiated with confidence—"the printing these Travels will probably be of great value to you," he writes—and the immediate success of *Travels* bore him out entirely. Since the bitter satire in his book was directed rather toward mankind at large than toward specific political enemies, the secrecy surrounding its publication was somewhat unwarranted. The Morgan Library owns two other pseudonymous letters by Swift regarding *Travels*, Motte's letter to "Sympson" accepting *Travels*, and one of the copies of *Travels* (another is in the Forster Collection of the Victoria and Albert Museum) that contain manuscript corrections by Charles Ford.

London Augt 8.th 1726 S^r^ My Cousin M^r^. Lemuel Gulliver entrusted me some Years ago with a Copy of his Travels, whereof that which I here send you is about a fourth part, for I shortned them very much as you will find in my Preface to the Reader. I have shewn them to several persons of great Judgment and Distinction, who are confident they will sell very well: And although some parts of this and the following Volumes may be thought in one or two places to be a little Satyrical, yet it is agreed they will give no Offence, but in that you must Judge for your self, and take the Advice of your Friends, and if they or you be of another opinion, you may let me know it when you return these Papers, which I expect shall be in three Days at furthest. The good Report I have received of you makes me put so great a trust into your Hands, which I hope you will give me no Reason to repent, and in that Confidence I require that you will never suffer these Papers to be once out of your Sight. . . .

Sr

London Augt. 8th. 1726

My Cousin Mr. Lemuel Gulliver entrusted me some Years ago with a Copy of his Travels, whereof that which I here send you is about a fourth part, for I shortned them very much as you will find in my Preface to the Reader. I have shewn them to several persons of great Judgment and Distinction, who are confident they will sell very well: And although some parts of this and the following Volumes may be thought in one or two places to be a little Satyrical, yet it is agreed they will give no Offence, but in that you must Judge for your self, and take the Advice of your Friends, and if they or you be of another opinion, you may let me know it when you return these Papers, which I expect shall be in three Days at furthest. The good Report I have recived of you makes me put so great a trust into your Hands, which I hope you will give me no Reason to repent, and in that Confidence I require that you will never suffer these Papers to be once out of your Sight.

As the printing these Travels will probably be of great value to you, so as a Manager for my Friend and Cousin I expect you will give a due consideration for it, because I know the Author intends the Profit for the use of poor Sea=men, and I am advised to say that two Hundred pounds is the least summ I will receive on his account, but if it shall happen that the Sale will not answer as I expect and believe, then whatever shall be thought too much even upon your own word shall be duely repaid.

Perhaps you may think this a strange way of proceeding to a man of Trade, but since I begin with so great a trust to you, whom I never saw, I think it not hard that you should trust me as much. Therefore if after three days reading and consulting these Papers, you think it proper to stand to my agreement, you may begin to print them, and the subsequent parts shall be all sent you one after another in less than a week, provided that immediatly upon your Resolution to print them, you do within three days deliver a Bank Bill of two hundred pounds, wrapt up so as to make a parcel to the Hand from whence you receive this, who will come in the same manner exactly at 9 a clock at night on Thursday which will be the 11th Instant.

If you do not aprove of this proposal deliver these Papers to the person who will come on thursday

If you chuse rather to send the Papers make no other Proposal of your own but just barely write on a piece of paper that you do not acept my offer.

I am

Sr

your Humble Servant

Richard Sympson

67

Jonathan Swift

Autograph letter signed with initials, dated 17 July 1735, to John Boyle, fifth Earl of Orrery. 3 pp. 184 x 149 mm. MA 455.

Swift was an exile in his homeland. "As to my native country," he wrote to a friend, "I happened by a perfect accident to be born here . . . and thus I am a Teague, or an Irishman, or what people please, although the best part of my life was in England." Though accident accounted for his Irish birth, it was due to the political nature of ecclesiastical preferment that Swift spent most of his life in Dublin as Dean of St. Patrick's Cathedral. In spite of his disliking for Ireland, he fought actively against English abuses of the Irish and, by the date of this letter, had become something of a national hero. The letters written in the latter part of Swift's life breathe a spirit of isolation and melancholy, prompted partly by his distance from English friends, partly by the onset of disease. In this letter to the Earl of Orrery, an Irishman who lived mainly in London, Swift talks of making his will and settling his small fortune on the city of Dublin "in trust for building and maintaining an Hospital for Ideots and Lunaticks." Orrery had recently sent him a copy of *Poems on Several Occasions* by John Hughes (published posthumously in 1735), a gift which provoked a characteristically acerbic reply from Swift: "I have be[en] turning over Squire Hughes's poems, and his puppy Publisher one Duncomb's Preface and Life of the Author. This is all your fault. I am put out of all Patience to the present Set of Whifflers, and their new fangled Politeness. . . . The Verses and prose are such as our Dublin third rate rime[r]s might write just the same for nine hours a day till the coming of Antichrist."

[Starting with line 10:] Stay my Lord, it continues Wednesday still, and I have be[en] turning over Squire Hughes's poems, and his puppy Publisher one Duncomb's Preface and Life of the Author. This is all your fault. I am put out of all Patience to the present Set of Whifflers, and their new fangled Politeness. Duncombs Preface is 50 Pages upon celebrating a fellow I never once heard of in my Life, though I lived in London most of the Time that Duncomb makes him flourish. Duncomb ~~sent me~~ put ~~Short~~ a short note in loose paper to make me a present of the two Volumes and desired my pardon for putting my Name among the Subscribers I was in a rage when I looked and found my Name; but was a little in countenance when I saw Your Lordships there too. The Verses and prose are such as our Dublin third rate rime[r]s might write just the same for nine hours a day till the coming of Antichrist. I wish I could send them to you by post for your Punishment.—Pray My Lord as you ride along, [illegible deletion] compute how much the Desolation and Poverty of the People have encreased since your last Travells through your dominions, Although I fancy we suffer a great deal more twenty miles round Dublin than in any of the remoter parts, except your City of Cork, who are starving (I hope) by their own Villany. . . .

is as arrogant as ever, and Dr Delany costs two Thirteens to be visited in wet weather, by which I shall be out of pocket nine pence when I dine with Him. — This Moment (Wednesday Six a clock evening July 16) Mr Philips sent me word that he Landed with his Bishop this morning, and hath sent me 2 Volumes of Poetry just reeking, by one John Hughes Esqr. Your Lordship may know that I never begin to write a Letter when it is post day, but when I have time. However, I will let you wait till to morrow, and hope to pick up some fine things from Mr Philips. So adieu My Lord, till to morrow, Which will be Thursday the 17th. — Stay my Lord, it continues Wednesday Still and I have be turning over Squire Hughes's poems, and his puppy Publisher one Duncomb's Preface and Life of the Author. This is all your fault. I am put out of all Patience to the present Set of Whifflers, and their new fangled Politeness. Duncombs Preface is 50 Pages upon celebrating a fellow I never once heard of in my Life, though I lived in London most of the time that Duncomb makes him flourish. Duncomb sent me a short note in loose paper to make me a present of the two Volumes and desired my pardon for putting my Name among the Subscribers I was in a rage when I looked and found my Name; but was a little in countenance when I saw Your Lordships there too. The Verses and prose are such as our Dublin third rate rimers might write just the same for nine hours a Day till the coming of Antichrist. I wish I could send them to you by post for your Punishment. — Pray My Lord as you ride along, compute how much the Desolation and Poverty of the People have encreased since your last Travells through your dominions, Although I fancy we suffer a great deal more twenty miles round Dublin than in any of the remoter parts, except

your City of Cork, who are starving (I hope) by their own Villany. Since you left the Town there hath not been one Ryot either in the University nor among the Cavan Bail, which causeth a great Dearth of News, nay not so much as a Review, and but two or three bloody Murders. My Lady Acheson is undone for want of Quadrille: As to my own Domestick. My old Woman can hardly roast my Chicken, she hath so many pains in her bones, and my favorite Dog your Acquaintance is in the same condition by his own fault, by pursuing one of his fellow servants round the Vineyard field, who yerked him a kick in the back, which forced him to keep his bed for some days, but is now better. His Physician is a Cobler of ninety two, who is likewise a Dog-Doctor —

Thursday 17. This being Post day I have a great mind not to finish my Letter, but defer it as usuall; onely my head being tolerable, and my [illegible] on, being invited to dine with the Lord Mayor as a Free[illegible] Drapier and builder of a future hospital, I will rid my self of your Lordship, although you and some other Business have prevented me from seeing Mr Philips, I suppose he is before this time attending on his Patron the Bishop. However I will carry this Letter with me in hopes of new additions. I called at my Lady Acheson, and in came Philips very hearty and has some excellent Storys piping hot from London, which I have intreated him to send You. His Bishop is full of Disease, but Philips pronounces him the best man alive, and he does not value the Chaplainship the thousand part so much as the agreeable manner that it was given This you will agree to be a compliment perfectly new, as new as any of my polite Conversation. I will keep you no longer, but remain My Dear Lord with more expression than the remainder of this paper will hold

ever Your &c J. S.

William Congreve
1670–1729

Autograph letters, one signed, dated 4 December 1702 and ca. March or April 1710, to Joseph Keally. 2 pp. The earlier letter, MA 3388, is the gift of Miss Julia P. Wightman in honor of Charles Ryskamp.

Unlike Vanbrugh, Congreve was content to rest after the labors of his dramatic career had ended. As Swift, an old schoolmate at Kilkenny and Trinity College, Dublin, remarked:

> Thus, *Congreve* spent, in writing Plays,
> And one poor Office, half his Days.

Dryden had proclaimed Congreve his dramatic heir, but the year of Dryden's death (1700) also marked the effective end of Congreve's active literary life. After 1691, when his novel *Incognita* was published, he rose to immediate fame with *The Old Batchelour* (1692), *The Double-Dealer* (1693) and *Love for Love* (1695). But the "moderate success" of *The Way of the World* (1700), his finest work and possibly the greatest Restoration comedy, drove him into retirement. He worked briefly with Vanbrugh at the Queen's Theatre, but for the most part he lived the life of a gentleman, supported not by "one poor Office," but by several government appointments. The last half of his life Congreve devoted to his friendships, literary and other. These two letters were written to one of Congreve's oldest friends, Joseph Keally, like Swift an Irish schoolmate and a companion during the days when Congreve had considered entering the law. The good humor that played between them is evident in Congreve's ascribing a Latin quotation from Ovid to "Jack Allen. Epist. 3^{d}."

The British Library and the Public Record Office, London, preserve the greatest number of Congreve's letters.

December 4^{the} 1702 Dear Keally I had not time to answer y^{rs} before; but I carryd the enclosed for y^{r} brother to the Secretarys office the next morning & put it into the Portugall Pacquett. I have no great faith in y^{r} promises yet I am willing to expect y^{r} performance & hope you will celebrate the ensuing festivall in Arundell Street great revolutions have been there since the Death of Sapho. things not to be entrusted to frail paper and pacquett boats. My service to inhuman Robin [wh]ose letters I always punctually answerd. an exactnesse I woud not have you observe at this time for—nil mihi re[scribas attamen ipse] veni—Jack Allen. Epist. 3^{d} [Y^{rs} Will: Congreve]

I sent to you by 9 a clock this morning but you were gon out. I went and made y^{r} Compliment to Lady Wharton & she will be glad to see you when you please. I fasted till 3 in hopes you might have come this way. pray let me know how you are disposed to morrow Yrs W Congreve thursday afternoone.

186

December 4th: 1702

Dear Keally

I had not time to answer yrs before; but I carryed the enclosed for yr brother to the Secretarys office the next morning & put it into the Portugall pacquett. I have no great faith in yr promises yet I am willing to expect yr performance & hope you will Celebrate the ensuing festivall in Arundell street great revolutions have been there since the Death of Sapho. things not to be entrusted to frail paper and pacquett boats. my service to inhuman Robin whose letters I allways punctually answer. an exactness I would not have you observe at this time for—nil mihi rescribas attamen ipse veni— Jack: Allen. Epist: 3d. Yrs Wm Congreve

I sent to you by 9 a clock this morning but you were gon out. I went and made yr Complement to Lady Wharton & she will be glad to see you when you please. I waited till 3 in hopes you might have come this way. pray let me know how you are disposed to morrow.

Yrs Wm Congreve

Thursday afternoon

69

COLLEY CIBBER
1671–1757

Manuscript "Bill for ye Stage," signed, undated, but written after 16 February 1716, also signed by Robert Wilks and Barton Booth. 1 p. 274 x 171 mm.

To his great misfortune, Colley Cibber's finest role was a nondramatic one, for he is the antihero and archdunce of Pope's revised *Dunciad*, a figure of even greater dullness than Lewis Theobald, the Shakespearean editor. In the "Advertisement to the Reader" of *The Dunciad*, Pope (behind the initials of William Warburton) explained that the change in heroes from Theobald to Cibber came about because Cibber had published in 1742 "a ridiculous book against [Pope], full of Personal Reflections which furnished him with a lucky opportunity of improving *This Poem* . . . ." The book was Cibber's pamphlet, entitled, in the true Cibberian manner, *A Letter from Mr. Cibber to Mr. Pope, inquiring into the MOTIVES that might induce him in his SATYRICAL WORKS, to be so frequently fond of Mr. CIBBER's Name*. Who could resist such a maladroit invitation to abuse its author? Certainly, Pope could not, and the world is indebted to Cibber for providing *The Dunciad* with "the only thing it wanted, *a more considerable Hero*." The enmity of Pope notwithstanding, Cibber had a successful, if often ludicrous, career on the stage as a playwright of some distinction, a theater manager at Drury Lane and the finest actor of fops in his day. Today, Cibber is remembered not only as Pope's "lively Dunce," but as the author of an important, if inflated, autobiography, *An Apology for the Life of Mr Colley Cibber* (1740).

This "Bill for ye Stage" at Drury Lane is signed by the three joint managers of the theater, and records the plays that appeared between the eleventh and sixteenth of February 1716, the year before Cibber's feud with Pope began. The plays mentioned are *Lady Jane Grey*, by Nicholas Rowe, *The Spanish Fryar*, by John Dryden, *Cato*, by Joseph Addison, and *The Distressed Mother*, by Ambrose Philips. Among the items purchased are beer, tobacco, sugar and what is no doubt a type of make-up, "Gost White."

Sat 11 Feb: Bill for ye Stage

	l s c
Lady Jane Gray — —	0 - 0 - 0
Munday 13- Spanish Fryer.	
Gost White — — —	0 - 2 - 0
Tusday 14 Catto: bear & tobacco	0 - 0/ - 6
Sugar. — —	0 - 0 - 6.
Thirsday 16 Distrest Mother	
bear tobacco — —	0 - ~~6~~ - 6
~~*Sugar*~~	~~0 - 0 - 6.~~
~~*Charis & Coaches to ye Temple*~~	~~1 - 2 - 0~~

~~*Grost out in Last weaks bill*~~

~~*Sugar* — — — 0 - 2 - 6~~

1 - 10 - 6

0 - 5 - 6

five shills, & sixpence

C Cibber.

Rob. Wilks

B Booth

Sat 11 Feb: Bill for ye Stage

	l	s	d
Lady Jane Gray — —	0	0	0
Munday 13 Spanish Fryer.			
Bott White — —	0	2	0
Tusday 14 Catto: Bear & tobacco —	0	1	6
Sugar — — —	0	0	6
Thirsday 16 Distrest Mother			
Bear tobacco — —	0	1	6
~~Sugar~~ — — —	~~0~~	~~0~~	~~6~~
~~Chairs & Coaches to ye Temple~~	~~1~~	~~2~~	~~0~~
~~Crost out in Last weeks bill~~			
~~Sugar~~ — —	~~0~~	~~2~~	~~6~~
	1	10	6
		5	6

five shills, & six pence

C Cibber.

Robt Wilks

B Booth

Joseph Addison
1672–1719

Autograph letter signed, dated 2 November 1713, to Ambrose Philips.
2 pp. 192 x 155 mm.

The last months of 1713 were a time of rest for Addison. In April his play *Cato* had opened to the cheers of London. Pope and Lady Mary Wortley Montagu offered comments on the manuscript, Swift visited a rehearsal, and Addison's new friend George Berkeley helped him to bear the excitement of opening night at Drury Lane. As Samuel Johnson said, this was the "grand climacterick of Addison's reputation." Rewarding himself for this success and for his previous accomplishments as co-author with Steele of *The Spectator*, Addison went down to Bilton Hall in Warwickshire, the estate he had purchased in February 1713. Between "killing Hares and partridges" and planting trees, the new squire found time to write to Ambrose Philips, best known as the author of *Pastorals* (1709). In early eighteenth-century literary society, political borderlines were clearly marked and closely guarded; a writer could provoke hostilities by writing insipidly as well as by crossing party boundaries. Philips commited both sins. He had rejected Swift's offer of patronage on behalf of the Tories and come over to Addison and the Whig cause. His *Pastorals* called down upon him the exquisite wrath of Pope, who ensured Philips' immortality by satirizing him in a feignedly favorable number of the *Guardian* (No. 40). Addison's stature as the preeminent man of English letters in his day was proof against most such attacks, but Philips was fair game: thanks to Pope and his circle, he has come down to us as the source of the epithet "namby-pamby," descriptive of his simple verse.

Most of Addison's letters survive in the form of copies, made either by Addison himself or by clerks—as in the case of the letters preserved in the Public Record Office, London, and those in the Charterhouse, Surrey. The greatest number of autograph letters is found in the British Library.

[I] hope to walk with you under the shade of them, which will make me truly rejoice in my planting. I woud willingly see the year turned before I come to London and have already found all the Effects of good Air and Exercise in my Health. I don't know what to talk of in this barren place but ~~of~~ my self, and shall therefore only adde that I am with the most inviolable attachment Dear Sir Your most Faithfull and most Humble Servant J. Addison Pray give my most H. Service to all friends and ꝑticularly to Col. Brett. To Ambrose Philips Esqre at Button's Coffee-house Convent-Garden Frank J. Addison

Joseph Addison

1713

hope to walk with you under the shade of them,
which will make me truly rejoice in my plantations.
I woud willingly see the year turned before I
come to London and have already found all the
Effects of good Air and Exercise in my Health.
I don't know what to talk of in this barren
place but ~~of~~ my self, and shall therefore only
adde that I am with the most inviolable
attachment Dear Sir

Your most Faithfull
and most Humble Servant
J. Addison

Pray give my most
H. Service to all friends
and particularly to Col. Brett.

To Ambrose Philips Esq
at Button's Coffee-house
Covent-Garden

Frank
J. Addison

71

Sir Richard Steele
1672–1729

Autograph letter signed, dated 19 March 1714, to Sir Thomas Hanmer. 4 pp. 231 x 177 mm.

The last number (555) of the original series of *The Spectator* appeared on 6 December 1712 and the partnership of Addison and Steele was dissolved. Henceforth, each man gave more of his time to politics in his own way, Addison with his politically ambiguous *Cato*, applauded by Whig and Tory alike, and Steele with his politically explicit periodicals *The Guardian* and *The Englishman*. A Tory ministry was in power, dependent on Queen Anne's failing health, and debate over the Treaty of Utrecht had created political chaos. It was a most interesting time for literature, since national awareness of the struggle within Parliament depended on the propaganda of two Irishmen, Jonathan Swift for the Tories and Richard Steele for the Whigs, while Daniel Defoe threaded his way between their extreme positions. Defoe had already paid and Swift and Steele would pay for their alliances, Swift when Anne died in August 1714 and the Tory government fell, and Steele somewhat earlier, when he published his inflammatory pamphlet *The Crisis* on 19 January 1713/14.

When the Queen opened Parliament on the second week of March, the hunt for Steele was on. Within two weeks, charges of seditious libel were brought against him, and on the eighteenth the House of Commons voted for his expulsion from its chambers. The next day Steele wrote this letter to the Speaker, Sir Thomas Hanmer, requesting that "proper Questions" touching his "Reputation which is dearer to Me than my life" be put to Parliament. The request was denied. But a grant of three thousand pounds appeared, probably from deep within the Whig party, and Steele was relieved from the financial consequences of vociferously defending the Whig cause under his own name.

The largest collection of letters and manuscripts by Steele is in the British Library.

I writ what I writ with the laws in my View, and thought my self safe as long as I had them on my side. I am sure I did what I did in Order to preserve them, and they are now my refuge. It is some comfort to Me that my adversaries were reduced to the lamentable shift of saying that tho what I said were true I should be an ~~idle man~~ offender in saying it. ~~But~~ This is a monstrous position for Hell is the only place which can be destroyed by Truth. My Reputation which is dearer to Me than my life, is wounded by this Vote and I know no way to heal it, but by appealing to the laws of my Countrey that they may have their due effect in the protection of Innocence.

I therefore Humbly desire proper Questions may be put to bring about resolutions of this kind to wit

That Mr. Steele who is Expelled this House for — may be prosequuted at law for His said offence, & that no non pros. or noli prosequi may be admitted in His case.

That Mr. Steele is or is not *capable of being reelected into this present Parliament. . . .*

I writ what I writ with the laws in my view, and thought my self safe as long as I had them on my side. I am sure I did what I did in order to preserve them, and they are now my refuge. It is some comfort to me that my adversaries were reduced to the lamentable shift of saying that tho what I said were true I should be an offender in saying it. This is a monstrous position for Hell is the only place which can be destroyed by Truth. My Reputation which is dearer to me than my life, is wounded by this vote and I know no way to heal it, but by appealing to the laws of my Country that they may have their due effect in the protection of Inocence.

I therefore Humbly desire proper Questions may be put to bring about resolutions of this kind to wit

That Mr Steele who is Expelled this House for— may be prosequuted at law for his said Offence, & that no non pros. or noli prosequi may be admitted in his case.

That Mr Steele is or is not capable of being reelected into this present Parliament.

I am accused of undutifulnesse to the Queen. I hope it will appear to all the World I have not deserved that imputation. If I have through Weaknesse done any thing that will support such an accusation, I know she is Mercifull, and I who have erred (If I have erred) from a good motive shall be a proper object on which to

ISAAC WATTS
1674–1748

Autograph commonplace book, undated but written after 1698. 108 pp. 145 x 92 mm. MA 515.

The claim has often been made that Restoration drama represents the moral nadir of English literature. Jeremy Collier, the first and most telling proponent of this view, was a man of courageous principles, a rebel from the Anglican church in a very dangerous time for such eccentricity, and a skilled controversialist. Moreover, he gained the distinction of humbling some of England's greatest dramatists with his *Short View of the Immorality, and Profaneness of the English Stage* (1698). The ethical foundation of his attack could not be clearer: "The business of *Plays* is to recomend Virtue, and discountenance Vice; To shew the Uncertainty of Humane Greatness, the suddain Turns of Fate, and the Unhappy Conclusions of Violence and Injustice." One reader who took delight in Collier's at times farfetched search for sexual innuendo was Isaac Watts, also characterized by his piety and, unlike Collier, by his poetic ability. This small manuscript volume contains Watts's notes (largely transcriptions) on Collier's *Short View*. It is hardly surprising that England's greatest hymn writer should agree with the nonjuring self-appointed censor of the stage. "Had I thought," Watts concludes in his final "Reflexion," "this book had so many things in generall well said, most of w:ch I have transcribd, & so many particular Citations of all sorts & pretty reflexions on 'em—. . . I think t'had been much more advisable for me to have had ye Book it self. . . ."

A Short View of ye Immorality & Profaneness of the English Stage, &c.—by Jer: Collier. M.A. Epitomiz'd, the quotations omitted, *8º 1698.*

Introduc: The business of Plays is to recommend Vertue & discounten: Vice; Tragedy is designed to show ye uncertainty of humane Greatness, suddain turns of State, unhappy conclusions of Violence & Injustice; Comedy to expose ye Singularitys of Pride & Fancy, to make Folly & Falshood Contemptible, & to bring every thing that's ill under Infamy & Neglect. The Poets have in a great measure the springs of thought & Inclination in their power. Show, Music, action, & Rhetoric are moving Entertainm^ts & Rightly employd would be very significant. But these Advantages are now in the Enemys hand, & under a very dangerous management. . . .

A Short View of ye
Immorality & Profaneness of
the English Stage, &c. —

8o: 1698. | by Jer: Collier. M.A.
Epitomiz'd. { the quotations omitted.

Introduc: The business of Plays
is to recommend Vertue & discounten:
Vice; Tragedy is designed to show ye Uncertainty of humane
Greatness, suddain turns of State, unhap-
-py conclusions of Violence & Injustice; Comedy to expose ye Singularitys of Pride & fancy, to make
ffolly & ffalshood Contemptible, & to —
bring every thing that's ill under Infamy &
Neglect. || The Poets have in a great mea-
-sure the springs of thought & Inclination
in their power. Show, Music, action, & Rhe-
-toric are moving Entertainmts. & Rightly em-
-ploy'd would be very significant. But —
these Advantages are now in the Enemys
hand, & under a very dangerous manage-
-ment. Like Cannon seiz'd, they are point-
-ed the wrong way, & by ye Strength of ye
Defence the Mischief is made the greater.
Some of ye Stage Advocates pretend the Authors Remarks on their Poetry are forreign to the business
On the Contrary he conceives it very defensible to
disarm an adversary if it may be, & Disable
him from Doing mischief. To expose that which
would

73

HENRY ST. JOHN, FIRST VISCOUNT BOLINGBROKE
1678–1751

Autograph letter unsigned, dated 12 September 1724, to Charles Ford.
3 pp. 191 x 133 mm.

In person and in print Bolingbroke aroused extreme reactions. Pope, who knew him well, considered him a celestial being; Johnson, upon learning of the publication of his *Works* (1754), edited by David Mallet, called him "a scoundrel, for charging a blunderbuss against religion and morality; a coward, because he had not resolution to fire it off himself, but left half a crown to a beggarly Scotchman, to draw the trigger after his death" (Johnson had not read Bolingbroke). Along with Robert Harley, first Earl of Oxford, Bolingbroke was the principal loser when the Tory government collapsed in 1714 and a vindictive Whig government came in. Oxford was imprisoned and Bolingbroke fled to France, where he took up philosophical studies. The rest of his life was largely a search for his former power, first in the Old Pretender's ranks, then in the service of Walpole, who soon became a bitter enemy. The author of numerous works on philosophy and history, he is more important as an influence on other authors.

This amusing letter testifies to his love for Swift, who, he argues, was really detained in Ireland only by his affection for Esther Johnson, his "Stella." Here he tries to persuade Charles Ford to assist him in his efforts to bring Swift to France: "when ye Dean therefore has Sung all Stellas perfections over in Sonnet, Ode, Pastoral &c, his Devil having no more employm^{t} will certainly run away with him. You may know enuff of ye black art perhaps to direct this Devils flight into France."

I know not whether to be pleas'd or sorry that Stella has so many good quallitys. ye Easy howrs wch she procures to our friend are reasons for the first; and his attachment to Ireland, which I believe owing to his attachm^{t} to her, ~~are~~ is a Reason~~s~~ for ye latter. my cheif hopes are plac'd on his inconstancy. I have known Several persons of lively imaginations, fond of their houses, & their gardens, as long as there were improvements to be made, and as these houses & gardens were incitements to their fancy, & continual Subjects for ye Exercise of it. But ye same Persons grew tir'd of y^{m} when they were once adorn'd beyond a possibillity of being so anymore. the Deans fancy is like that Devil wch a certain Conjurer had rais'd, and which threaten'd to carry him away, if he left him a moment unemploy'd. . . .

those necessary lessons which we would not learn voluntarily in ye School of prosperity.

I know not whether to be pleas'd or sorry that Stella has so many good quallitys. ye Easy hours wch she procures to our friend are reasons for the first; and his attachment to Ireland, which I believe owing to his attachmt to her, is a Reason for ye latter. my cheif hopes are plac'd on his inconstancy. I have known several persons of lively imaginations, fond of their houses, & their gardens, as long as there were improvements to be made, and as these houses & gardens were incitements to their fancy, & continual subjects for ye exercise of it. But ye same persons grew tir'd of ym when they were once adorn'd beyond a possibillity of being so any more. the Deans fancy is like that Devil wch a certain Conjurer had rais'd, and which threaten'd to carry him away, if he left him a moment unemploy'd. When ye Dean therefore has sung all Stellas perfections over in sonnet, Ode, Pastoral &c, his Devil having no more employmt will certainly run away with him. You may know enuff of ye black art perhaps to direct this Devils flight into France. A Person whose affairs carry'd her this Summer into England, will be oblig'd to return thither again in the beginning of ye winter. she will joyn all her skill in negromancy with yrs, and I have been inform'd by some of the best conjurers in Europe that there is a certain plastick virtue in petty coats of great efficiency in all cases of this kind.

this person regrets her not having been able to see you oftner, hopes to repair the loss at her next journey & assures you of her humble services.

Sep: ye 12th.

THOMAS PARNELL
1679–1718

Autograph letter signed, co-written with Alexander Pope, dated 19 May [1714], to Charles Ford. 3 pp. 180 x 142 mm. MA 561.

Like Swift, Parnell was an Irishman, a clergyman and a member of the Scriblerus Club. Goldsmith says of him, "Pope himself was not only excessively fond of his company, but under several literary obligations to him for his assistance in the translation of Homer." Parnell did compose an "Essay on the Life, Writings, and Learning of Homer," which appeared in the first volume of Pope's *Iliad* (1715), but there can be little question about who owed whom the greater debt. Though nine years younger than Parnell, Pope corrected much of his verse and prepared the first collection of his poetry, published by Lintot in 1722. Parnell's muse was a humorous and facile one, befitting the author of "The Flies, An Eclogue," and "The Book-Worm":

Come hither, Boy, we'll hunt to Day
The *Book-Worm*, ravening Beast of Prey.

This letter to Charles Ford, a close friend of Swift, was written by Pope and Parnell (Pope's hand can be seen at the top left) and signed with a joint signature. They addressed their letter, a marvelous piece of whimsy, "From the Romantic World," Pope's section written "By Sunshine," Parnell's "By Moonshine."

& now he Sinkes beneath our Horizon leaving some illustrated tracks of his former beauty behind him, which as they insensibly wear away are succeeded by the silver gleams of his palefacd delegate. From the dark tops of the hills She emerges into Sight to run her inconstant race over the Azure firmament. The Starrs wait around her as a numerous train of Inamorato's who confess the flames of love at the Sight of the celestiall Goddess; the fixed Starrs seem to stand amazd to behold her, ~~&~~ while the Planets dance in her presence & wink upon her as a Sett of more familiar gallants. But now while I look behold a new & more melancholly Scene, a darkning cloud intercepts her Streaming glorys, She goes behind it as a ~~lady~~ matron mounting up into a mourning chariot, & now & then peeps through it as a pretty ~~young~~ widdow looking through her crapes. [illegible deletion] Darkness ~~spreads~~ has now spread its veil over the variety of this terrestriall creation for which rejoyce ye quarrelling Oyster wenches whom it parts & ye fondling Lovers who are to meet in it but what will ye Do ye Mooncalves who have stayd late in company in hopes to go home by the light of this second luminary. . . .

Gold, and the Leaves of the Trees turn'd up with the same. But the God, better pleas'd with the Water-Tabby of the Ocean, is resolv'd to enrich it withall his Spangles. & now he sinks beneath our Horizon leaving some illustrated tracks of his former beauty behind him, which as they insensibley wear away are succeeded by the silver gleams of his palefac'd delegate. From the dark tops of the hills she emerges into sight to run her inconstant race over the Azure firmament. The Stars wait around her as a numerous train of Inamorato's who confess the flames of love at the sight of the celestiall Goddess, the fixed Stars seem to stand amaz'd to behold her, while the Planets dance in her presence & wink upon her as a sett of more familiar gallants. But now while I look behold a new & more melancholly scene, a darkning cloud intercepts her streaming glorys, she goes behind it as a ~~lady~~ matron mounting up into a mourning chariot, & now & then peeps through it as a pretty ~~young~~ widdow looking through her crapes. ~~[illegible]~~ Darkness ~~spreads~~

has now spread its veil over the variety of this terrestiall creation for which rejoyce ye quarrelling Oyster wenches whom it parts & ye fondling Lovers who are to meet in it but what will ye do ye Mooncalves who have stay'd late in company in hopes to go home by the light of this second Luminary.

By this time it is evident that we have written the day down & the night allmost through which makes it no feign'd excuse but a reall reason for us upon the account of want of time to conclude with professing our selves Your Most Aff: Frd^s

& Hum: Ser^{ts}

By Moonshine. May 19.

Pope Parnell

75

Edward Young
1683–1765

Autograph letter signed, dated 10 April 1750, to Samuel Richardson. 1 p. 180 x 114 mm. MA 2967. Purchased as the gift of Mrs. W. Rodman Fay.

Though the extant correspondence between Richardson and Young is relatively laconic (unlike Richardson's copious letters to his female admirers), it had a firm basis in affection. Young assisted the novelist as *Clarissa* neared completion, and Richardson took unusually fine care of his friend's works as they went to press. The two men first began exchanging letters in 1744, when Richardson's printing shop started work on the last three "Nights" of Young's blank-verse poem, *Night Thoughts*. Now perhaps best known for Blake's illustrations, *Night Thoughts* (and *Conjectures on Original Composition*, published in the form of a letter to Richardson) brought the poet a European reputation of vast proportions. While Young lived in retirement at Welwyn in Hertfordshire, his works were translated into French and German and appropriated by the young romantics of a later generation. The melancholy nature of his greatest poem was reflected in the morbid piety of his quiet closing years. Best of all Richardson's readers, he could appreciate Clarissa's obsession with the tomb.

In this letter Young thanks Richardson for a copy of *The Universal History*. Since this was a monumental work in numerous volumes, spawned by a coalition of printers to which Richardson belonged, it is likely that Richardson sent Young only the most recently completed volume. The Mrs. Hallows to whom he refers was his housekeeper.

Dear S^{r} I thank you for ye Universal History, & y^{r} very kind Present; Mr Stevens at ye Temple Gate will soon have money of mine in his hands, if He has not allready, & He will pay You for the History. Mine & Mrs Hallows Love & Service to You & Yours. My Eye makes writing Uneasie to me, pardon therefore the Shortness of my Letter. I am Dear S^{r} very Affectionately Yrs E Young Ap:10. 17~~4~~50.

B

L. 66.

127
1750

April 10 1750

Dear Sr

I thank you for ye Universal History, & ye very kind Present; Mr Stevens at ye Temple Gate will soon have money of mine in his hands, if He has not allready, & He will pay you for the History. Mine & Mrs Hallows Love & Service to You & Yours. — My Eye makes writing uneasie to me, pardon therefore the Shortness of my Letter.

I am Dear Sr

Affectionately Yrs

E Young

Ap: 10.
1750

ALLEN BATHURST, FIRST EARL BATHURST
1684–1775

Autograph poem "On the Death of Mr Southern," dated May 1746.
1 p. 120 x 165 mm.

By the date of this poem, 1746, Bathurst had lost most of the literary friends he had encouraged and protected for years. Congreve, Prior, Gay, Swift, Pope and now Southerne had all died, leaving in print and in their letters a rich legacy of affection for Bathurst. His numerous benefactions to an entire generation of poets and dramatists were perhaps best repaid by Pope in his *Epistle to Bathurst*:

> Oh teach us, BATHURST! yet unspoil'd by wealth!
> That secret rare, between th'extremes to move
> Of mad Good-nature, and of mean Self-love.

Like the Earl of Burlington, he represented for Pope and many others an exemplar of the proper use of riches. At Cirencester and Riskins (Richings), Bathurst's estates, Pope habitually rested, translated Homer and directed the planting of the gardens. His bower in Oakley Wood at Cirencester was, he said, "the place of all others I fancy," for life in company with Bathurst had many pleasures: "I write an hour or two every morning, then ride out a hunting upon the Downes, eat heartily, talk tender sentiments with Lord B. or draw Plans for Houses and Gardens, open Avenues, cut Glades, plant Firrs, contrive waterworks, all very fine and beautiful in our own imagination."

Thomas Southerne's dramatic career had virtually closed by 1700, though he produced several unsuccessful plays after that date. Like Bathurst, who in his old age came to know Sterne, Southerne lived a very long time, spanning the gap between Dryden, whom he assisted in the 1690s, and Gray, who met him near Burnham in 1736. As Bathurst here observes, the playwright had faded from public notice; and, in turn, the past had faded away from him; for, as Gray discovered, Southerne had lost his memory. The melancholy of this poem is both a tribute to an old friendship and the result of Bathurst's feeling that one of the greatest periods of English literature had come to an end.

On the Death of Mr Southern. May 1746./ Prais'd by the Grandsires *of the present Age,/ Shall* Southern *pass unnoted off the Stage?/ Who, more than half a Century ago,/ Caus'd from each Eye the tender Tear to flow;/ Does not his Death one gratefull Drop demand,/ In Works of Wit the* Nestor *of our Land?/* Southern *was* Drydens *Friend: Him Genius warm'd,/ When* Otway *wrote, &* Betterton *perform'd./ He knew* poor 'Nat, *[*] while regular his Fire:/ Was* Congreve's *Pattern e'er* He *rais'd Desire;/ Belong'd to* Charles's *Age, when Wit ran high,/ And liv'd so long but to behold it* die.

**Nat Lee. Mr Southerne, in a Lr. published a few Years ago, gives him this Epithet & says it was bestowd on him by all his friends after he had the misfortune of loosing his Senses.*

On the Death of Mr Southern. May 1746.

Prais'd by the *Grandsires* of the present age,
Shall *Southern* pass unnoted off the Stage?
Who, more than half a Century ago,
Caus'd from each Eye the tender Tear to flow,
Does not his Death one gratefull Drop demand,
In Works of Wit the *Nestor* of our Land?
Southern was *Drydens* Friend: His Genius warm'd,
When *Otway* wrote, & *Betterton* perform'd.
He knew *poor Nat*, while regular his Fire:
Was *Congreve's* pattern e'er *He* rais'd Desire;
Belong'd to *Charles's Age*, when Wit ran high,
And liv'd so long but to behold its *die*.

* Nat Lee. Mr Southerne in a Lr published a few Years ago, giving him this Epithet & says it was bestow'd on him by all his friends after he had the misfortune of loosing his Senses.

77

JOHN GAY
1685–1732

Autograph letter signed, dated 5 October [1713], to William Fortescue. 3 pp. 180 x 115 mm. MA 983.

As a literary form, burlesque thrives when generic expectations are strongest, a spirit of mockery playing within acknowledged bounds of strict conformity. This description applies also to a master of burlesque in the early eighteenth century, John Gay. Surrounded by worldly men capable of great earnestness (as well as great humor)—Pope, Swift, Bolingbroke and Arbuthnot—Gay seems never to have seen a need for utter sobriety; his powerful friends loved him and watched over him. After Gay's death, Pope recalled that "he was the most amiable by far, his qualities were the gentlest." When he wrote this letter to William Fortescue, a distant cousin and friend of Pope, Gay had already formed a lifelong bond with the writers who, with him, would create the Scriblerus Club in November 1713. Staying at the Duchess of Monmouth's estate in Hertfordshire, Moor Park, he was able to enjoy the aristocratic life for which he was so well suited: riding, hunting and then dilating wittily on the day's experiences. Here he explains to Fortescue the difficulty of describing a hunt in French: "when I would tell you that we owed our Game to Dogs called Pointers, I was obliged in a tedious Circumlocution to tell you that we had Dogs that lying themselves down, would direct us to the Birds."

Approximately seventy autograph letters by Gay still survive, the majority in the British Library, and many, like this one, contain fragments of verse. The mock-heroic poem from which he quotes here, *The Fan*, was not a great success, in spite of possible revisions by Pope, but it gave a clear indication of the talent that would soon produce *The Shepherd's Week* (1714) and the splendid *Trivia: or, the Art of Walking the Streets of London* (1716).

What thought what pompous Numbers can express/ Th'inconstant Equipage of female Dress?/ How the strait Stays the Slender Waste constrain,/ Or How t'adjust the Mantoe's Sweeping train?/ What Fancy can the Petticoat Surround/ With the capacious hoop of Whalebone bound?/ But Stay, presumptuous Muse, nor Boldly dare,/ The Toilette's sacred Mysteries Declare;/ Let a just distance be to Beauty paid,/ None Here must Enter but the trusty Maid./ Should you the Wardrobe's Magazine Rehearse,/ And glossy Mantoes rustle in thy Verse,/ Should you the rich Brocaded Suit unfold/ Where rising flowr's grow stiff with frosted Gold,/ The dazled Muse Would from her Subject stray,/ And in a Maze of Fashions lose her Way.

Adieu Dear Mr Fortescue. Octr. 5. Term begins the latter end of this Month. J Gay

-known tongue. Here's a Melancholy prospect before my eyes; I am now looking upon the Grove, which is now every day losing its Shade; and alas! what is a Grove without a Shade, the leaves fall; the Bowling-Green is Wet, the Roads are Dirty and I almost wish to be in London, where Pope hath been all this Summer, & Budgell is still of the same Opinion when I last saw him which is about a Month since that all the Ladies are Rascals. I have just finish'd a Poem which I wrote since I came to Moorparke, as I sent you a Specimen of the Rural Sports, I here send you a Sample of this new Production. The Poem is upon a Fan, wherein I have in some measure followed Virgil's & Homer's Shields, in the Description of its painting & invention; I have introduced Gods & Goddesses & others of little inferior Dignity. tis in english about 700 lines, but in Goodness I am afraid not above 100. when you see it I don't question but you will give me your impartial Opinion, till then take this; tis part of a Digression about Dress.

What thought what pompous Numbers can express
Th' inconstant Equipage of female Dress?
How the strait Stays the slender Waste constrain,
Or How t' adjust the Mantoe's sweeping train?
What Fancy can the Petticoat surround
With the capacious hoop of Whalebone bound?
But stay presumptuous Muse, nor Boldly dare,
The Toilette's sacred Mysteries Declare;
Let a just distance be to Beauty paid,
None Here must Enter but the trusty Maid.
Should you the Wardrobe's Magazine Rehearse,
And glossy Mantoes rustle in thy Verse,
Should you the rich Brocaded suit unfold
Where rising flow'rs grow stiff with frosted Gold,
The dazled Muse would from her Subject stray,
And in a Maze of Fashions lose her Way.

Adieu

Dear M.r Fortescue

Oct.r 5

J Gay

Term begins the latter end of this Month.

John Gay

George Berkeley
1685–1753

Autograph letter signed, dated Gravesend, 5 September 1728, to Thomas Sherlock, Bishop of London. 2 pp. 228 x 187 mm. MA 3258. Purchased as the gift of Mrs. Walter H. Page and Miss Julia P. Wightman.

George Berkeley had unbounded faith in the future of the New World and looked there for another golden age such as Europe had "bred when fresh and young." Thus there is more than a hint of apocalpyse in his poem "On the Prospect of Planting Arts and Learning in America":

Westward the course of empire takes its way;
  The first four acts already past,
A fifth shall close the drama with the day;
  Time's noblest offspring is the last.

In 1728, two years after this poem is believed to have been written, Berkeley sailed for America in order to found a college in Bermuda for the training of clergy. He and his bride of a month were aboard ship in the Thames estuary when he wrote the letter shown here to the Bishop of London, explaining his reasons for immediate departure: "It shou'd seem therefore that the intermediate time may be passed with more advantage in America where I can see things with my own eyes and prepare matters for the rendering our college more useful." Berkeley had planned to wait in Rhode Island until the necessary funds were gathered; unfortunately, the money never arrived and the college was never established. Still, the voyage to America was not lost time. In Newport his wife bore him a son and a daughter (who died in infancy) and there Berkeley preached and wrote *Alciphron, or the Minute Philosopher*. Though he returned to England in 1732, he remained interested in New England throughout his life and made important gifts of books and money to Yale University.

I intend to join them. Going to Bermuda without either money or associates I cou'd not think of. I shou'd have made but a bad figure and done no good. Staying here wou'd have been no less disagreeable and to as little purpose, since all I cou'd do here was finished except receiving the money which may as well be done by others. It shou'd seem therefore that the intermediate time may be passed with more advantage in America where I can see things with my own eyes and prepare matters for the rendering our college more useful. I humbly recommend the undertaking & my self to your Lordship's protection & prayers and remain with all duty and respect My Lord Yr. Lordship's most obedient & most devoted humble Servt. G: Berkeley

I intend to join them. Going to Bermuda without either money
or associates I cou'd not think of. I shou'd have made but a bad figure and done no good. Staying here wou'd have been no less
disagreeable and to as little purpose since all I cou'd do here
was finished except receiving the money which may as
well be done by others. It shou'd seem therefore that the intermediate time may be passed with more advantage in
America where I can see things with my own eyes and
prepare matters for the rendering our college more
useful. I humbly recommend the undertaking
& my self to Your Lordship's protection & prayers
and remain with all duty and respect

My Lord

Yr. Lordship's most
obedient & most
devoted humble
Servt. G. Berkeley

P.L.

Allan Ramsay
1686–1758

Autograph manuscript of "Henry to Emma," undated and unsigned. 2 pp. 267 x 194 mm. MA 3102. Purchased as the gift of Mrs. Hugh Bullock.

The position of a Scots-speaking gentleman of letters in the eighteenth century was a difficult one. London made literary reputations and London exacted its own linguistic decorum. Few Scottish writers were content with local fame, and the literary history of the eighteenth century records many examples of men who came south to make their reputations in English, so many that it became a standing joke between Johnson and his Scottish biographer, James Boswell. Allan Ramsay remained north of the Tweed, however. A wigmaker by profession, he turned to bookselling when he discovered a local market for his own verse. As a poet, he does not now enjoy high renown—he is remembered for a few lyrics and a very popular pastoral play, *The Gentle Shepherd* (1721)—but his influence in the literary world of Edinburgh was enormous. He edited several volumes of Scots poetry, among them *Scots Songs* (1719), *The Tea-Table Miscellany* (1724–7) and *The Evergreen* (1724–7), a collection of Scots poetry written before 1600. His bookshop became a center for literary men in Scotland; and Ramsay took the lead in a form of poetic nationalism. Like Burns later, however, he also wrote English verse of no particular distinction. This poem, "Henry to Emma," probably dates from early in his career, for it is an imitation of Matthew Prior's poem "Henry and Emma, a Poem Upon the Model of the Nut-brown Maid," published in 1708.

The finest collections of Ramsay manuscripts are in the British Library, the National Library of Scotland (which owns the manuscript of *The Gentle Shepherd*) and the University of Edinburgh.

Henry to Emma/ To Thee O Emma Lovelyest of thy kind/ whose dear Idea fills thy Henry's Mind/ Thy Henry who each Soft reflection moves/ delights to tell his Fair how much he Loves/ ~~words want full Power or description/~~ but descriptive[3] Words[2] ~~and~~ Phrases chosen best/ will faill to paint the Movements of my breast/ where thou allone oer Evry Passion ~~Reigns~~ sways/ And each with Joy almighty Love obeys/ Tho Now extended tracts of Hills and plains/ between my Fair & me augment my Pains/ yet Hope by Day & Welcome Dreams by Night/ give me the best reliefe and most delight./ Thus on the Greenland Coast without a Smile/ The Britton Lours a voluntire Exile/ in Cold inhospitable rocky Caves/ or on the yet more dangerous Icy waves/ Yet when on warm Brittania's flowry Dales/ with Joy he thinks and hopes the prosp'rous gales/ Shall bear him to his wishd for Native Shore/ his Heart beats Joyously and greifes No More

Henry To Emma

To thee O Emma Lovelyest of thy kind
whose dear Idea fills thy Henry's Mind
Thy Henry who each soft reflection moves
delights to tell his Fair how much he Loves
~~words want full power or description~~
but descriptive Words, ~~and~~ Phrases chosen best
will faill to paint the Movements of my breast
where thou allone oer Every Passion ~~Reigns~~ sways
and each with Joy allmighty Love obeys
Tho now extended tracts of Hills and plains
between my fair & me augment my Pains
yet Hope by Day & Welcome Dreams by night
give me the best reliefe and most delight.
Thus on the Greenland Coast without a smile
the Britton Lours a voluntire Exile
in Cold inhospitable rocky Caves
or on the yet more dangerous Icy waves
yet when on warm Brittania's flowry Vales
with Joy he thinks and hopes the prosp'rous gales
shall bear him to his wishd for native shore
his Heart beats Joyously and greifs no more

Alexander Pope
1688–1744

Autograph manuscript of "An Essay on Man," Book I, undated but written ca. 1731. 11 pp. 227 x 186 mm. MA 348.

Pope wrote *An Essay on Man* in the declarative mood and published it anonymously. More than any other poem by him, it draws away from the tangible world, the domain of particular personalities, of nuance and irony, of satiric potential, and turns toward the universal realm of Truth. In 1723 the former Tory leader Henry St. John, Viscount Bolingbroke, returned from political exile in Paris and settled at Dawley Farm, not far from Pope's home at Twickenham. The two men renewed their earlier acquaintance and became close friends. When Joseph Spence remarked in 1744 that Bolingbroke seemed too good for this world, Pope agreed: "when the comet appeared to us a month or two ago I had sometimes an imagination that it might possibly be come to our world to carry him home, as a coach comes to one's door for other visitors." Bolingbroke's influence over Pope was great, partly because he thought he saw in him a nobler turn of mind than that which had created the first version of *The Dunciad*, published in 1728. Under Bolingbroke's philosophical guidance Pope began to compose *An Essay on Man*, the ethical center of his writings. In a letter to Swift written in August 1731, Bolingbroke described the poem in its current state: it then consisted of three epistles, the first of which "considers man, and the Habitation, of man, relatively to the whole system of universal Being. . . ." In the section of manuscript shown here Pope justifies man's place in the scale of being; this passage (roughly corresponding to lines 207 to 242 in the published version) is the classical early eighteenth-century expression of the middle state of man.

The Morgan Library houses the most complete and earliest draft of all four epistles of *An Essay of Man*, which was published in 1733 and 1734. Another draft of this poem is in the Houghton Library, Harvard University.

[Starting with recto page:] The bliss of Man (could Pride that blessing find)/ Is, not to know nor think beyond Mankind;/ No self-confounding Faculties to share;/ No Senses stronger than his brain can bear./ Why has not Man a microscopic Eye?/ For this plain reason, Man is not a Fly:/ What the advantage, if his finer eyes/ Study a Mite, not comprehend the Skies?/ His Touch, if tremblingly alive all o'er,/ To smart, and agonize at ev'ry pore?/ Or quick Effluvia darting thro his brain,/ Dye of a Rose, in Aromatic pain?/ If Nature Thunder'd in his opening Ears,/ And stunnd him with the Music of the Spheres,/ How w^d he wish that Heav'n had left him still/ The whisp'ring Zephyr and the purling Rill?/ Who finds not Providence all-good ~~all~~ & wise,/ Alike in what it gives, & what denies? . . .

See, thro whole Life

Behold, thro all a gradual Scale arise,
Of Sensual, and of mental Faculties!
14- ~~How wide the~~ vast Range of Sense, from ~~human~~ Man's imperial race
To the green Myriads in the peopled Grass!
~~How many~~ What Modes of Sight ~~between~~ betwixt each wide extreme,
The Mole's dim Curtain & the Lynx's Beam!
vel delend | ~~Degrees~~ Of Smell, the headlong Lioness between,
And Hound, sagacious on the tainted green!
Of Hearing, from the Life that fills the Flood,
To that which warbles thro the vernal Wood!
In the nice Bee, what sense so subtly true
From poisnous herbs extracts the healing Dew!
The Spiders touch, how exquisitely fine,
Feels at each thread, and lives along the line!
How Instinct varies! what a Hog may want
Compar'd with thine, half-reas'ning Elephant!
Twixt that Instinct, and Reason, what a nice Barrier,
For ever sep'rate, yet for ever near!
15- Remembrance and Reflexion, how allied!
What thin partitions Sense from Thought divide!
And middle natures, how they long to join,
Yet never pass th' Insuperable Line!
Without this just Gradation, could they be
Subjected these to those or all to thee?
The Pow'rs of all subdu'd by thee alone,
Is not thy Reason all those pow'rs in one?

The

The bliss of Man (could Pride that blessing find)
Is, not to know nor think beyond Mankind;
No self-confounding Faculties to share;
No Senses stronger than his brain can bear.
Why has not Man a microscopic Eye?
For this plain reason, Man is not a Fly:
What the advantage, if his finer eyes -16
Study a Mite, not comprehend the Skies?
His Touch, if tremblingly alive all o'er,
To smart, and agonize at ev'ry pore?
Or quick Effluvia darting thro his brain,
Dye of a Rose, in aromatic pain?
If nature Thunder'd in his opening Ears,
And stunn'd him with the Music of the Spheres,
How w^d he wish that Heav'n had left him still
The whisp'ring Zephyr and the purling Rill?
Who finds not Providence all-good, & ~~all~~-wise,
Alike in what it gives, & what denies?

See, thro' this Air, this Ocean & this Earth,
All Matter quick, and bursting into Birth.
Above, how high progressive Life ~~must~~ may go? (17
Around, how wide? how deep extend below?
Vast Chain of Being! which from God began,
Ethereal Essence, Spirit, Substance, Man,
Beast, Bird, Fish, Insect: what no Eye can see,
No Glass can reach! From Infinite to Thee!
From Thee to Nothing! — On superior Pow'rs
Were we to press, inferior ~~might~~ might on ours:

Or

Alexander Pope

Autograph manuscript draft of the poem "Of Taste: An Epistle to the Earl of Burlington," undated but written ca. 1730–1. 2 pp. 302 x 186 mm. MA 352.

An Essay on Man was but the first part of a much larger ethical work—Pope's "Opus Magnum"—conceived under Bolingbroke's aegis and never completed in its entirety. Pope told Spence that *An Essay on Man* was to the rest of the proposed "Ethick Epistles" what "a Scale of Miles [is] to a book of Maps." Though the Scale is essential, the Maps are much more interesting; for the former is an outline of possible virtues, the latter, his *Epistles to Several Persons*, a graphic depiction of available vices and actual examples of moral good. Richard Boyle, third Earl of Burlington, shared with Pope a tremendous effect on the arts of architecture and gardening in the early eighteenth century. Under Burlington's sponsorship the architectural principles of Palladio acquired a new currency; he encouraged and funded works on Palladio and Inigo Jones and was the patron of the architect William Kent, who lived at his home. Burlington also built the lovely neo-Palladian villa at Chiswick, just downstream from Pope's house at Twickenham which he helped design. This manuscript represents a very early stage in the composition of the poem which was variously called "Of Taste," "Of False Taste" and "Of the Use of Riches," and which was first published in 1731. The *Epistle to the Earl of Burlington* celebrates the aesthetic that he and Pope advocated: a belief in proportion, in the decorum that nature provides.

> To build, to plant, whatever you intend,
> To rear the Column, or the Arch to bend,
> To swell the Terras, or to sink the Grot;
> In all, let Nature never be forgot:

[Starting with line 23:] Oft' have You hinted to your Brother Peer,/ A certain truth, which many buy too dear:/ Something there is, that should precede Expence,/ Something to govern Taste itself—'tis Sense;/ Good Sense, which only is the Gift of Heav'n,/ And tho' no Science, yet is fairly worth the Seven:/ ~~'Tis in yourself you must this Light perceive,/~~ A Light, wch in yourself y^{u} must perceive/ ~~Jones & Lenôtre have it not to give./ For Gibs & Bridgeman~~ have it not to give/ Jones & Lenôtre/ To build, to plant, whatever you intend,/ To rear the Column, or the Arch to bend,/ To swell the Terras, or to sink the Grot;/ In all, let Nature never be forgot:

OF *TASTE*:

AN

EPISTLE

To The

EARL of BURLINGTON.

'Tis strange, we think, that Misers still employ
Their Cares to gather Wealth they ne'er enjoy:
Is it less strange, the Prodigal should waste
His Wealth to purchase what he ne'er can taste?
~~Not for himself, but Fountain, Gems he buys;~~
Pictures, of price for Mohun, or for Guise;
For Topham, Drawings & far-sought Designs;
For Curio, Statues, dirty Gods, and Coins;
Rare Monkish Manuscripts for Herne alone;
And Books for Mead, & Butterflies for Sloan.
Think we all these are for Himself? No more
Than his fine Wife, my Lord, or finer Whore.
For what has Virro built, and painted, planted?
Only to show how many Tastes he wanted.
What brought Sir Shylock's ill-got Wealth to waste?
Some Dæmon whisper'd, "Knights should have a Taste".
Heav'n visits with a Taste the wealthy Fool,
And needs no Rod, but Mo—s with a Rule.
See sportive Fate, to punish aukward Pride,
Bids Dado build, and reads him such a Guide;
A ~~[illegible]~~ Sermon! at each Years Expence,
That never Coxcomb reach'd Magnificence.

Not for himself he sees, or hears, or eats,
Artists must chuse his Pictures, Music, Meats;
He buys for Topham Drawings & Designs,
For Pembroke Statues & for Curio Coins;
Rare Monkish — and Books

Must Bishops, Lawyers, Statesmen, have ye Skill
To build, to plant, judge Paintings, w^t ye Skill
Then why not twist Heat and Treaties
Bridgman explain ye Gospel, Gibs Draw Laws?

Oft have You hinted to your Brother Peer,
A certain truth, which many buy too dear:
Something there is, that should precede Expence,
Something to govern Taste itself—'Tis Sense;
Good Sense, which only is the Gift of Heav'n,
And tho' no Science, fairly is worth the Seven:
A Light, wch in yourself y^u must perceive,
Jones & Le Nôtre have it not to give.
To build, to plant, whatever you intend,
To rear the Column, or the Arch to bend,
To swell the Terras, or to sink the Grot;
In all, let Nature never be forgot:

Con-

ALEXANDER POPE

Autograph letter signed, dated 25 December 1738, to William Fortescue. 4 pp. 226 x 182 mm. MA 561.

Alexander Pope flourished, in part necessarily so, behind a succession of satiric masks and rhetorical strategies, and to expect him to drop these completely in his letters is to expect too much. His correspondence seemed to find its way into print, with or without his connivance, and many of his letters were written with just that end in mind. This letter to his friend William Fortescue, written on Christmas Day 1738, is both a public and a private epistle. Pope suggests that Fortescue show his laudatory paragraph about the munificent Ralph Allen to him as a means of answering "a Letter I lately had from him, inviting me to Bath." (Allen was a patron of Pope and Fielding; Squire Allworthy in *Tom Jones* was modeled on him.) Pope then moves into a more personal mode, full of friendly feelings for the absent Fortescue; but his style soon swells as he looks back over the past. "Mine are *poor* Vanities," he writes, "a few of the *worst sort* of Laurels. I began my Life without any Views, & hope to end it without any Regretts. I have raised no Estate, nor aimd at it . . . I shall dye poor but not dishonourd; and if no body weeps for me, nobody will curse my Memory." This is the rhetorically pious Pope of the *Epistle to Dr. Arbuthnot*, in which he invokes the memory of his father, from whose manner of living his own life differed so much:

> Born to no Pride, inheriting no Strife,
> Nor marrying Discord in a Noble Wife,
> Stranger to Civil and Religious Rage,
> The good Man walk'd innoxious thro' his Age.

The largest collection of Pope's autograph letters is in the British Library.

[Starting with line 9:] As you are at Bath, I hope you are acquainted with the Best Man there, and indeed one of ye Best Men any where, Mr Allen: If you do not know him Well, *you will not know him* Enough*; and pray let me lay one Obligation upon you as you have layd many on me, in making you know him better. Shew him this paragraph in my Letter, & it will answer a Letter I lately had from him, inviting me to Bath, whither I need no Inviting while Either of you are there, could I supersede what I think a duty: If ever you draw my Affections ~~farther~~ nearer Devonshire than the Bath, you will have cause to think y^{r}self very Powerfull; for there's no Journey I dread like it, not even to Rome, tho both ye Pope & Pretender are there. The last ten miles of Rock between Malborow & Bath almost killed me once, & I really believe the Alps are more passable than from thence to Exeter. Jervas has written his Wife a most Poetical Letter of his Travels over them, upon wch I intend to Ground my letter to him. If you send me yours, in folio, I'll fill it up, or add another Sheet to it. Y^{r} Chimney piece I'll take care of; but God knows I little expect ever to sit by its side. I must be content to see the Light of y^{r} Countenance by a London or Twitnam Fire, at which places I have set up my Rest. I smile at You w^{n} you talk to me of our* mutually *renouncing the* Pomps *of ye World. pray when was I a Partaker of them? . . .*

by attending you to Bath, wch I wd infallibly have done.

I shd be glad to hear first, that your journey was well & safely performd, & the Effect of ye Waters after, as you can give me that satisfaction. Yr Compliments to the two Ladies I have made, ye Evening I receivd yr kind Letter, & I made my best efforts to have got just to see you that Evening, but it was too cold, & too late, for my sad infirm Carcase, which ill corresponds with ye Motions of my Heart.

As you are at Bath, I hope you are acquainted with the Best Man there, and indeed one of ye Best Men any where, Mr Allen: If you do not know him Well, you will not know him Enough; and pray let me lay one Obligation upon you as you have layd many on me, in making you know him better. Shew him this paragraph in my Letter, & it will answer a Letter I lately had from him, inviting me to Bath, whither I need no inviting while Either of you are there, could I supersede what I think a duty. If ever you draw my affections ~~farther~~ nearer Devonshire than the Bath, you will have cause to think yrself very Powerfull; for there's no Journey I dread like it, not even to Rome, tho both ye Pope & Pretender are there. The last Ten miles of Rock between Malbrow & Bath almost killed me once, & I really believe the Alps are more passable than from thence to Exeter. Jervas has writ her his Wife a most Poetical Letter of his Travels over them, upon wch I intend to ground my letter to him. If you send me yours, in folio, I'll fill it up, or add another Sheet to it. Yr Chimney piece I'll take care of; but God knows I little expect ever to sit by its Side. I must be content to see the Light of yr Countenance by a London or Twitnam Fire, at which places I have set up my Rest. I smile at you wn you talk to me of our mutually renouncing the Pomps of ye World. pray when was I a Partaker of them? What Ribans, what Titles, what Furs, yea what Coifs, did I ever wear, or attempt to wear? Mine are poor Vanities, a few of ye worse sort of Laurels. I began my Life without any Views, & hope to end it without any Regretts. I have raised no Estate, nor aimd at it, tho I inherited none. I have livd decently, & not servilely, that's enough for me: I shall dye poor, but not dishonourd; and if nobody weeps for me, nobody will curse my Memory. Let Greater Men say this, if they can, & let them be Good if they dare; ~~but~~ but alas, they hardly dare to be Quiet. Their Trust is in other mens Meanness & Vices, or they wd not be what we call Great. Your situation is a happy one, as it makes

Samuel Richardson
1689–1761

Autograph letter signed, dated 1 February 1749/50, to Miss Frances Grainger. 2 pp. 216 x 180 mm. MA 1024.

Miss Frances Grainger must have just finished reading *Clarissa. Or, The History of a Young Lady*... when she wrote to Samuel Richardson about the relative merits of Miss Howe's suitor, Hickman, and Clarissa's raptor, Lovelace. The final three volumes of *Clarissa* (published in seven volumes beginning in 1747) appeared in early December 1748. As he composed his novels Richardson customarily sought the opinions of his friends and family. This process seems to have involved him in some perplexity as he tried to sort out conflicting advice about *Clarissa*. One suggestion was nearly unanimous, however: shorten the novel, which had grown to thirty manuscript volumes before it reached its final form. The author ignored his friends' advice, for each passage he tried to omit turned out to contain a "beauty." Richardson's most difficult decision was to let Clarissa Harlowe, like Little Nell almost a century later, go to her death against the wishes of sentimental readers. Sensibly, he felt it advisable to print a postscript explaining his choice of endings.

Like his heroes and heroines, Richardson was a prolific letter writer, a useful propensity for an author of epistolary novels; more than five hundred autograph letters survive, most in the Forster Collection of the Victoria and Albert Museum, South Kensington. His correspondence with Miss Grainger began in December 1748, when she was twenty-two, and it thrived on controversy. She advanced dangerous attitudes not only about Lovelace—such as her "generous, tho' hazardous Hope of Reforming a Lovelace by [her] example"—but also about Richardson himself. In this letter he deftly and paternally deflects the love she had expressed for him in her most recent letter.

[Beginning with last paragraph on verso page:] And thus, Madam, are we at last agreed. I congratulate myself upon it; and repeat, that I admire you in Twenty Places, of the Letter before me. Never fear, my dear Miss Grainger, that I can give you up. Your Papa is very kind to me. I love not writing for Writing['s] Sake; but if, as you flatter me, I can do any Service to the Young Ladies I have the Honour to be acquainted with, I have a real Pleasure in it; For this purpose, more than for any private one, was Clarissa written. And as Miss Grainger has a numerous Acquaintance among her own Sex, who can doubt of the Extensive Influence of her Example?—And could we make our future Daughters not worse than their Mothers, that may be of more Benefit to the next Age than can easily be imagind.

I read to my good Wife, the distinguishing Honour you do me in acknowledging a Love for me. She thanks you most sincerely for your Favour to me: And as I have the Pleasure of receiving it in a filial Sense, I will subscribe my self my Dear Miss Grainger, Paternally Yours S. Richardson Febr. 1. 1749/50. I have lent to a worthy Divine, who had read the first Red Cover'd Volume, the Second. As soon as it is return'd, it shall attend you.

shall be encouraging. Yet the dear Creatures will have more Awe than I wish them to have. But if I was not all this: If I had visible and great Faults, I should hope, that the good Son of Noah rather than the bad ones, would be their Example.

So, Madam, you see, that I am not in Love with the Word Authority, any more than you. But my Dear, let me say, since you put the Case (and very prettily and laudably you put it) of your own Conduct as a Mother, that I should rather, much rather, have you disclaim it (shew your Aversion to it, in your strong Word) as a Mother, than as a Daughter. It would be more generous at least. Don't you think, my dear Miss Grainger, that it would? And permit me to add, that when in one place you say, that you have from Principle some of Clarissa's Notions of Duty, as to concealing or extenuating Parents Faults, I am not so fully convinced of this good Principle, by another, where you tell me, that were you to judge by your own Heart, the Exertion of the Parents Authority, you are sure, would have a revolting Effect upon you; — and you should be a worse Girl than Miss Howe. "Don't let your Confession of this, you request, confirm "my Opinion of your being half a Rogue." Dear Miss Grainger! — Do you not think, that you'll come very well off, if I account you, at this Rate, but half a one?

I am afraid, greatly afraid, my Dear, that you are a young Lady, that had all your Will till Eight Years of Age. You'll excuse me for this Personality. I had not Personality in my Head before.

Your Mamma will tell me, that you are not a Clarissa, in this Particular — I came not home till near 9 o'Clock last Night; but I will attend your Mamma very soon; and we will try this Cause, if you please, at her Bar.. And yet I am apt to credit every thing that a Lady says of herself.

To what you say of faulty Parents, and their Suspicions, needless Vigilance, Tyranny, &c. I entirely subscribe. I must repeat to this purpose, my Reference to you of the Bona Fide of Lovelace. But I never understood, that our Debate on the filial Duty was confined on your Part to sensible Daughters and wrong-headed Mothers; on mine, to wise Parents and foolish Children. The general Duty, The general Right and Wrong, was my View to lay down. Particular Cases were to claim their Exemptions from the general Rule. The Mrs. Woodford would have been condemned by these Exemptions; Miss Woodford, so far as she deserved Acquittal, would have been acquitted. The Tenor of the whole History of Clarissa is this on both Sides. And once more, I must say, to my dear Miss Grainger, that had she attended to it, as more than a Romance, she would have found it so; and spared her self some Trouble. With your intriguing, extravagant, uncontroulable, gaming Daughters I have nothing to do. Those Parents most heartily do I pity who are cursed with such, if by their early Indulgence, which you so laudably condemn, and by their own bad Examples, they have not contributed to their Wickedness (Follies is too light a Word for such). If they have, or by a negligent or faulty Education, let them, unpitied, take the Consequence of their own Faults.

And then, Madam, are we at last agreed. I congratulate my self upon it; and repeat, that I admire you in Twenty Places of the Letter before me. Never fear, my dear Miss Grainger, that I can give you up. Your Papa is very kind to me. I love not writing for Writing Sake; but if, as you flatter me, I can do any Service to the young Ladies I have the Honour to be acquainted with, I have a real Pleasure in it; For this purpose, more than for any private one, was Clarissa written. And as Miss Grainger has a numerous Acquaintance among her own Sex, who can doubt of the Extensive Influence of her Example? — And could we make our future Daughters not worse than their Mothers, that may be of more Benefit to the next Age than can easily be imagined.

I read to my good Wife, the distinguishing Honour you do me, in acknowleging a Love for me. She thanks you most sincerely for your Favour to me: And as I have the Pleasure of receiving it in a filial Sense, I will subscribe my self my Dear Miss Grainger,

Paternally Yours

Febr. 1. 1749/50.

S. Richardson

I have lent to a worthy Divine, who had read the first Red Cover'd Volume, the Second. As soon as it is return'd, it shall attend you.

Samuel Richardson

Samuel Richardson

Autograph manuscript of the "History of Mrs Beaumont a Fragment in a letter from Dr. Bartlett, To Miss Byron," undated, possibly written ca. 1754–5. 19 pp. 190 x 150 mm. MA 377.

Richardson was a master of claustrophobic situations. Bound by virtue and the wishes of their families, threatened by the unwanted addresses of Squire B. and Lovelace, the heroines of *Pamela* and *Clarissa* seem continually to be retreating from house to house, room to room, until the only escape is marriage or death. Another heroine of this sort, Miss Hortensia Beaumont, survives only in this autograph manuscript, written in the form of a letter from Dr. Bartlett to Harriet Byron, both characters in Richardson's last novel, *Sir Charles Grandison*. The fictional Miss Beaumont was the daughter of a merchant, left when her father died to be raised by her uncle, who defrauds her of her fortune and tries to force her into marriage with one of his clerks. She flees the family, declines the advances of an extremely shy man who would marry her in the midst of her woes, and eventually travels to Italy.

Conjectures abound about Miss Beaumont. It has been suggested that this fragment of her history was excised from *Sir Charles Grandison* (the manuscript of which is lost), and there is evidence to believe that Richardson considered writing a novel based on her adventures after he finished *Grandison* (1754). The most interesting conjecture, made by Richardson's first biographer, Mrs. Barbauld, suggests that Miss Beaumont was a real woman with whom the author was once in love. Indeed, Richardson occasionally dropped hints to friends about an early love affair, and the description of the modest "Mr. R" corresponds to Richardson's description of himself as a youth: "When I was young, I was very sheepish." Miss Beaumont is perhaps the only one of Richardson's heroines to decline a suitor for being excessively modest.

Mrs. Winwood, the pious, the patient, Mrs. Winwood, was the only Person to whom the young Sufferer could open her Heart. And she continually inculcated in her Mind the Doctrines of Resignation which she herself to her great Comfort, daily practised.

At last the Insults she met with being not to be borne; among the rest, the unmarried Daughters insisting upon the Young Lady's Attendance upon them, in their Dressing-Rooms, the afflicted Hortensia desired a patient Audience of her Uncle alone.

He, tho' ungraciously, granted her Request: And she laid before him the Hardships she laboured under from the Ill-Nature of her Cousins, and their Demands upon her for attending them.

His Answer, delivered with great Coldness, was, "He knew no Harm in young Ladies doing kind Offices for one another. He doubted not but her Cousins would be as ready to oblige her, as she was them."

She wept. It was far otherwise, she said. He must know it was far otherwise. . . .

Mrs. Winwood, the pious, the patient, Mrs. Winwood, was the only Person to whom the young Sufferer could open her Heart. And she continually inculcated on her Mind the Doctrines of Resignation which she herself to her great Comfort, daily practised.

At last the Insults she met with being not to be borne; among the rest, the unmarried Daughters insisting upon the young Lady's Attendance upon them, in their Dressing-Rooms, the afflicted Hortensia desired a patient Audience of her Uncle alone.

He, tho' ungraciously, granted her Request: And she laid before him the Hardships she laboured under from the Ill-Nature of her Cousins, and their Demands upon her for attending them.

His Answer, delivered with great Coldness, was, "He knew no Harm in young Ladies "doing kind Offices for one another. He doubted not but her Cousins would be as ready "to oblige her, as she was them."

She wept. It was far otherwise, she said. He must know it was far otherwise.

"That, he said, was calling upon him to bear Testimony against his own Chil-"dren.

She had hoped, she replied, that she might have been considered as one of his Children.

"So she had been, and still was; tho' he must needs say, that of late she had sh-"herself a pretty pert one."

Who I! who I, my Uncle, a pert one! – Indeed I have been treated as if I were so. But I know not my self if I am.

She called out for Instances, that she might rectify her Conduct.

"What signified recriminating?" She was a very young Creature; and, for the Sake "of her Father's Memory, he was desirous to overlook common Failings."

My Father's Memory! repeated she, profoundly sighing. But, Sir, after a Pause, if my Aunt will have the Goodness to countenance the poor Orphan a little more when my Cousins use me ill, and chide them when she thinks them blameable, instead of smiling at their Insults and Ridicule, I shall not, for the future, have so much Reason to complain as I have now.

"She called herself Orphan, he replied, to reflect upon him and her Aunt. Stranger "was a good-natured Woman; and it was hard if she might not be allowed to smile "at the Jests of young Folks with young Folks."

She wept. He knew, she said, that was not the Case. She never dared to jest with them: Nor was her Situation of late such, as disposed her to jest.

He could hardly contain himself on this. His Conscience allowed him to take the Hint in the severest Sense; yet had not Strength enough with him, to make his Resentment yield to Justice. He stormed.

She was terrified: But resuming some little Courage; I am unhappy indeed, said she. I hoped to raise to my self a Protector in my Uncle; and intended not to offend him. I must not call my self an Orphan; What can I call myself? – I am

too

85

Lady Mary Wortley Montagu
1689–1762

Autograph manuscript of "born to be slaves our Fathers freedom sought" and "Venus to ye courts above," written ca. 1734. 2 pp. 193 x 152 mm. MA 347.

When Joseph Spence met Lady Mary in Italy in 1741, he called her "the most wise, most imprudent; loveliest, disagreeablest; best natured, cruellest woman in the world." This accurately summarizes the vicissitudes of her reputation. As she herself said, "it was my fate to be much with the wits"; she was esteemed as an intellectual, a poet, a woman of brilliant social qualities and a champion of inoculation against smallpox (from which she herself had suffered). But her greater renown was that of a malicious wit, suited indeed to her sparring partner, Alexander Pope. His friendship for her had intensified during her residence in Constantinople (where her husband was ambassador from 1716 to 1718) into mildly erotic ardor, a feeling which she repulsed with laughter. Their feud sputtered into print on Pope's side first; Lady Mary made her response, among other places, in a manuscript poem mimicking *An Essay on Man*, in which Pope supposedly says to Bolingbroke:

> You, learned Doctor of the publick Stage,
> Give gilded poison to corrupt the Age;
> Your poor Toad-eater I, around me scatter
> My scurril jests, and gaping Crouds bespatter.

Lady Mary's true fame arose shortly after her death with the publication of her letters, many of them written from abroad where a great part of her life had been spent. Shown here is an epigram probably written for the 1734 elections and a verse compliment to Lady Mary, copied in her own hand, by an unknown author. The manuscripts and letters of Lady Mary Wortley Montague remain largely in private hands, primarily among the Wortley manuscripts owned by the Earl of Harrowby.

---

born to be slaves our Fathers freedom sought/ & wth their blood ye valu'd treasure bought/ We their mean ofspring our own bondage plot/ & born to Freedom for our chains we vote

Venus to ye courts above/ confirm'd y^t you were born for Love/ For this endu'd wth every grace/ Minerva's wit, her own dear face/ A Heart sincere, O matchless prize/ The thoughts apparent in ye Eyes/ Eyes wch glow wth warm desire/ Melting wishes, gentle Fire/ this own'd; does yr perfections prove/ ~~H~~ I am ye Object of y^r Love?/ ~~O~~ Nor that the Fopling you can mend/ Whose follys ~~you~~ only you defend/ is cause that quiting masks & plays/ in solitude you spend y^r days.

So haughty Patriots missing of their Aim
left their Devotion to their Royal Dame
yet still desirous in some court to shine
paid their addresses to ye Princes shrine

Pagina mendax
Quon alios spesque metusque necant

born to be slaves our Fathers freedom sought
& wth their blood ye valu'd treasure bought
we their mean offspring our own bondage plot
& born to Freedom for our chains we vote

Venus to ye courts above
confirm'd yt you were born for Love
For this endu'd wth every grace
Minervas wit, her own dear face
a Heart sincere. O matchless prize
The thoughts apparent in ye Eyes
Eyes wch glow wth warm desire
~~melting~~ wishes, gentle Fire
this own'd; does yr perfections poore
Who am ye Object of yr Love?
Or that the Fonling you commend
whose follys ~~warmly~~ you defend
is cause that quiting marks & plays
in solitude you spend yr days

Philip Dormer Stanhope, fourth Earl of Chesterfield 1694–1773

Autograph letter unsigned, dated Bath, 5 November 1739, to his son Philip. 3 pp. 226 x 184 mm.

Certain stereotypes about the eighteenth century seem all-pervasive: it is unjustly considered an age of shallow grace and punctilious immorality. No author has fostered or suffered by these imputations more than that complex and sophisticated figure, Lord Chesterfield. Nineteenth-century reaction to him may be summed up in a single quotation from Dickens' *Barnaby Rudge*, in which John Chester (modeled on Chesterfield) contemplates *Letters Written by the . . . Earl of Chesterfield, to his Son, Philip Stanhope* (1774): "in every page of this enlightened writer, I find some captivating hypocrisy which has never occurred to me before, or some superlative piece of selfishness to which I was utterly a stranger." Chesterfield was not half the devil he is portrayed as being. The young Philip Stanhope, the natural son of Chesterfield and Mlle. de Bouchet, whom he met while he was ambassador at The Hague, proved to be an ungainly youth, shy and lacking in the address so necessary for worldly advancement in the eighteenth century. The letters from Chesterfield to his son were not intended for publication, nor do they provide a generalized scheme of education: they offer specific advice designed to counter specific tendencies in young Philip. Even Samuel Johnson, who contributed so much to Chesterfield's ill repute by writing a largely unjust letter about his lack of support for the *Dictionary*, admitted that, with the immorality removed, the *Letters to His Son* "should be put into the hands of every young gentleman." The letter shown here is a fine example of the affection and humanity with which Chesterfield wrote to his son, who was seven at the time this letter was written.

Bath. Nov: ye 5th 1739 Dear Boy I am glad to hear that you went to see the Lord Mayor's show, for I suppose it amus'd you, and besides, I would have you see every thing. It is a good way of getting knowledge, especially if you enquire carefully (as I hope you always do) after the meaning, and the particulars of every thing you see. You know then, to be sure, that the Lord Mayor is the Head of the City of London, and that there is a new Lord Mayor chosen every year. That the city is govern'd by the Lord Mayor, the Court of Aldermen, and the common councill. There are six and twenty Aldermen, who are the most considerable tradesmen of the City; the Common councill is very Numerous, and consists likewise of Tradesmen, who all belong to the several companys, that you saw march in the procession, with their colours and Streamers. The Lord Mayor is chosen every year out of the Court of Aldermen. There are but two Lord Mayors in England; one for the city of London, and the other for the city of York. The Mayors of other Towns, are only call'd Mayors, not Lord Mayors. People who have seen little, are apt to stare sillily, and wonder at every new thing they see, but a Man, who [illegible deletion] has been bred in the world, looks at every thing with coollness and sedateness, and makes proper observations, upon what he sees.

Bath Nov: yᵉ 5ᵗʰ 1739

Dear Boy

I am glad to hear that you went to see the Lord Mayor's show, for I suppose it amus'd you, and besides, I would have you see every thing. It is a good way of getting knowledge, especially if you enquire carefully (as I hope you always do) after the meaning, and the particulars of every thing you see. You know then, to be sure, that the Lord Mayor is the Head of the City of London, and that there is a new Lord Mayor chosen every year. That the city is govern'd by the Lord Mayor, the Court of Aldermen, and the common councill. There are six and twenty Aldermen, who are the most considerable tradesmen of the City; the Common council is very Numerous, and consists likewise of Tradesmen. who all belong to the several companys, that you saw march in the procession, with their colours and Streamers. The Lord Mayor is chosen every year out of the Court of Aldermen. There are but two Lord Mayors in England; one for the city of London, and the other for the city of York. The Mayors of other Towns, are only call'd Mayors, not Lord Mayors. People who have seen little, are apt to stare sillily, and wonder at every new thing they see, but a Man, who [redacted] has been bred in the world, looks at every thing with coolness and sedateness, and makes proper observations, upon what he sees.

87

JAMES THOMSON
1700–1748

Autograph manuscript of the poem "Come, dear Eliza, quit the Town," undated but written ca. 1743. 1 p. 229 x 185 mm. MA 1575. Purchased as the gift of the Fellows.

In 1743 Thomson applied himself not only to correcting and enlarging his most famous poem, *The Seasons*, but also to winning the heart of Miss Elizabeth Young, who, like himself, hailed from Scotland. He was rather more successful at the former task. *The Seasons* seemed to swell with each passing year, as did its popularity. A masterpiece of blank verse when the dominant form was the heroic couplet, it is a topographical extension of the patriotic themes that run through Thomson's other works, *Liberty* and *Britannia* among them. The diction of Augustan England, so compact in Pope's verse, is stretched by Thomson along a looser syntax which reflects the discursive nature of the poem:

> Hence from the busy Joy-resounding Fields,
> In chearful Error, let us tread the Maze
> Of Autumn, unconfin'd; and taste, reviv'd,
> The Breath of Orchard big with bending Fruit.

Elizabeth Young inspired a different sort of verse, more closely akin to the lyrics of the stage, for which Thomson also wrote. This charming poem did not have its intended effect, however. "Eliza" married an admiral, and when Thomson published the poem he effaced her memory by substituting the name "Amanda." Contemporary opinion of "Eliza" differed radically from the poet's: one writer considered her "as regular a red-haired, 'rump-fed ronyon' as ever startled the passing traveller into wondering whether she were man or woman."

Song./ 1 Come, dear Eliza, quit the Town,/ And to the rural Hamlets fly:/ Behold, the wintry Storms are gone;/ A gentle Radiance glads the Sky.

2 The Birds awake, the Flowers appear,/ Earth spreads a verdant couch for thee;/ 'Tis Joy and Music all we hear,/ 'Tis Love and Beauty all we see.

3 Come, let us mark the gradual Spring,/ How peeps the Bud, the Blossom blows;/ Till Philomel begin to sing,/ And perfect May to swell the Rose.

4 Let us secure the short Delight,/ And wisely crop the blooming day;/ Too soon our Spring will take it's Flight:/ Arise, my Love, and come away.

Song

1

Come, dear Eliza, quit the Town,
And to the rural Hamlets fly:
Behold, the wintry storms are gone;
A gentle Radiance glads the sky.

2

The Birds awake, the Flowers appear,
Earth spreads a verdant Couch for thee;
'Tis Joy and Music all we hear,
'Tis Love and Beauty all we see.

3

Come, let us mark the gradual Spring,
How peeps the Bud, the Blossom blows;
Till Philomel begin to sing,
And perfect May to swell the Rose.

4

Let us secure the short Delight,
And wisely crop the blooming day;
Too soon our Spring will take it's Flight:
Arise, my Love, and come away.

DAVID MALLET
1705?–1765

Autograph letter signed, dated Hanover-Square, 2 November 1762, to John Stuart, third Earl of Bute. 3 pp. 197 x 161 mm.

David Mallet was a Scotsman who anglicized his original name, Malloch, because southerners could not pronounce it, and who has been described as a "whiffler in poetry." He also managed extremely well the unwieldy process of securing patronage from the nobility of England. This letter is shown not because of any peculiar literary merit but because it represents a type of epistle which must have been written hundreds of times in the eighteenth century, usually with far less success than this one found. Before 1762, Mallet had produced several plays, including *Alfred*, written with his close friend and fellow Scotsman, James Thomson. The play to which he alludes here, *Elvira*, did not win much acclaim, even though it was staged by Garrick. Along with some well-directed flattery, *Elvira* did, however, affect the mind of the Earl of Bute, to whom this letter is addressed, for in 1763 Mallet received the post of inspector of exchequer-book in the outports of London, a sinecure he enjoyed for only two years before his death. A perfect index of the inequities wrought by the system of literary patronage is the fact that Samuel Johnson had received through Lord Bute the year before a pension from George III for the same sum that Mallet "earned" in his nominal post: £300.

In that case, I would venture to beg a second favor; a leisure hour, if any of yours at present can be such, first to hear it red. You will then judge, and your Lordship is able to judge in the last appeal, whether it will deserve the patronage I am here soliciting. Should you find reason to deny me this distinction, I will readily mortify my own vanity into your opinion: and, what you will find equally true, my Lord, that denial will not make the smallest alteration in the high regard and honest attachment with which I am Your Lordship's most faithful humble servant D. Mallet. George-Street, Hanover-Square, ~~Oct~~ Novr. 2d, 1762.

and abettors, I will do myself this honor, if
you think it agreable. In that case, I would
venture to beg a second favor; a leisure
hour, if any of yours at present can be such,
first to hear it red. You will then judge,
and your Lordship is able to judge in the
last appeal, whether it will deserve the
patronage I am here soliciting. Should you
find reason to deny me this distinction,
I will readily mortify my own vanity into
your opinion: and, what you will find
equally true, my Lord, that denial will
not make the smallest alteration

in the high regard and honest attachment
with which I am

Your Lordship's
most faithful
humble servant
D. Mallet.

George Street,
Hanover-Square,
Nov.r 2d, 1762.

89

Henry Fielding
1707–1754

Autograph receipt signed, dated 11 June 1748, to Andrew Millar for the purchase of the copyright of "Tom Jones". 1 p. 82 x 199 mm. MA 789.

The eighteenth century produced many distinctive authorial voices—one naturally thinks of Pope, Johnson and Sterne—but none is more engaging than Fielding's. By 1748, the date of the receipt shown here, he had mastered even more literary forms than Defoe. His relentlessly satiric plays provoked Sir Robert Walpole's administration to introduce a theatrical licensing act in 1737, effectively forcing him to turn to another genre. His experience in the theater was not lost, however. As a dramatist, Fielding had specialized in "rehearsal plays," based on Buckingham's *The Rehearsal* (1671). These are essentially plays within plays, for in them an author watches his work being rehearsed and comments upon its action as it occurs. This double perspective proved to be a very useful literary and satiric tool, and Fielding employed it again, in a slightly different manner, in *The History of Tom Jones, A Foundling*. Though the garrulous and intrusive narrator is a familiar convention of romance, Fielding perfected the technique, stepping into the midst of his novel to instruct, to cajole and to entertain, as he explains in Chapter Two: "Reader, I think proper, before we proceed any farther together, to acquaint thee, that I intend to digress, through this whole History, as often as I see Occasion: Of which I am myself a better Judge than any pitiful Critic whatever. . . ." Fielding found an appreciative Reader, for the first edition of *Tom Jones* was completely sold out before its advertised publication date in February 1749.

June 11 1748 Recd of Mr. Andrew Millar Six hundred Pounds being in full for the Sole Copy Right of a Book called the History of a Foundling in Eighteen Books. And in Consideration of the Said Six Hundred Pounds I promise to assign over the Said Book to the Said Andrew Millar his Executors and assigns for ever when I shall be thereto demanded. Hen: Fielding

The Said Work to contain Six Volumes in Duodecimo.

£ s d.

£: 600; 00, 00:

June 11 1748

Recd of Mr. Andrew Millar Six hundred Pounds being in full for the sole Copy Right of a Book called the History of a Foundling in Eighteen Books. and in Consideration of the said Six Hundred Pounds I promise to assign over the said Book to the said Andrew Millar his Executors and assigns for ever when I shall be thereto demanded.

£ s d
£:600:00:00.

Hen: Fielding

The said work to contain six Volumes in Duodecimo.

Henry Fielding

Autograph manuscript of legal notes entitled "Of Outlawry in Criminal Causes," undated but written probably ca. 1745. 22 pp. 316 x 176 mm. From the Collection of Mrs. Donald F. Hyde.

Besides being a novelist, playwright, theater manager, journalist and puppeteer, Fielding was also a justice of the peace. When Walpole imposed his theatrical licensing act in 1737, the former dramatic satirist enrolled at the Middle Temple. Needless to say, Fielding approached his legal career with the same energy he had applied to his dramatic career. Lawbooks began to pile up and manuscript extracts and notebooks based on them began to multiply. As always, publication was not far from his mind; the manuscript shown here, "Of Outlawry in Criminal Causes," may have been intended for a work entitled *An Institute of the Pleas of the Crown*, advertised in 1745 but never published. Appropriately, Fielding's first legal appointment was to the Commission of the Peace for Westminster, more specifically to the justice court in Covent Garden, the scene of so much of his dramatic labor. He and his blind half-brother, Sir John Fielding, who succeeded him in 1754, played an important part in the history of criminal justice in London.

Manuscripts by Fielding are unusually scarce, and of those that survive, the most important are legal in nature. The most significant collection of Fielding manuscripts is that from which the one shown here comes, the Hyde Collection in Somerville, New Jersey.

Chapt. 1. Of Outlawry in Criminal Causes. 1. Upon [illegible deletion] Indictment [illegible deletion] for Treason, Felony; [illegible deletion] ~~or Trespass~~ or Trespass vi et armis if the Deft be not in Custody Prowfs of Outlawry lies. But if he be once in Custody of ① Record, as where the Sheriff returns ② cepi to the ③ Capias, if he afterwards escape, the Sheriff shall be punished, but no ④ exigent awarded. @χ a. H.H. PC. vol. II 202. //This refers to ye fifth page back . . .

Chapt 5. Of Outlawry in Criminal Causes.

1. Upon ~~an~~ Indictment ~~[illegible]~~ for Treason, Felony, ~~[illegible]~~ or Trespass vi et armis ~~or trespass~~ if the Deft be not in Custody Process of Outlawry lies. But if he be once in Custody of Record, as where the Sheriff returns cepi to the Capias, if he afterwards escape, the Sheriff shall be punished, but no Exigent awarded. (a) ✕ — This refers to 5th fifth page back — a. H. H. P C. vol II 202.

2. In order to prosecute a Criminal to an Outlawry there must be either first an Appeal ~~of~~ the Party injured wch was formerly usual in all ~~Cases of~~ Felonies but hath of late been totally discontinued unless in ~~Murder~~ ... or 2dly an Indictment ~~either originally [illegible]~~ ~~[illegible]~~ of Record in the Court whence the Writ issues (b) ... — This refers to y fifth page back — (b) H. H. P C. I. 5 ... Bract C 3 c 12 de Cor

~~3. The Court of B R either on an Indictment found before them or removed by Certiorari.~~

3. If an Indictment be found in B R or removed into that Court by Certiorari, a Capias issues to the Sheriff of the County where the Deft is indicted, and on the Sheriff's Return that he is not found in his Bailywick ~~[illegible]~~ an Exigent shall go unless it be testified that ~~he~~ the Deft is in some other County, then a Capias and Exigent shall issue into that County, ~~&c~~ (c) — (c) H. H. P C II 19[illegible]

4) Justices of Oyer and Terminer may ~~[illegible]~~ Capias & Exigent & so proceed to outlaw any person indicted before them This

(1) The Reason of this is that no Averment is suffered agt the Truth of a Record. (2) When a Sheriff arrests a Man on a Writ he endorses on the Back of it cepi corpus I have taken the Body, and at ye Day wch ye Writ is returnable he sends it back ~~[illegible]~~ endorsed, which ye Endorsement or Return of the Sheriff becomes likewise part of the Record. (3) The Writ commanding him to arrest the Body. (4) This is explained a little below. (5) In Latin Appellum, i e a Call. a Term taken from the Civil Law and means a calling upon another to answer some allegation in a Court of Justice, in which the Plaintiff or caller is named Appellant, the Deft or person called on is the Appellee. (6) ... [illegible]

91

Samuel Johnson
1709–1784

Autograph manuscript of "The Life of Pope," undated but written in 1780. 184 pp. 227 x 189 mm. MA 205.

In the entire range of English criticism no voice speaks with more good sense and natural authority than Johnson's, partly because of his vigorous style and partly because of the ethical emphasis of much of his criticism. His best critical writings are grounded in biography; for he affirmed, with some qualifications, Cicero's belief in the direct relationship between moral and literary harmonies. Casual though they be, Johnson's *Lives of the Most Eminent English Poets* (published separately in 1781) offered him the opportunity to assess in print the preceding century of verse. He called them "little lives, and little Prefaces" but they are the central critical achievement of the eighteenth century. By the time his "Life of Pope" was published, a younger generation had begun seriously to reconsider the merits of Pope's reputation. New poets had grown up since Pope's death in 1744; and, uncertain that he might not have been a mere versifier, they posed a problem which Johnson solved resoundingly at the conclusion of his "Life." "After all this," he assured his audience, "it is surely superfluous to answer the question that has once been asked, Whether Pope was a poet? otherwise than by asking in return, If Pope be not a poet, where is poetry to be found?" Shown here is Johnson's comparison of Pope with Dryden, remarkable for the justice with which he discriminates the relative virtues of two of England's greatest poets: "The flights of Dryden therefore are higher, but Pope continues longer on the wing. Of Dryden's fire the blaze is brighter, of Pope's the heat is regular and constant."

Of Genius, that power which constitutes a Poet, that quality without which judgement is cold, and knowledge is inert, that ~~whic~~ energy which collects, combines, amplifies, and animates, the superiority must, with some hesitation, be allowed to Dryden. It is not to be inferred that of this poetical vigour Pope had only a little, because Dryden had more, for every other writer since Milton, must give place to Pope, and even of Dryden it ~~can only~~ must be said that ~~though~~ he has brighter paragraphs, ~~he has~~ but not better poems. Dryden's performances were hasty, either elicited by some external occasion, or extorted by domestick necessity. he ~~compsosed~~ composed with ~~little~~ out consideration, and published with ~~little~~ out correction. What his mind could supply at call, or gather in one excursion was all that he sought, and all that he gave. The dilatory caution of Pope enabled him to condense his ~~thoughts~~ sentiments, ~~and~~ to multiply his images, and to accumulate whatever study might produce, or chance might supply. The flights of Dryden therefore are higher, but Pope continues longer on the wing. Of Dryden's fire the blaze is brighter, of Pope's the heat is regular and constant. Dryden often ~~exceeds~~ surpasses expectation, and Pope never falls below it. Dryden is read with frequent astonishment, and Pope with perpetual delight.

Of Genius, that power which constitutes a Poet, that quality without which judgement is cold, and knowledge is inert, that ~~active~~ energy which collects, combines, amplifies, and animates, the superiority must, with some hesitation, be allowed to Dryden. It is not to be inferred that of this poetical vigour Pope had only a little, because Dryden had more, for every other writer since Milton, must give place to Pope, and even of Dryden it ~~can only~~ must be said that ~~though~~ he has brighter paragraphs, ~~he has~~ but not better poems. Dryden's performances were always hasty, either excited by some external occasion, or extorted by domestic necessity. he ~~composed~~ composed with~~out~~ ~~little~~ consideration, and published with~~out~~ ~~little~~ correction. What his mind could supply at call, or gather in one excursion was all that he sought, and all that he gave. The dilatory caution of Pope enabled him to condense his ~~thoughts~~ sentiments, ~~and~~ to multiply his images, and to accumulate whatever study might produce, or chance might supply. The flights of Dryden therefore are higher, but Pope continues longer on the wing. Of Dryden's fire the blaze is brighter, of Pope's the heat is regular and constant. Dryden often ~~exceeds~~ surpasses expectation, and Pope never falls below it. Dryden is read with frequent astonishment, and Pope with perpetual delight.

Samuel Johnson

Autograph letter signed, dated 11 December 1782, to Mrs. Hester Lynch Thrale. 3 pp. 190 x 158 mm. MA 204.

In spite of what Mrs. Thrale called his "natural roughness of manner," Johnson was a creature formed for society: "I think scarce any temporal good equally to be desired with the regard and familiarity of worthy men." The Club, founded in 1764, was an institution which guaranteed Johnson (weekly at first and then fortnightly) the conversation of worthy men like Sir Joshua Reynolds, Oliver Goldsmith, Edmund Burke, David Garrick, James Boswell and Edward Gibbon. By the date of this letter to Mrs. Thrale, The Club's membership had quadrupled from its original number of eight, and in the midst of this august body of men, even Johnson paid unusual attention to the quality of his discourse. "We had yesterday a very crouded Club," he writes here to Mrs. Thrale, "St Asaph, Fox, Bourke [Burke], Althrop, and about sixteen more. And the talk was of Mrs Siddons [the actress]. Can you talk skilfully of Mrs Siddons? I had nothing to say. There was talk of Cecilia [Fanny Burney's second novel],—and I did better." Because *Cecilia* was mentioned, Mrs. Thrale sent this letter to Fanny Burney, who endorsed it, "This letter from Dr. Johnson to Mrs. Thrale was kindly sent to me at the time she received it; and was never reclaimed." It eventually found a place in her collection of letters from Dr. Johnson as "No. 6," and thus was not included by Mrs. Thrale in her published correspondence with Johnson.

We had yesterday a very crouded Club. St Asaph, Fox, Bourke, Althrop, and about sixteen more. And the talk was of Mrs Siddons. Can you talk skilfully of Mrs Siddons? I had nothing to say. There was talk of Cecilia,—and I did better.

Then I went to the Painters distribution of prizes. Sir Joshua made his Speech. The king is not heard with more attention.

I have very sorry nights, and therefore but chearless days. But I hope things will mend with us all. Let me continue to be, Dear Madam, Your most humble Servant Sam: Johnson Dec. 11. 1782

inclined to think him right. Therefore, dear Lady, hope the best. The best is indeed very bad, so bad that hope can hardly be joined with it. Let us however remember with gratitude that the worst, is but negative; it will not be distress.

We had yesterday a very crowded Club. Sir Joseph, Fox, Burke, Althorp, and about sixteen more. And the talk was of Mrs Siddons. Can you talk skilfully of Mrs Siddons? I had nothing to say. There was talk of Beattie, and I did better.

Then I went to the Painters distribution of prizes. Sir Joshua made his Speech. The King's is not heard with more attention.

I have very sorry nights, and therefore but cheerless days. But I hope things will mend with us all. For me continue to be,

Dear Madam,

Your most humble Servant

Sam: Johnson

Dec. 11. 1782

93

Samuel Johnson

Autograph prayer, dated 1 January 1784. 2 pp. 184 x 115 mm. MA 206.

Beneath Johnson's positive manner lay a brooding concern with religion, characteristic not only of his own troubled mind, but of the perplexity with which the eighteenth century as a whole faced the problem of faith. The counsel given at the end of Johnson's *Vanity of Human Wishes*—"Implore his aid, in his decisions rest,/ Secure whate'er he gives, he gives the best"—was not easily taken, even by its author. New Year's, Easter and his birthday were annual occasions for introspection and for the composition of prayers intended both to ease his conscience and to overcome the "scruples" which "encumber and obstruct my mind." This prayer was written on the first of January 1784, the last year of Johnson's life, in the midst of "a very severe winter" during which he "was confined to the house in great pain, being sometimes obliged to sit all night in his chair. . . ."

Most of the manuscripts of Johnson's prayers are in the library of Pembroke College, Oxford; other major collections are in the Bodleian Library, Oxford, and in the Hyde Collection, Somerville, New Jersey.

1784 Jan. 1 p.m. 11. O Lord God, heavenly Father, by whose mercy I am now beginning another year, grant, I beseech thee that the time which Thou shalt yet allow me, may be spent in thy fear and to thy glory, give me such ease of body as may enable me to be useful, and remove from me all such scruples and perplexities as encumber and ~~perplex~~ obstruct my mind, and ~~so enable help~~ help me so to pass by the direction of thy Holy Spirit through the remaining part of life that I may be finally received to everlasting joy through Jesus Christ, our Lord. Amen.

1784
Jan. 1. p.m. 11.

O Lord God, heavenly Father,
by whose mercy I am now beginning
another year, grant, I beseech thee
that the time which Thou shalt
yet allow me, may be spent in thy
fear and to thy glory, give me
such ease of body as may enable
me to be useful, and remove from
me all such scruples and perplexities as encumber and ~~perplex~~ obstruct my mind, and ~~to~~ ~~enable~~ help me
to pass by the direction of thy
Holy Spirit through the remaining part of life that I may be
finally received to everlasting joy
through Jesus Christ, our Lord.
Amen.

David Hume
1711–1776

Autograph letter signed, dated Lisle Street, 25 July 1766, to Madame La Présidente de Meinières. 3 pp. 324 x 270 mm. MA 668.

When David Hume and Jean-Jacques Rousseau landed at Dover on 11 January 1766, it seemed as though the French philosopher might at last enjoy a peaceful exile (he had fled from France in 1762 after the publication and condemnation of *Emile*) and the English philosopher might earn vicarious celebrity as his host. Instead, their brief friendship and bitter quarrel provided one of the great philosophical sideshows of the eighteenth century. After an attempt to share Hume's Lisle Street home, Rousseau retreated to the country where he hoped to escape the crush of notoriety. Isolated at Wooton Hall in Derbyshire, the author of *Emile* conceived the neurotic fantasy that Hume had formed a conspiracy with the sole intention of humiliating him before the English people. Of course, Hume was innocent of such charges; he had been campaigning with declining patience for a pension on Rousseau's behalf. When he learned of his supposed friend's accusations, he was furious; both sides took to print, the papers were filled with the scandal of Rousseau's prodigious and characteristic paranoia, and Boswell, who had seduced Rousseau's mistress (and was then subjected to a comic *éducation sentimentale*), devised a caricature of the entire episode.

This letter from Hume to a Parisian friend outlines the origins of his quarrel with Rousseau, but it errs on one point: no part of the fracas would be a "high Panegyric" on either man. Hume soon regained his balance, however. He had completed his *History of England* in 1761 and been lionized at Paris, where he enjoyed intellectual renown of a sort he had not seen for some years in England; following this dismal conflict with Rousseau, he joined Pitt's administration as Under-Secretary of State to General Conway. Approximately 350 autograph letters by Hume survive, primarily in the Royal Society of Edinburgh.

[Starting with second paragraph:] You desire an Account of my Transactions with M. Rousseau, which are certainly the most unexpected and most extraordinary in the World. I shall endeavour to abridge them as much as possible. It is needless to give you a long ~~Account~~ Detail of my Behaviour towards him while he lived here and in this Neighbourhood, the Marks of Affection and Attachment which I gave him, my Compliance with all his Humours, my constant Occupation in his Service. I was blamed by all my Friends for giving him so much of my Time and Care, and was laughed at by others. All the Letters, which I wrote to any part of the World, were honourable and friendly for him; and he, on his part, gave me the warmest Testimonies of Gratitude, seemed transported whenever he saw me, and after he went to the Country, he wrote me Letters, which I have happily preserved, and which contain Expressions of Friendship that even the Energy of his Pen cou'd not carry farther. I settled him in a most beautiful Country, with a very honest Gentleman of about 7000 Pounds Sterling a Year, and who at my Entreaty takes 30 pounds a Year of board for ~~M. Rousseau~~ him & his Gouvernante. The Gentleman himself lives at about 20 Miles distance; from him; so that every thing seemed, as if it were contrived to make ~~him~~ our Philosopher happy and easy. I was also very fortunate in my Negotiations for his Pension ....

5

Lisle Street Leicester Fields 25 of July 1766

Tho' I have great Reason, Madam, to be ashamed, when I am prevented by you, in writing, I own, that your Letter gave me a sensible Pleasure: I am happy in retaining some Share in your Memory and Friendship; and I hope, that the same Disposition will incline you to have Indulgence for me in my very culpable Silence. But my Indolence in this particular is unaccountable even to myself. You know, I lived almost with M. de Montigny, and his Family and that there are no Persons in the World for whom I have a greater Value: Yet except one Letter to Mde Dupré, I have given them no Testimony of my Gratitude or Esteem. I cannot possibly ~~give~~ tell a stronger Instance of my ill Behaviour in this particular.

You desire an Account of my Transactions with M. Rousseau, which are certainly the most unexpected and most extraordinary in the World. I shall endeavour to abridge them as much as possible. It is needless to give you a long Detail of my Behaviour towards him while he lived here and in this Neighbourhood, the Marks of Affection and Attachment which I gave him, my Compliance with all his Humours, my constant Occupation in his Service. I was blamed by all my Friends for giving him so much of my Time and Care, and was laughed at by others. All the Letters, which I wrote to any part of the World, were honourable and friendly for him; and he, on his part, gave me the warmest Testimonies of Gratitude, seemed transported whenever he saw me, and after he went to the Country, he wrote me Letters, which I have happily preserved, and which contain Expressions of Friendship that even the Energy of his Pen coud not carry farther. I settled him in a most beautiful Country, with a very honest Gentleman of about 7000 Pounds Sterling a Year, and who at my Entreaty takes 30 pounds a Year of board for ~~M. Rousseau~~ him & his Gouvernante. The Gentleman himself lives at about 20 Miles distance from him; so that every thing seemed, as if it were contrived to make ~~him~~ our Philosopher happy and easy. I was also very fortunate in my Negotiations for his Pension. I first consulted himself: He gave his Consent: He wrote the same thing to Lord Mareschal. I then applyed to the Ministers, particularly to General Conway, Brother to Lord Hertford: I was favoured by their ~~Concurrence~~ Compliance; only on Condition, that the Affair shoud remain a Secret. I introduced Rousseau to them, who thanked them for their Goodness. The Affair was not brought to a full Conclusion before he went to the Country by reason of General Conway's Sickness; but was soon after finished. I informed Rousseau: He wrote to M. Conway, that he coud not take the Pension as long as the King was resolved to keep it a Secret. I then desired M. Rousseau to recollect, that he was informed of this Circumstance from the beginning, and that he not only agreed to it but was pleased with it; and I entreated him to return

To Mme. de Meinières

to

Laurence Sterne
1713–1768

Autograph manuscript of a sermon on "Penancies," preached on 8 April 1750. 29 pp. MA 418.

For better or worse, Sterne was a clergyman as well as an author; this meant that like Homenas in his "Fragment in the Manner of Rabelais" he usually "had to preach next Sunday—knowing Nothing at all of the Matter." To Sterne, however, the "Matter" came more easily than it did to Homenas, and when *Tristram Shandy* brought him immediate notoriety he stood ready to profit from it by the publication of his sermons. The first two volumes of *The Sermons of Mr. Yorick* were published in 1760; in 1765 Sterne, with plans for volumes three and four in his head, wrote to Garrick, "I have had a lucrative winter's campaign here—Shandy sells well—I am taxing the publick with two more volumes of sermons, which will more than double the gains of Shandy—It goes into the world with a prancing list of *de toute la noblesse*." The manuscript shown here is that of a sermon on penances, in which Sterne argues, on plausible grounds, "That God never intended to debar Man of Pleasure, under certain Limitations" and that stringent asceticism is therefore as much an error as hedonism. *The Sermons of Mr. Yorick* offended some readers, but not Thomas Gray, whose comment upon them gives an indication of the balance they maintain between piety and impropriety: "they are in the style I think most proper for the Pulpit, & shew a very strong imagination & a sensible heart: but you see him often tottering on the verge of laughter, & ready to throw his perriwig in the face of his audience."

Among the other Sterne manuscripts in the Morgan Library is a series of twelve love letters to Catherine Fourmantel, a "letter-book" containing twenty-eight letters to and from Sterne, and a contemporary manuscript, once thought to be in Sterne's hand, of *A Sentimental Journey*.

From this representio~~ns~~ of Things, ~~It seems plain~~ we are led to this demons^ve^ Truth—then That God never intended to debar Man of Pleasure, under certain Limitations—

Travellers on a Business of the last & most important Concern, may be allowed to please their Eyes with the natural and artificial Beauties of the Country they are passing thro' without reproach of forgetting the main Errand They ~~a~~were sent upon: And if They are not led out of their Road, by variety of Prospects Edifices & Ruins, would it not be a senseless Piece of Severity to shut their Eyes ag^st^ such Gratifications—

From this representation
of Things, we are led to this demonst.^e Truth, ~~It seems plain~~ then
That God never intended to
debar Man of Pleasure, under
certain Limitations –

Travellers on a Business
of the last & most important
Concern, may be allowed to
please their Eyes with the
natural and artificial Beau-
-ties of the Country they are
passing thro' without reproach
of forgetting the main Errand
They ^w are sent upon: And if
They are not led out of their
Road by variety of Prospects –
Edifices & Ruins, would it
not be a senseless Piece of
severity to shut their Eyes
ag.^st such Gratifications –

LAURENCE STERNE

Autograph manuscript of "A Fragment in the Manner of Rabelais," written ca. 1759. 23 pp. 190 x 110 mm. MA 1011.

To those who search for harbingers of the modern spirit, no eighteenth-century figure seems as auspicious as Laurence Sterne, for no work broke through the conventional order of eighteenth-century narrative as radically as did his masterpiece *Tristram Shandy* (1760–7). The apparent chaos of that novel reflects the eccentricity of its author, whose bizarre character was set off all the more starkly by the clerical nature of his surroundings. By 1759—the probable date of the manuscript shown here—his thinly veiled local satire entitled *A Political Romance* had been suppressed and Sterne had begun to contemplate a more extensive but equally impertinent literary work. "A Fragment in the Manner of Rabelais" may represent one of Sterne's initial attempts at a method, if not a theme, which eventually matured into the innovative technique of *Tristram Shandy*. The subject of "A Fragment" must have been dear to Sterne's heart; several men with Rabelaisian names and clerical obligations discuss the possibility of writing a "Kerukopædia," that is, a work on the art of composing sermons, while, in an adjoining room, a colleague named Homenas cribs his sermons from the works of Dr. Samuel Clarke. "A Fragment" was first printed in *The Letters of the Late Rev. Mr. Laurence Sterne* (1775), edited by his daughter. Needless to say, the bawdry of Sterne's fragment, though barely up to Rabelaisian standards, was excised throughout.

Chap. 2[d] In which the Reader will begin to form a Judgment, of what an Historical, Dramatical, Anecdotical, Allegorical and Comical Kind of a Work, He has got hold of.—

Homenas who had to preach next Sunday [before God knows whom]—knowing Nothing at all of the Matter—was all this while ~~Rogering~~ at it as hard as He could drive in the very next Room: . . .

Chap. 2^d

In which the Reader will begin to form a Judg=ment, of what an Histori=cal, Dramatical, Anecdo=tical, Allegorical and Comi=cal Kind of a Work, He has got hold of. —

Homenas who had to preach next Sunday [before God knows whom] — know=ing Nothing at all of the Matter — was all this while ~~[illegible]~~ at it as hard as He could drive in the very next Room: for having

97

William Shenstone
1714–1765

Autograph draft of letter signed, dated The Leasowes, 24 May 1751, to Lady Henrietta Luxborough. 7 pp. 242 x 190 mm.

To that "sullen and surly speculator," Dr. Johnson, the art of landscape gardening seemed "rather the sport than the business of human reason." The thousands of persons who flocked to William Shenstone's *ferme ornée* at his childhood home, The Leasowes, in Worcestershire, would not have disagreed with the urban Doctor's opinion, but they would have remarked what a pleasurable sport it was. Following the aesthetic lead of Alexander Pope, the greatest of eighteenth-century English poet-gardeners, Shenstone began "to point his prospects, to diversify his surface, to entangle his walks, and to wind his waters" about 1739. He consumed a life of retirement by writing poetry and detached *pensées*, and by pouring his funds into the highly complex and allusive art of gardening. He added to his grounds and walks fragmentary ruins, urns and seats, recalling here a line from Pope and there a picture by Poussin, while he dedicated an entire grove to Virgil; the phrase *et in Arcadia ego* summed up the whole. Shenstone's major disappointment in his work was the rival claim of the neighboring estate at Hagley, built on a far more lavish scale by George Lyttleton, to whom Fielding dedicated *Tom Jones*. This letter was written to Shenstone's close friend, Lady Luxborough, a fellow gardener in her own small way; Shenstone had just nursed his brother back to health and he requests the loan of Francis Coventry's popular novel, *The History of Pompey the Little: or the Life and Adventures of a Lap-Dog* (1751).

Shenstone occasionally wrote preliminary drafts of his letters, and this letter to Lady Luxborough is an example of one. The copy that was actually posted is now in the British Library, where the largest collection of Shenstone's letters can be found.

[Starting at bottom of verso page:] Wou'd your Ladyship be so kind as lend me Pompey ye little? I have read, as I said before, nothing but Physick-Books for this last Six-weeks, & I want now to be indulg'd with somewhat more amusing. I wont pretend to your Ladyship y^t^ I am a very great Physician, *but I consider myself as qualify'd to make ye best* Nurse *of any body in the three kingdoms—I hope soon to be able to adjust a time when I may have ye long-wish'd for Happiness of waiting on your Ladyship at the Leasows. In ye mean time I am to return my Brother's Thanks wth my own for every obliging Instance of y^r^ regard, & to subscribe myself inviolably your Ladyships most dutifull & obedient Servt Will: Shenstone.*

Brother will occasion him much wordly Perplexity as well as Concern, at present. I would otherwise prep him to spend a week with us at the Leasows. as some kind of Relief to him, & a great Pleasure to us. I think a Change of Place after such an Affliction is very often of no small service. That Book of Mr. Pearsalls w.ch your Ladyship subscrib'd for, is come out, I hear; but I have had no Copies sent yet. Your Ladyship, I know, intended to oblige me by your Subscription, & That Point you can never fail to obtain. More I am not at Liberty to say. You will please to mention this Publication to Mr. Hall. I sent his Name, tho' I'm not sure y.t he subscrib'd; but I knew he wou'd be y.e readiest of Men to serve an old School fellow— Wou'd your Ladyship be so kind as lend me Pompey y.e little? I have

read, as I said before, nothing but Physick-Books for this last Six-weeks, & I want now to be indulg'd with somewhat more amusing. I wont pretend to your Ladyship y.t I am a very great Physician, but I consider myself as qualify'd to make y.e best Nurse of any body in the three Kingdoms— I hope soon to be able to adjust a time when I may have y.e long-wish'd for Happiness of waiting on your Ladyship at the Leasows. In y.e mean time I am to return my Brothers Thanks w.th my own for every obliging Instance of y.r regard, & to subscribe myself inviolably your Ladyships most

dutifull & obedient Serv.t

Wil: Shenstone.

William Shenstone

THOMAS GRAY
1716–1771

Autograph manuscript of his ode "On the Death of a favourite Cat drown'd in a China-Tub of Gold-Fishes," dated by Carolina Pery about 1757. 2 pp. 157 x 102 mm. MA 3389. Purchased as the gift of Miss Julia P. Wightman in honor of Charles Ryskamp.

Gray once complained to his friend Richard West that he suffered from white melancholy (or, as he called it, "Leucocholy")—"a good easy sort of state"—and black melancholy, which carried with it a conviction that whatever was "frightful" would certainly take place. The latter was the mood that led him to write to Wharton, "It is indeed for want of spirits, as you suspect, that my studies lie among the Cathedrals, and the Tombs, and the Ruins." But there was another side to Gray, perfectly suited in its frivolity to his friendship with Horace Walpole. In February 1747 Walpole's favorite cat, Selima, had drowned in a goldfish bowl, and Walpole requested a dirge for his stricken pet. Gray's response is a masterpiece of light humor and delicate moralizing:

From hence, ye Beauties, undeceiv'd
Know, one false Step is ne'er retrieved,
And be with Caution bold.
Not all, that strikes your wand'ring Eyes,
And heedless Hearts is lawful Prize,
Nor all, that glisters, Gold.

Two years after Gray's death, Walpole informed William Mason that he was having a "Gothic carved pedestal" made, upon which was mounted the china tub in which Selima drowned; the first stanza of Gray's poem adorned the front of the pedestal, which is still preserved at Strawberry Hill. The manuscript shown here is the latest of three manuscripts of the poem.

On the Death of a favourite Cat drown'd in a China-Tub of Gold-Fishes.

'Twas on a lofty Vase's Side,/ Where China's gayest Art had dyed/ The azure Flow'rs that blow,/ Demurest of the tabby Kind,/ The pensive Selima reclined/ Gazed on the Lake below./ Her conscious Tail her Joy declared,/ Her fair round Face, her snowy Beard,/ The Velvet of her Paws,/ Her Coat, that with the Tortoise vies/ Her Ears of Jet, & Emerald Eyes,/ She saw & purr'd Applause./ Still had she gazed, but midst the Tide/ Two angel Forms were seen to glide,/ The Genii of the Stream:/ Their scaly Armour's Tyrian Hue/ Thro' richest Purple to the View/ Betray'd a golden Gleam./ The hapless Nymph with Wonder saw;/ A Whisker first, & then a Claw,/ With many an ardent Wish,/ She stretch'd in vain to reach the Prize:/ What Female-Heart can Gold despise?/ What Cat's averse to Fish?...

On the Death of a favourite Cat drown'd in a China-Tub of Gold-Fishes.

'Twas on a lofty Vase's Side,
Where China's gayest Art had dyed
The azure Flow'rs that blow,
Demurest of the tabby Kind,
The pensive Selima reclined
Gazed on the Lake below.
Her conscious Tail her Joy declared,
Her fair round Face, her snowy Beard,
The Velvet of her Paws,
Her Coat, that with the Tortoise vies
Her Ears of Jet, & Emerald Eyes,
She saw & purr'd Applause.
Still had she gazed, but midst the Tide
Two angel Forms were seen to glide,
The Genii of the Stream:
Their scaly Armour's Tyrian Hue
Thro' richest Purple to the View
Betray'd a golden Gleam.
The hapless Nymph with Wonder saw;
A Whisker first, & then a Claw,
With many an ardent Wish,
She stretch'd in vain to reach the Prize:
What Female-Heart can Gold despise?
What Cat's averse to Fish?
Presumptuous Maid! with Eyes intent
Again she stretch'd, again she bent,
Nor knew the Gulph between.
Malignant Fate sat by, & smiled.
The slippery Verge her Feet beguiled:
She tumbled headlong in.
Eight times emerging from the Flood
She mew'd to ev'ry watry God
Some speedy Aid to send.
No Dolphin came, no Nereid stir'd,
Nor cruel John, nor Susan heard;
A Fav'rite has no Friend!

Volti sub:

99

THOMAS GRAY

Autograph manuscript of "The Fatal Sisters," unsigned, undated but written ca. 1761. 3 pp. 203 x 159 mm. MA 3390. Gift of Mr. and Mrs. Robert Cremin.

The origins of English poetry fascinated Gray. At least as early as 1752, he had begun shaping in his mind a history of English poetry to be based on a plan devised by Alexander Pope. Like many of Gray's projects, the history was laid aside, and he eventually abandoned it in deference to the progress Thomas Warton had made toward such a work. (Warton's *History of English Poetry* was published between 1774 and 1781.) Gray's history would have begun with "the poetry of the *Galic* (or Celtic) nations, as far back as it can be traced." When James Macpherson's controversial *Fragments of Ancient Poetry* appeared in 1760, Gray remarked in a letter to his childhood friend Thomas Wharton that he had "gone mad about them," though he strongly doubted their authenticity. About the same time, Gray's own research into early Norse and Welsh verse prompted him to write "The Fatal Sisters," "The Descent of Odin" and "The Triumph of Owen." Based largely on Latin translations of original poems, they were published in 1768.

This manuscript of "The Fatal Sisters" is apparently unrecorded. It shares many features with the version in Gray's Commonplace Book at Pembroke College, Cambridge, and with Wharton's transcription of the poem; but there are significant differences. The headnote varies substantially from these manuscript versions and from the published text. Several other variants within the poem indicate that this may be the earliest of the surviving manuscripts of "The Fatal Sisters."

About the year 1029 Sigurd, Earl & Sovereign of the Orkney-Islands, with a fleet of ships & a considerable body of troops went to the assistance of Sigtryg with the silken beard, King of a part of Ireland, who was then engaged in a war against his Father-in-law, Brian the Good, King of Dublin. Sigtryg was defeated, & the Earl with almost all his forces cut in pieces: but the other army lost all the advantage of the victory by the death of Brian, who fell in the action.

On Christmas-Day (the day of the Battle) a Native of Caithness in Scotland beheld at distance a troop of Persons on horseback riding full-speed towards a neighbouring hill & seeming to enter into it. his curiosity led him to follow them, till (looking thro' an opening in the rocks) he could discern twelve gigantic figures resembling Women: they were all employ'd in weaving; & as they wove, they sung the following magic song.

Now the storm beings to lour/ (Haste, the loom of Hell prepare!)/ Iron-sleet of arrowy shower/ Hurtles in the darken'd air./ Glitt'ring launces are the loom,/ Where the dusky warp we strain,/ Weaving many a Soldier's doom,/ Orkney's woe, & Randver's bane. ...

About the year 1029 Sigurd, Earl & Sovereign of the Orkney-Islands, with a fleet of ships & a considerable body of troops went to the assistance of Sigtryg with the silken beard, King of a part of Ireland, who was then engaged in a war against his Father-in-law, Brian the Good, King of Dublin. Sigtryg was defeated, & the Earl with almost all his forces cut in pieces: but the other army lost all the advantage of the victory by the death of Brian, who fell in the action.

On Christmas-Day (the day of the Battle) a Native of Caithness in Scotland beheld at distance a troop of Persons on horseback riding full-speed towards a neighbouring hill & seeming to enter into it. his curiosity led him to follow them, till (looking thro' an opening in the rocks) he could discern twelve gigantic figures resembling Women: they were all employ'd in weaving; & as they wove, they sung the following magic song.

Now the storm begins to lour
(Haste, the loom of Hell prepare!)
Iron-sleet of arrowy shower
Hurtles in the darken'd air.
Glitt'ring launces are the loom,
Where the dusky warp we strain,
Weaving many a Soldier's doom,
Orkney's woe, & Randver's bane.
See the griesly texture grow,
('Tis of human entrails made)
And the weights, that play below,
Each a gasping Warrior's head;
Shafts for shuttles dipt in gore
Shoot the trembling cords along:
Sword, that once a Monarch bore,
Keep the tissue close & strong!

100

David Garrick
1717–1779

Autograph letter signed, undated but written ca. 22 April 1768, to Mrs. Hannah Pritchard. 4 pp. 230 x 186 mm. MA 161.

David Garrick may fairly be said to have dedicated his life to the memory of Shakespeare. Writing to the actor William Powell, who had just left his Drury Lane company for Colman's rival Covent Garden, he offered paternal advice: "above all, never let your *Shakespear* be out of your hands, or your Pocket—Keep him about you, as a Charm—the more you read him, the more you'll like him, & the better you'll Act him." The culmination of Garrick's adulation of the Bard came in the summer of 1769 when he staged a Shakespeare Jubilee at Stratford. The project consisted of moving all of literary London down to the banks of the Avon for three days in September, during which time banquets, balls, horseraces and fireworks would be conducted in honor of Shakespeare. Unfortunately, rain came after the first day, but before the skies darkened, Garrick was declared the Steward of the Jubilee. (One of the Steward's most important acts was to pay the festival's deficit of 2,000 pounds.) All in all, it was a remarkable commemoration of the Bard, but an even more remarkable testimony to the wonderful vanity of Garrick.

The letter shown here contains an epilogue written in 1768 for the final performance of Mrs. Hannah Pritchard, one of the finest actresses in Garrick's company. Fittingly, her last role was Lady Macbeth; and, in closing, she addressed the audience in Garrick's words:

> Merits You have, to other Realms unknown;
> With all their Boastings, *Shakespear* is Your Own!

The largest single group of Garrick letters is in the Forster Collection of the Victoria and Albert Museum, South Kensington.

Mrs Pritchard's Farewell./ The Curtain dropt—my Mimic life is past;/ That Scene of Sleep & terror was my last:/ From which, this moral profit Mortals reap,/ That tho the Senses *may,* Guilt *cannot sleep./ */ Could I in* such *a Scene, my* Exit *make,/ When all my better Feelings are* awake?/ ~~*Are*~~ *Which beating* Here, *superiour to all art,/* ~~*And*~~ Burst *in full tides,* ~~*burst*~~ *from a most gratefull heart?/ Before I go,* ~~*this still*~~ *and this lov'd Spot forsake,/ The all I have to give, my* Wishes *take:/ Upon your hearts may no Affliction weigh,/ Which cannot by the Stage be chas'd away;/ And may the Stage, to please each virtuous mind,/ Grow ev'ry day more pure, & more refin'd;/ Refin'd from grossness, not by foreign Skill,/ Weed out the poyson, but be* English *still.*

**I now appear Myself—distress'd dismay'd/ More than in All the Characters I've play'd—*

Mrs Pritchard's Farewell.

* The Curtain dropt — my Mimic life is past;
That Scene of Sleep & terror was my last:
[From which, this moral profit Mortals reap,
That tho the Senses may, Guilt cannot sleep.]
*Could I in such a Scene my Exit make,
When all my better Feelings are awake?
~~Are~~ Which beating Here, superiour to all art,
~~And~~ Burst in full tide, ~~Burst~~ from a most gratefull heart?

Before I go, ~~this stage~~ and this lov'd Spot forsake,
The all I have to give, my Wishes take:
Upon your hearts may no affliction weigh,
Which cannot by the Stage be chas'd away;
And may the Stage, to please each virtuous mind,
Grow ev'ry day more pure, & more refin'd;
Refin'd from grossness, not by foreign Skill,
Weed out the poyson, but be English still.

* I now appear myself — dischg'd disrob'd
Mere free [illegible] all the Characters I've play'd —

I will see You on Monday Night,
don't let any body see them till
You & I have conn'd 'Em Over.

If You will make yr Daughter
Palmer write two or 3 lines (to
morrow before 12 o'Clock & send
them to my house) to let me know
how They strike You or what You
could wish about Em, I shall
receive them the same Night
& be oblig'd to her & to You

most Sincerely
Yours
D. Garrick

If you can't read
my hand well, let
Hopkins take a Copy
immediately for You, to study by.

HORACE WALPOLE, FOURTH EARL OF ORFORD 1717–1797

Autograph manuscript of his "Reminiscences," dated 13 January 1789, a fair copy made from an earlier draft dated 31 October 1788. 27 ff. 324 x 200 mm. MA 493.

By the time Walpole met the Berry sisters in the autumn of 1788, he was seventy, still a bachelor, and disabled by gout; they were twenty-three and twenty-four. He considered them "the best-informed and the most perfect creatures I ever saw." "They are exceedingly sensible," he wrote to Lady Ossory, "entirely natural and unaffected, frank, and, being qualified to talk on any subject, nothing is so easy and agreeable as their conversation." To them, Walpole was not so much the author of *A Catalogue of the Royal and Noble Authors of England* (1758), *Anecdotes of Painting in England* (1762–3) or *The Castle of Otranto* (1765) as a kind and affectionate friend and an actor among remarkable scenes that had occurred before their births. At their request he entered upon one of his favorite exercises, telling tales about people he had known. His stories were such a success that he yielded to their "wishes that I woud commit those passages (for they are scarce worthy of the title even of anecdotes) to writing." *Reminiscences* is in fact a loose collection of Walpole's rambling memories of the men and women who frequented the courts of George I and George II. Mary Berry later edited the *Works of Lord Orford* (1798) and it was she who first published his *Reminiscences*, though she was obliged to expunge several passages in which Walpole had dealt indecorously with figures of noble magnitude. On the page shown here, he records "an admirable reply of the famous Lady Mary Wortley Montagu" to a remark made by the Duchess of Marlborough. The Morgan Library owns not only both drafts of *Reminiscences*, but also nearly all of Walpole's correspondence with the Berrys.

The finest collection of Walpole manuscripts is that assembled by the late W. S. Lewis in Farmington, Connecticut.

She appeared in the court of justice, and with some wit and infinite abuse treated the laughing Public with the spectacle of a Woman who had held the reins of Empire metamorphosed into the Widow Blackacre. Her Grandson in his suit demanded a sword set with diamonds given to his Grandsire by the Emperor. "I retained it, said the Beldame, lest he shoud pick out the diamonds & pawn them."

I will repeat but one more instance of her insolent asperity, which produced an admirable reply of the famous Lady Mary Wortley Montagu. Lady Sundon had received a pair of diamond earrings as a bribe for procuring a considerable post in Queen Caroline's family for a certain Peer; & decked with those jewels, paid a visit to the old Duchess, who as soon as She was gone, said, "what an impudent Creature, to come hither with her bribe in her ear!" "Madam, replied Lady Mary Wortley, who was present, how shoud people know where wine is ~~wine is~~ sold, unless a bush is hung out?"...

She appeared in the court of justice, and with some wit and infinite abuse treated the laughing Public with the spectacle of a Woman who had held the reins of Empire metamorphosed into the Widow Blackacre. Her Grandson in his suit demanded a sword set with diamonds given to his Grandsire by the Emperor. "I retained it, said the Beldame, lest he shoud pick out the diamonds & pawn them."

I will repeat but one more instance of her insolent asperity, which produced an admirable reply of the famous Lady Mary Wortley Montagu. Lady Sundon had received a pair of diamond earrings as a bribe for procuring a considerable post in Queen Caroline's family for a certain Peer; & decked with those jewels, paid a visit to the old Duchess, who as soon as She was gone, said, "what an impudent Creature, to come hither with her bribe in her ear!" "Madam, replied Lady Mary Wortley, who was present, how shoud people know where wine is ~~wine is~~ sold, unless a bush is hung out!"

The Duchess of Buckingham was as much elated by owing her birth to James 2d. as the Marlborough was by the favour of his Daughter. Lady Dorchester, the Mother of the former, endeavoured to curb that pride, & one shoud have thought took an effectual method, tho one few Mothers woud have practiced; "you need not be so vain, said the old Profligate, for you are not the King's Daughter, but Colonel Graham's." Graham was a fashionable Man of those days, and noted for dry humour. His legitimate Daughter the Countess of Berkshire was extremely like to the Duchess of Buckingham: "well! well! said Graham, Kings are all-powerfull, and one must not complain, but certainly the same Man begot those two Women." To discredit the Wit of both Parents the Duchess never ceased labouring to restore the House of Stuart, & to mark her filial devotion to it. Frequent were her journies to the Continent for that purpose. She always stopped at Paris, visited the Church where lay the unburied body of James, and wept over it. A poor Benedictine of the Convent observing her filial piety, took notice to her Grace that the velvet pall that covered the Coffin was become threadbare—and so it remained!

Finding all her efforts fruitless, and perhaps aware that her plots were not undiscovered by Sr Robert Walpole, who was remarkable for his intelligence, She made an artfull double, & resolved to try what might be done thro him himself. I forget how She contracted an acquaintance with Him—I do remember that more than once He received letters from the Pretender Himself, which probably were transmitted thro Her. Sr Robert always carried them to George 2d, who endorsed and returned them. That negotiation not succeeding, the Duchess made a more home push. Learning his extreme fondness for his Daughter [afterwards Lady Mary Churchill] She sent for Sr Robert and asked him if he recollected what had not been thought too great a reward to Lord Clarendon for restoring the Royal Family? He affected not to understand her—"was not he allowed, urged the Zealous Duchess, to match his Daughter to the Duke of York!" Sr Robert smiled, & left Her.

Sr Robert being forced from Court, the Duchess thought the moment favorable, & took a new journey to Rome—but conscious of the danger She might run of discovery, She made over her Estate to the famous Mr Pulteney [afterwards Earl of Bath] and left the Deed in his Custody. What was her astonishment when on her return She redemanded the Instrument—It was mislaid—He coud not find it—He never coud find it! The Duchess grew clamorous—at last his Friend

102

Samuel Foote
1720–1777

Autograph letter signed, dated [27 May 1768] to David Garrick.
1 p. 187 x 152 mm.

The improvident and "Facetious Mr Foote" discovered his talent for mimicry while at Oxford and parlayed it into a lifelong career, becoming the gadfly of his generation. His popularity began with libelous dramatic trifles like "Tea at 6:30" and "Chocolate in Ireland." Repeated financial reverses did nothing to hinder his irrepressible spirit, nor did the loss of a leg in 1766: he merely remarked that he would be able to imitate the one-legged George Faulkner (the publisher and friend of Swift) all the better. The highly imitable Samuel Johnson escaped representation by Foote only by offering to remove his other leg. Nonetheless, he was amused by Foote's antics: "The first time I was in company with Foote was at Fitzherbert's. Having no good opinion of the fellow, I was resolved not to be pleased; and it is very difficult to please a man against his will. I went on eating my dinner pretty sullenly, affecting not to mind him. But the dog was so very comical, that I was obliged to lay down my knife and fork, throw myself back upon my chair, and fairly laugh it out. No, Sir, he was irresistible." In this delightful letter to David Garrick, Foote proposes to breed a dog owned by Mr. Barrel with one of Garrick's; Garrick, however, no longer owned his dogs, and wrote back, in a letter also in the Morgan Library: "I am Sorry that I cannot oblige ye Young Lady with one of my breed, for they were most Efficaciously Gallant—."

Mr Barrel has prevaild on me to pimp for a four legd favorite of his and to send a Card to one of your little Gentlemen to beg the favor of his Company: for a day: or two, Mr Barrel will send a Chair at any appointed hour Y^{r} most Devoted Servt Saml Foote Fryday

Mr Barrel has prevail'd on me to Pimp for a four leg'd favorite of his and to send a Card to one of your little Gentlemen to beg the favor of his Company for a day or two, Mr Barrel will send a Chair at any appointed hour

yr most devoted Sert

Saml Foote

Fryd an

From "Dramatic Memoirs"

Samuel Foote 1720-1777

103

Gilbert White
1720–1793

Autograph letter signed, dated 14 November 1775, to his brother John White. 3 pp. 200 x 161 mm. MA 3322. Gift of Mr. and Mrs. Robert Cremin.

On 4 October 1783, Gilbert White took a census of the souls in his cure; they numbered 676, to which he might have added the entire plant and animal kingdom in the parish of Selborne. As far as White was concerned, only one thing was lacking: "It has been my misfortune never to have had any neighbours whose studies have led them towards the pursuit of natural knowledge . . . a kind of information to which I have been attached from my childhood." In an age so deeply given to the communication of knowledge in epistolary form, White's lack of naturalist neighbors was no serious bar to advancement in the study of natural history and a positive advantage when he began to consider publication. The familiar letter could be many things in the late eighteenth century; in *The Natural History of Selborne*, published in 1788 as a series of letters to Thomas Pennant and Daines Barrington, White made it an outwardly formal vehicle for the exchange of scientific information. But at the heart of each of the ninety-one letters that make up *The Natural History of Selborne* and its second part, *The Antiquities of Selborne*, there lies White's sense of the edifying mystery presented daily by nature:

> Such baffled searches mock man's prying pride,
> The GOD of NATURE is your secret guide!

White's brother John, to whom the letter shown here was written, was also a naturalist and the author of *Fauna Calpensis*, a work on the natural history of Gibraltar, part of the manuscript introduction to which is now in the Morgan Library, along with several drawings for that work. In this letter to his brother, White provides advice on the subject of preparing *Fauna Calpensis* for the printer and offers appropriately fraternal counseling about moderation in all things, including study: "study beyond a man's strength is a most pernicious sort of debauch."

The manuscript of *The Natural History of Selborne* is now in the Gilbert White Museum, Selborne, Hampshire.

Selborne: Nov: 14.:75 Dear Brother, Your letter of Octr 14: hit me most exactly at Oriel: no rifle-man could have taken a truer aim. I am glad to find that you have finished your Fauna, & that more for the sake of y^{r} health *that y^{r}* fame, *since I find you are become quite intemperate in y^{r} pursuits of that sort, not remembering that study beyond a man's strength is a most pernicious sort of debauch: & you might as well think of drinking for 12 hours together, as of writing for 12 hours together. You do not use to manage y^{r} health in this manner. I am not very sorry that you have smarted* a little. — *In y^{r} introductory part you will probably pay all proper attention to* comparative *views between this climate, & lat: 36. Engravings will take a deal of time; so I trust you will set them a going; & will bring y^{r} work to Town in the spring, & try if you can dispose of it to advantage. As your work will be bulky enough, perhaps you need not use a great deal of y^{r} meteorology: tables of that nature are in general little attended-to: yet some will be necessary. . . .*

Dear Brother, Selborne: Nov: 14. 75.

Your letter of Oct: 14: hit me most exactly at Oriel: no rifle-man could have taken a truer aim. I am glad to find that you have finished your Fauna, & that more for the sake of yr *health* that yr *fame*, since I find you are become quite intemperate in yr pursuits of that sort, not re-:membering that study beyond a man's strength is a most pernicious sort of debauch: & you might as well think of drinking for 12 hours together, as of writing for 12 hours together. You do not use to manage yr health in this manner. I am not very sorry that you have smarted *a little*. — In yr introductory part you will probably pay all proper attention to *compara-:tive* views between this climate, & lat: 36. Engravings will take a deal of time; so I trust you will set them a going; & will bring yr work to Town in the spring, & try if you can dispose of it to advantage. As your work will be bulky enough, perhaps you need not use a great deal of yr meteorology: tables of that nature are in general little attended to: yet some will be necessary. Look into Sr Will: Monson's *naval tracts* for the influx & reflux of the sea at the streights of Gib: Brown, I conclude, will be yr best artist for yr birds. A perspective frontis-:piece of the scene of action, I conclude, will be ne-:cessary. As to my own work, wanting yr vigor & dis-:patch, I fall into the other extreme: I heap up materials but finish nothing. — Pray send Jack's letter: I shall always

TOBIAS GEORGE SMOLLETT
1721–1771

Autograph letter signed, dated Chelsea, 20 July 1759, to William Strahan. 1 p. 233 x 190 mm. MA 1229.

Like many other men of his time, the Scotsman Smollett arrived in London with a play in his pocket and the example of a hundred Grub Street hacks before him. The adventures that befall the heroes of his picaresque novels seem at times no more haphazard and comic than his own progress in literary London. For years, he tried to stage his play *The Regicide* ("it is a Scotch Story, but it won't do," said Garrick in 1747); he attributed his failure to the enmity of the theater managers. For a time, he seems to have been an active pawn in the competition between booksellers: his *History of England* was written largely with the purpose of deflating the sales of David Hume's popular *History of England*. By 1759 he had also published three novels, *Roderick Random*, *Peregrine Pickle* and *Ferdinand Count Fathom*, and translated the works from which he derived the form of these novels: *Don Quixote* and *Gil Blas*. At the date of the letter shown here, Smollett's most important contribution to English letters was the *Critical Review*, which he edited between 1756 and 1763. It too was created in response to a rival, the *Monthly Review*. Though the *Critical Review* handled its authors roughly, Samuel Johnson felt it was founded on the "best principles." Even so, just four months before this letter was written Smollett was convicted for a libel printed in his periodical. Typically, he writes here to the printer Strahan attempting to patch up a misunderstanding, probably caused by "inveterate Enemies" like Ralph Griffiths, editor of the *Monthly Review*, whose work Strahan also printed.

Dear Sir, I should have answered the Letter you sent me some time ago; but conscious of my own Innocence with respect to some Insinuations therein contained, & of your Entertaining some Jealousy which I knew Time and my Conduct would easily dissipate; I thought it would have been unnecessary to vindicate myself any other way, from a suspicion I had not justly incurred. I can say with a safe Conscience, that with respect to Mr Strahan, I never once deviated from Those Thoughts which every honest man ought to entertain for an old friend to whom he has been essentially obliged: you Will never find any Just Reason to believe me capable of acting in another Manner. I rejoice as much as ever in your Prosperity, & only regret that you are so little connected with me & so much with Some Persons who I know to be my inveterate Enemies. The first, is not owing to any fault in me; nor do I impute the other to any abatement in your friendship for me, but to inevitable chances in the Course of Business. I wish you a great deal of Pleasure in your purposed Excursion; & shall take it kind, if when at Edr, you will visit Commissary Smollett to whom & his Lady you will present my best respects. I repeat it that there is no Person on Earth who wishes you better, than does Dear Sir your obliged friend & servt T. Smollett Chelsea July 20 1759

Dear Sir

I should have answered the Letter you sent me some time ago; but
conscious of my own Innocence with respect to some Insinuations therein
contained, & of your entertaining some Jealousy which I knew Time and
my Conduct would easily dissipate; I thought it would have been unnecess-
-ary to vindicate myself any other way, from a suspicion I had not justly
incurred. I can say with a safe Conscience, that with respect to Mr Strahan
I never once deviated from those Thoughts which every honest man ought
to entertain for an old friend to whom he has been essentially obliged: you
will never find any just Reason to believe me capable of acting in another
manner. I rejoice as much as ever in your Prosperity, & only regret that you are so
little connected with me & so much with some Persons who I know to be my
inveterate Enemies. the first, is not owing to any fault in me; nor do I impute
the other to any abatement in your friendship for me but to inevitable chances in
the Course of Business — I wish you a great deal of Pleasure in your proposed
Excursion; & shall take it kind, if when at Edr, you will visit Commissary
Smollett to whom & his Lady you will present my best respects. I repeat it
that there is no Person on Earth who wishes you better, than does

Dear Sir

Your obliged friend & Servt

T. Smollett

Chelsea July 20 1759

105

CHRISTOPHER SMART
1722–1771

Autograph letter signed, dated King's Bench Prison, 26 April 1770, to Dr. Charles Burney. 1 p. 199 x 159 mm. Anonymous loan.

Dr. Charles Burney was making preparations for a trip to Italy to conduct research for his *General History of Music* (1776–89) when he received this letter from Christopher Smart. The two men had been friends since 1744 when they were both new to London, Burney apprenticed to the composer Thomas Arne and performing as "a supernumerary Violin or Tenor" in the orchestra of Drury Lane, Smart still affiliated with Cambridge University. Together they published a ballad: "Lovely Harriote. A Crambo Song." During Smart's most successful years as a periodical writer and poet in the volatile world of Grub Street, Burney was detained by illness at King's Lynn, Norfolk; by the time Burney was able to return to London permanently, Smart had been confined in Bethlehem Hospital (Bedlam) for madness that took the form of religious mania. When Smart was finally freed in 1763, Burney was among the first of his friends to assist in organizing a relief fund for the poet half-buried in obscurity by debt and insanity. The efforts of his friends were not enough; he died in 1771 in the prison from which this letter was written.

Smart's gratitude to his old friend is best recorded in *Jubilate Agno*, the poet's masterpiece, not discovered until 1939: "God be gracious to Arne his wife to Michael & Charles Burney." Like his other great poem, *A Song to David* (1763), *Jubilate Agno* was probably composed in Bedlam. Very few of Smart's manuscripts survive: the autograph manuscript of *Jubilate Agno* and two autograph letters to Burney are at Harvard. In other collections there are gathered only a small handful of letters, none more poignant than this one summarizing years of pain.

King's Bench Prison April 26th 1770. Dr Sr After being a fortnight at a spunging house, one week at the Marshalsea in the event of all things, I am this day safely arrived at the King's Bench.—Seven years in Madhouses, eight times arrested in six years, I beg leave to commend myself to a benevolent & providing friend Yrs affectionately Christopher Smart.

King's Bench Prison
April 26th 1770.

Dr Sr

After being a fortnight
at a spunging house one week
at the Marshalsea in the course
of all things, I am this day
safely arrived at the King's
Bench. — Seven years in
Madhouses, eight times
arrested in six years, I beg
leave to commend myself to
a benevolent & Providing
friend Yrs affectionately

Christopher Smart.

William Mason
1742–1797

Autograph manuscript, signed, of "The Rise of Fashion an Epistolary Tale to Miss Cotesworth," dated August 1747. 8 pp. 232 x 178 mm.

1747 was the year in which Mason first made the acquaintance of Thomas Gray, known to him as "Scroddles," whose life he would later write. This manuscript suggests that besides meeting Gray and gaining election to a Pembroke College fellowship in that year, Mason was also paying addresses to a Miss Cotesworth, about whom little is known. He thought well enough of her to send her a copy of Wenceslaus Hollar's *Ornatus Muliebris Anglicanus or The Severall Habits of English Women . . . , as they are in these times, 1640* (London, 1640), prefaced by a tale of his own composition. Mason achieved moderate fame as a poet (indeed, Gray's praise for his "Ode to a Water Nymph" eased the beginnings of their friendship) but for a different sort of verse than this. *The Rise of Fashion* is a charming poem written, as he says, in the manner of Prior, but imitating along the way John Gay's digression on fashion in *The Fan*, Ovid's *Metamorphoses* and the *Aeneid*. Though this sounds quite pompous in the abstract, it is really an amusing tale about the birth of Fashion, begat in a sea-grotto by Proteus on Venus:

I can't well tell, my lovely reader,
The time of a cælestial Breeder:
But tis enough, the reck'ning ended,
That Miss was born, and Venus mended.

The Rise of Fashion an Epistolary Tale to Miss Cotesworth

I wish these Prints may chance to come/ Just as you dress for Rout, or Drum;/ If so (while Betty at your back/ Or pins your gown, or folds your sack)/ 'Twill entertain you much to place/ Each figure twixt yourself, & glass;/ And see how much an hundred years/ Have metamorphosd female geers—/ "Sure, Sir, our Grandames all were mad:/ "Lard what an air the Creatures had!/ "The Awkard Things! not half a waist;/ "And that all frightfully unlacd!/ "O hideous! what a shocking taste." . . .

Here Pegasus might win his race/ Oer mecklin, and oer brussels Lace;/ Here might he take pindaric bounces/ Oer floods of furbelows, and flounces;/ Gallop on lutestring plains; invade/ The thick-wove groves of rich brocade,/ And leap oer Whalebones stiff barrier./ —But here I bridle his carreer,/ And sagely think it most expedient/ Thus to conclude, your most obedient—/ W. Mason August 1747

The Rise of Fashion

an

Epistolary Tale

to

Miss Cotesworth

I wish these Prints may chance to come
Just as you dress for Rout, or Drum;
If so (while Betty at your back
Or pins your gown, or folds your sack)
Twill entertain you much to place
Each figure twixt yourself & glass;
And see how much an hundred years
Have metamorphosd female geers—
"Sure, Sir, our Grandams all were mad:
"Lard what an air the Creatures had!
"The Awkard Things! not half a waist;
"And that all frightfully unlacd!
"O hideous! what a shocking taste."

Here Pegasus might run his race
Oer mechlin, and oer brussels Lace;
Here might he take pindaric bounces
Oer floods of furbelows, and flounces;
Gallop on lutestring plains; invade
The thick-wove groves of rich brocade,
And leap oer Whalebones stiff barrier.
—But here I bridle his career,
And sagely think it most expedient
Thus to conclude, your most obedient—

W. Mason.

August 1747

107

EDMUND BURKE
1729–1797

Autograph letter signed (retained draft), dated 29 July 1782, to Fanny Burney. 2 pp. 230 x 187 mm.

In Burkean terms, the principle that moves the plot in most novels might be stated thus: "the generation of mankind is a great purpose, and it is requisite that men should be animated to the pursuit of it by some great incentive." As great incentives went in the eighteenth century, money did almost as well as love, at least in the novels of Fanny Burney. While Burke deliberated in the House of Commons on more important themes than sexual economy, he also managed to stay abreast of that subject by reading contemporary fiction. In 1778 he had sat up all night to read Fanny Burney's *Evelina;* when *Cecilia* appeared in 1782 he devoted three days to its five volumes and wrote with gravely measured praise to its author, "There are few, I believe I may say fairly, there are none at all, that will not find themselves better informed concerning human Nature, & their stock of observation enrichd by reading your Cecilia." His only criticism was that the characters might be too "numerous," but even this objection was delicately withdrawn: "I fear it is quite in vain to preach oeconomy to those who are come young to excessive & sudden opulence." On her part, Miss Burney was nearly overcome by a letter ("no such a one was ever written before") from the man she considered second in the kingdom only to Johnson; and, according to the custom (perhaps most exuberantly displayed in the preface to Crabbe's *Poems* of 1807), she printed Burke's letter as the preface to subsequent editions of *Cecilia.*

The largest collection of Burke manuscripts is in the Sheffield Central Library.

Madam, I should feel exceedingly to blame, if I could refuse to myself, the natural satisfaction, & to you, the just but poor return, of my best thanks for the very great instruction & entertainment I have received from the new present you have bestowd on the publick. There are few, I believe I may say fairly, there are none at all, that will not find themselves better informed concerning human Nature, & their stock of observation enrichd by reading your Cecilia. They certainly will, let their experience in Life & manners be what it may. The arrogance of age must submit to be taught by youth. [illegible deletion] You have crowded into a few small volumes an incredible variety of Characters; most of them well planned, well supported, & well contrasted with each other. If there be any fault in this respect, it is one, in which you are in no great danger of being imitated. Justly as your Characters are drawn, perhaps they are too numerous;—but I beg pardon; I fear it is quite in vain to preach oeconomy to those who are come young to excessive & sudden opulence. . . .

Madam,

I should feel exceedingly to blame, if I could refuse to myself, the natural satisfaction, & to you, the just but poor return, of my best thanks for the very great instruction & entertainment I have received from the new present you have bestowed on the publick. There are few, I believe I may say fairly, there are none at all, that will not find themselves better informed concerning human Nature, & their stock of observation enriched by reading your Cecilia. They certainly will, let their experience in Life & manners be what it may. The arrogance of age must submit to be taught by youth. [illegible] You have crowded into a few small volumes an incredible variety of Characters; most of them well planned, well supported, & well contrasted with each other. If there be any fault in this respect, it is one in which you are in no great danger of being imitated. Justly as your Characters are drawn, perhaps they are too numerous. But I beg pardon; I fear it is quite in vain to preach oeconomy to those who are come young to excessive & sudden opulence.

I

I might trespass on your delicacy if I should fill my Letter to you with what I fill my conversation to others. I should be troublesome to you alone, if I should tell you all I feel & think, on the natural vein of humour, the tender pathetick, the comprehensive & noble moral; & the sagacious observation, that appear quite throughout that extraordinary performance. In an age distinguished by producing extraordinary Women, I hardly dare to tell you where my opinion would place you amongst them. I respect your modesty, that will not endure the commendations which your merit forces from every body.

I have the honour to be with great gratitude, respect, & Esteem

Madam

your most obedient

& most humble Servt

Edm Burke

Whitehall July 29. 1782.

My best compliments & congratulations to Doctor Burney on the great honour acquired to his family.

Oliver Goldsmith
1730?–1774

Autograph manuscript of "The Captivity: An Oratorio," undated but written ca. 1764. 18 pp. 199 x 150 mm. MA 162.

During Passion Week and on Wednesdays and Fridays in the Lenten season, London theaters were customarily dark, although violations of this practice forced the government to reaffirm the old custom with an order in 1737. In an attempt to keep Covent Garden open on those nights the composer Handel tried the experiment of presenting religious oratorios, which had first appeared on London stages some years before. Though tickets were expensive, the oratorios were popular. Handel's *Judas Maccabeus*, *Messiah* and *Samson* were especially successful and later writers adhered closely to his pattern: Old Testament stories supported by "pleasing" airs and "majestically grand" choruses. The literary merit of these works was best described by Handel himself: "The music is good, damn the words!"

Goldsmith's *The Captivity: An Oratorio* is perhaps an exception to Handel's description. Based on the story of the Babylonian captivity (II Kings 25), it was purchased by the publisher Dodsley (probably in conjunction with another publisher, Newbery) on 31 October 1764 for ten guineas. *The Captivity* survives in two autograph versions, one formerly owned by Dodsley (and now in the possession of Sir John Murray) and one formerly owned by Newbery (shown here). The relationship between these two manuscripts is as complex as a textual relationship between only two manuscripts can be; the Newbery-Morgan manuscript is the more heavily revised of the two, but the Dodsley-Murray version is probably slightly superior. *The Captivity* was never performed and was not published in its entirety until 1820. Two songs from it were published with Goldsmith's *The Haunch of Venison* in 1776. Only six significant poetical manuscripts by Goldsmith are known to exist, among them a fair copy of *The Haunch of Venison* in the Berg Collection of The New York Public Library.

Israelitish Woman/ Air/ As panting flies the hunted hind/ Where brooks refreshing stray/ ~~Where~~ And rivers through the valley wind/ That stops the hunter's way

Thus we O Lord alike ~~opprest deprest~~ distrest/ For streams of mercy Long/ ~~Those~~ Streams which cheer the sore opprest/ And overwhelm the Strong. . . .

Israelitish Woman

Air

As panting flies the hunted hind
Where brooks refreshing stray
~~Where~~ And rivers through the valley wind
That stops the hunter's way

Thus we O Lord alike ~~oppress depress~~ distrest
For streams of mercy long
~~Those~~ streams which cheer the sore opprest
And overwhelm the strong.

1st Prophet. Recit.

But whence that shout! Good heavens! Amazement all
See yonder tower just nodding to the fall
Behold, an army covers all the ground
~~They sap the wall, and~~ 'Tis Cyrus here that pours destruction round
And now behold the battlement recline
O God of Hosts the victory is thine.

Chorus of Captives.

Down with them Lord to lick the dust
Thy vengeance be begun
Serve them as they have serv'd the just
And let ~~Behold~~ thy will be done.

1st Priest Recit.

All all is lost. ~~O whither shall we fly~~ The Syrian army fails
Cyrus the conqueror of the world prevails

109

Oliver Goldsmith

Autograph letter unsigned, undated but written ca. 25 December 1773, to Mrs. Catherine Bunbury. 4 pp. 225 x 185 mm. MA 1297.

Goldsmith was one of the delicate, disordered spirits of the eighteenth century. Endowed with enormous abilities, he struggled through his short life against what often seemed to be constitutional irresponsibility. In the chaotic world of Grub Street he had frequently to be guided to comparative safety by strong friends like David Garrick and Samuel Johnson. Nine months before the date of this letter, his most popular play, *She Stoops to Conquer, or, The Mistakes of a Night*, was staged by George Colman at Covent Garden. From the receipts of three author's benefit nights, Goldsmith realized over £500, enough to allay his creditors for a short time. And though he, like Colman, feared for the success of a comedy "not merely sentimental," he was rewarded with critical and popular praise for his play: "altho' it differed most essentially in manner, stile, and finishing from those which have of late years been received, and encouraged almost to adoration, its own excellence prevailed, laughter sat on every face . . . and repeated plaudits showered down on the author."

Just over forty-five autograph letters by Goldsmith exist, most of the later ones brief and businesslike. One of his last surviving letters (he died in early April 1774), this epistle in prose and verse fully recalls the humor and imagination that made him such a welcome member of Johnson's circle. Catherine Horneck, whom Goldsmith called "Little Comedy," married the caricaturist Henry William Bunbury in 1771; this letter is a response to her verse epistle inviting him down to Barton, Suffolk, the home of her brother-in-law. Her poem evokes the vivid impression Goldsmith must have made about London in his "Tyrian bloom satin grain and garter blue silk breeches":

> I hope my good Doctor you soon will be here
> And your spring velvet coat very smart will appear
> To open our ball the first day in the year.

First let me suppose what may shortly be true/ The company set, and the word to be Loo./ All smirking, and pleasant, and big with adventure/ And ogling the stake which is fixd in the center./ Round and round go the cards while I inwardly damn/ At never once finding a visit from Pam./ ~~I lay down my stake, I double that too,/ While some harpy beside me picks up the whole/~~ I lay down my stake, apparently cool,/ While the harpies about me all pocket the pool./ I fret [illegible deletion] in my gizzard yet cautious and sly/ I wish all my friends may be bolder than I./ Yet still they sit snugg, not a creature will aim/ By losing their money to venture at fame./ Tis in vain that at niggardly caution I scold/ Tis in vain that I flatter the brave and the bold/ All play in their own way, and think me an ass./ What does Mrs. Bunbury? I sir? I pass. . . .

And bring with you a wig that is modish and gay
To dance with the girls that are makers of hay.

The absurdity of making hay at Christmass you yourself seem sensible of. You say your sister will laugh, and so indeed she well may — the Lattins have an expression for a contemptuous kind of laughter; naso contemnere adunco that is to laugh with a crooked nose. She may laugh at you in the manner of the ancients if she thinks fit. But now I come to the most extraordinary of all extraordinary propositions which is to take your and your sister's advice in playing at Loo. The presumption of the offer raises my indignation beyond the bounds of prose it inspires me at once with verse and resentment. I take advice! And from who? You shall hear.

First let me suppose what may shortly be true
The company set, and the word to be Loo.
All smirking, and pleasant, and big with adventure
And ogling the stake which is fixd in the center.
Round and round go the cards while I inwardly damn
At never once finding a visit from Pam.
~~[illegible]~~
~~[illegible]~~
I lay down my stake, apparently cool,
While the harpies about me all pocket the pool.
I fret ~~[illegible]~~ in my gizzard yet cautious and sly
I wish all my friends may be bolder than I.
Yet still they sit snugg, not a creature will aim
By losing their money to venture at fame.
'Tis in vain that at niggardly caution I scold
'Tis in vain that I flatter the brave and the bold
All play in their own way, and think me an ass.
What does Mrs. Bunbury? I Sir? I pass.
Pray what does Miss Horneck? Take courage. Come do.
Who I! Let me see sir. Why I must pass too.
Mr. Bunbury frets, and I fret like the devil
To see them so cowardly lucky and civil.
Yet still I sit snugg and continue to sigh on
Till made by my losses as bold as a lion
I venture at all, while my avarice regards
The whole pool as my own. Come give me five cards.
Well done cry the Ladies. Ah Doctor that's good.
The pool's very rich. Ah. The Doctor is lood.
Thus foild in my courage, on all sides perplext,
I ask for advice from the lady that's next
Pray mam be so good as to give your advice
Dont you think the best way is to venture fort twice.
I advise cries the lady to try it I own.
Ah! The Doctor is lood. Come Doctor, put down.
Thus playing and playing I still grow more eager
And so bold and so bold, Im at last a bold beggar.
Now Ladies I ask if Law matters youre skill'd in
Whether crimes such as yours should not come before Fielding
For giving advice that is not worth a straw
May well be call'd picking of pockets in Law
And picking of pockets with which I now charge ye
Is by quinto Elizabeth death without Clergy.
What justice when both to the Old Baily brought
By the gods I'le enjoy it, tho' 'tis but in thought.
Both are placed at the bar with all proper decorum
With bunches of Fennel and nosegays before em.

Charles Churchill
1731–1764

Autograph letter signed, undated but written ca. September 1762, to David Garrick. 2 pp. 200 x 157 mm. From the Collection of Mrs. Donald F. Hyde.

Charles Churchill lived a short, strident life, reviving and virtually incorporating the abusive personal satire that had lapsed somewhat since the death of Pope in 1744. After entering orders according to his father's wish, Churchill quickly became England's most incongruous cleric. "The only thing I like my Gown for," he writes in the letter shown here, "is the exemption from challenges." He had great need of this benefit of clergy. His major satiric poems, *The Rosciad*, *The Ghost*, *The Author*, *The Duellist*, *Gotham* and *The Candidate*, appeared in rapid order between 1761 and 1764; with each publication Churchill's audience grew more astonished at his poetic power, his enemies more outraged at his satiric license. This letter to David Garrick catches Churchill in mid-stride, approaching the height of his powers. After requesting the "very particular favour" of a loan of forty or fifty pounds, he offers the dubious collateral of a fragment from his current work in progress, which was published in 1763 as *The Prophecy of Famine, A Scots Pastoral.* He also mentions the appearance of *The Ghost* and work on *An Epistle to William Hogarth*, the next stage in the escalating battle waged by Churchill and his close friend John Wilkes against the artist William Hogarth, who drew satiric caricatures of both men. Garrick tried to assist Churchill, not with a loan, but with advice which went unheeded: "I must intreat of You by ye Regard You profess to Me, that You don't tilt at my Friend Hogarth before You See Me . . . He is a great & original Genius . . . ."

Almost all of Churchill's letters and manuscripts (primarily his correspondence with Wilkes) is now in the British Library.

Jockey, whose manly high-bon'd cheeks to crown,/ With Freckles spotted flam'd the golden down,/ With mickle art could on the Bagpipes play,/ E'en from the rising to the setting day./ Sawney as long, without remorse, could bawl/ Hume's Madrigals, and ditties from Fingal,/ Oft at his strains all natural tho' rude,/ The Highland Lass forgot her want of food,/ And, whilst She scratch'd her Lover into rest,/ Sunk pleas'd, tho' hungry, on her Sawney's breast,

I have seen Hogarth's print; sure it is much unequal to the former productions of that Master of Humour. I am happy to find that he hath at last declar'd himself, for there is no credit to be got by breaking flies upon a wheel, . . .

Jockey, whose manly high-bon'd cheeks to crown,
With freckles spotted flam'd the golden down,
With mickle art could on the Bagpipes play,
E'en from the rising to the setting day;
Sawney as long, without remorse, could bawl
Home's Madrigals, and ditties from Fingal,
Oft at his strains, all natural tho' rude,
The Highland Lass forgot her want of food,
And, whilst she scratch'd her Lover into rest,
Sunk pleas'd, tho' hungry, on her Sawney's breast.

I have seen Hogarth's print, sure it is much unequal to the former productions of that Master of Humour. I am happy to find that he hath at last declar'd himself, for there is no credit to be got by breaking flies upon a wheel, But Hogarth's are Subjects worthy of an Englishman's pen.

Speedily will be published,

An Epistle to W. Hogarth by C. Churchill.

Pictoribus atq; Poetis,
Quidlibet audendi semper fuit aequa Potestas.

I was t'other day at Richmond, but lost much of the pleasure I had promis'd myself, being disappointed of seeing You. What is the use or meaning of the Pagoda — is it not improperly pronounced — it should certainly be Pago-da.

I long for the opening of the House on many accounts, but on none more than the opportunity it will give me of seeing that little Whimsical fellow Garrick, and that most agreeable of Women, to whom I am always proud of being remember'd, Mrs Garrick. Hubert I hear has got a weakness in his eyes. I am, Dr Garrick,

Yours most sincerely,

Charles Churchill.

Saturday Night.

William Cowper
1731–1800

Autograph letter signed, dated 10 December 1767, to Mrs. Maria Cowper. 3 pp. 202 x 163 mm. Promised gift of Mr. Charles Ryskamp.

Half the "poor transient night" of Cowper's life was spent dreading the dawn. From his second accession of despondency in 1763 until his death in 1800, he was subject to profound depression of spirits; a conviction of his personal damnation, the incapacity of God's grace, succeeded a brief but euphoric sense of salvation. Out of his isolation from God and his retirement in Olney and Weston Underwood, he fashioned his greatest poem, *The Task* (1785). Its title alludes to the request that led to its composition: that he write about anything, even a sofa. But behind the frivolity of its inception, *The Task* conceals a much deeper and more personal meaning. Barred from the benevolence of God, Cowper wrote about divine favor that could not be his; his task is to affirm for an audience what he cannot affirm for himself: the forgiveness of God. Today, *The Task* is read largely for its celebrated passages of natural description; ultimately, however, it is a poem of subjection to a fearsome God.

The letter shown here was written some two years after Cowper left Dr. Nathaniel Cotton's asylum at St. Alban's, where he had been treated for depression bordering on madness and where he became an Evangelical. Between 1765 and 1773 Cowper's correspondence is full of what he calls "the Language of a Christian Soul," utterly unlike the brighter and more famous letters written after 1776. The maddening irony of Cowper's life is that these sombre religious letters were written during a period of relative assurance and faith, while the more exuberant letters are, as Cowper said, merely brilliant reflections in a muddy pool. This letter also contains the only manuscript of what is surely one of Cowper's best-known poems—the hymn "Oh for a closer Walk with God," published in *Olney Hymns* (1779)—a poem about the religious yearning that was the central theme of Cowper's life.

[Starting with recto page:] I return you many Thanks for the verses you favor'd me with, which speak sweetly the Language of a Christian Soul. I wish I could pay you in kind, but must be contented to pay you in the best kind I can. I began to compose them yesterday morning before Daybreak, but fell asleep at the End of the two first Lines, when I awaked again the third and fourth were whisperd to my Heart in a way which I have often experienced.

Oh for a closer Walk with God,/ A calm & heav'nly Frame,/ A Light to shine upon the Road/ That leads me to the Lamb!

Where is the Blessedness I knew/ When first I saw the Lord?/ Where is the Soul:refreshing View/ Of Jesus in his Word?

What peacefull Hours I then enjoyd,/ How sweet their Mem'ry still!/ But they have left an Aching Void/ The World can never fill.

Return, O Holy Dove, Return,/ Sweet Messenger of Rest,/ I hate the Sins that made thee mourn/ And drove thee from my Breast. . . .

exemplary Patience under the sharpest Sufferings, her truly Xtian Humility and Resignation, I am more than ever inclined to believe that her Hour is come. Let me engage your Prayers for Her, and for me. You know what I have most need of upon an Occa:sion like this: Pray that I may receive it at His Hands from whom every good and perfect Gift pro:ceeds. She is the chief Blessing I have met with in my Journey since the Lord was pleased to call me, and I hope the Influence of her edifying and Excellent Example will never leave me. Her Illness has been a sharp Trial to me — Oh that it may have a sanctified Effect, that I may rejoice to Surrender up to the Lord my dearest Comforts the moment he shall require them. Oh! for no Will but the Will of my Heavenly Father! Doctor Cotton for whose advice we went together to St. Albans about a month since, seemed to have so little Expectation that medicine could help her, that he might be said to give her over. He prescribed however, but she has hardly been able to take his medicines. Her Disorder is a nervous Atrophy attended with violent Spasms of the Chest and Throat, and This is a bad Day with her; worse than common.

I return you many Thanks for the verses you favor'd me with, which speak sweetly the Language of a Christian Soul. I wish I could pay you in kind, but must be contented to pay you in the best kind I can. I began to compose them yesterday morning before Day:break, but fell asleep at the End of the two first Lines, when I awaked again the third and fourth were whisper'd to my Heart in a way which I have often experienced.

Oh for a closer Walk with God,
A calm & heav'nly Frame,
A Light to shine upon the Road
That leads me to the Lamb!

Where is the Blessedness I knew
When first I saw the Lord!
Where is the Soul:refreshing View
Of Jesus in his Word!

What peacefull Hours I then enjoy'd,
How sweet their mem'ry still!
But they have left an aching Void
The World can never fill.

Return, O Holy Dove, return,
Sweet Messenger of Rest,
I hate the Sins that made thee mourn
And drove thee from my Breast.

The dearest Idol I have known,
Whate'er that Idol be,
Help me to tear it from thy Throne,
And worship only Thee.

Then shall my Walk be close with God,
Calm and serene my Frame,
Then purer Light shall mark the Road
That leads me to the Lamb.

My dear Uncle
in the Bonds of that Love
which cannot be dissolved
Yours affectionately
Olney. Dec. 10. 67. Wm Cowper.

William Cowper

Autograph letter signed, dated 10 January 1786, to Lady Hesketh.
4 pp. 235 x 185 mm. MA 1345.

Unlike some poets—Pope, for example—whose public reputations include their private lives, Cowper died almost unknown to the public that loved his poetry. Though his cousin Lady Hesketh understood the need for an authorized biography, she intended to confine to the immediate circle of his friends any knowledge of what she considered the misfortune of his Evangelical beliefs and the undoubted tragedy of his periods of severe depression. William Hayley, the official biographer, respected her wishes, but when the first volume of his *Life and Letters of William Cowper* appeared in 1803, the reviewers abruptly brushed away the fragile web of Hayley's adulatory narrative and seized upon a previously unknown fact: Cowper was a brilliant correspondent. Within twenty years of his death, Cowper's reputation had almost completely reversed itself; his poetry had begun to fade, while he was justly hailed as one of the greatest of English letter writers. The attractions of Cowper's epistolary style—so adaptable and good-humored—ruined Lady Hesketh's plans to hide his miseries in oblivion, and today the details of his secluded life are better known than those of any other poet of his period.

The letter shown here was written just six months after Cowper resumed correspondence with Lady Hesketh following the publication and resounding success of *The Task*. Like so many of his letters it combines business—here, the problem of obtaining subscriptions for his projected translation of Homer—frivolity, and a brief mention of the religious melancholy from which he suffered daily and which plagued him during the writing of *The Task:* "In truth my Dear, had you known in what anguish of mind I wrote the whole of that poem . . . you would long since have wonderd as much as I do myself, that it turned out anything better than mere Grub Street."

The largest collections of Cowper's letters are in the Firestone Library at Princeton University and the British Library. The Morgan Library owns most of Cowper's correspondence with his former schoolmate Walter Bagot.

[Starting with first full paragraph:] It gave me the greatest pleasure that you found my friend Unwin, what I was sure you would find him, a most agreeable man. I did not usher him in with the marrow-bones and cleavers of high sounding Panegyric, both because I was sure that whatsoever merit he had, your discernment would quickly mark it, and because it is possible to do a man material injury by making his praise his harbinger. It is easy to raise expectation to such a pitch that the reality be it ever so excellent, must necessarily fall below it.

I account myself much indebted to M.r Burrows, of whom I have the first information from yourself, both for his friendly dispositions toward me, and for the manner in which he marks the defects of my Volume; an author must be tender indeed to wince on being touched so gently. It is undoubtedly as he says, and as you and my Uncle say. You cannot be all mistaken, neither is it at all probable that any of you should be so. I take it for granted therefore that there are inequalities in the composition, and do assure you my Dear, most faithfully, that if it should reach a second Edition, I will spare no pains to improve it. It may serve me for an agreeable amusement perhaps, when Homer shall be gone and done with. The first Edition of Poems has generally been susceptible of improvement. Pope I believe never published one in his life that did not undergo Variations, and his longest pieces, many. . . .

amazed, could they but conjecture that it is even possible I
may write to the King himself! My Dear I doubt not, at least
think it probable that you have hit upon the true cause of
the silence of your friend at Windsor, and found it in the dan-
-gerous illness of the Princess Elizabeth. So affectionate a
mother can have little leisure for poetry at such a season.
For my own part I shall be perfectly satisfied if I can have
liberty to dedicate either to Her Majesty or to His. I have
the profoundest respect for them both, and shall be sure
not to falsify my own sentiments, say whatsoever I may
on the occasion.

It gave me the greatest pleasure that you found
my friend Unwin, what I was sure you would find him, a
most agreeable man. I did not usher him in with the marrow-
-bones and cleavers of high sounding Panegyric, both be-
-cause I was sure that whatsoever merit he had, your discern-
-ment would quickly mark it, and because it is possible
to do a man material injury by making his praise his
harbinger. It is easy to raise expectation to such a pitch that
the reality be it ever so excellent, must necessarily fall be-
-low it.

I account myself much indebted to Mr. Burrows, of
whom I have the first information from yourself, both for his
friendly dispositions toward me, and for the manner in
which he marks the defects of my Volume; an author must
be tender indeed to wince on being touched so gently. It is
undoubtedly as he says, and as you and my Uncle say. You
cannot be all mistaken, neither is it at all probable that
any of you should be so. I take it for granted therefore that
there are inequalities in the composition, and do assure you
my Dear, most faithfully, that if it should reach a second
Edition, I will spare no pains to improve it. It may serve
me for an agreeable amusement perhaps, when Homer shall
be gone and done with. The first Edition of Poems was generally
been susceptible of improvement. Pope I believe never published
one in his life that did not undergo Variations, and his longest
pieces, many. I will only observe that inequalities there must
be always and in every work of length. There are the level parts

* Had not room here to be explicit on this subject. You will find me so
in a postscript that will reach you in an hour or two.

of every subject, parts which we cannot with propriety ever
attempt to elevate. They are by nature humble, and can only
be made to assume an awkward and uncouth appearance by
being mounted. But again I take it for granted, that this
remark does not apply to the matter of your objection. You
were sufficiently aware of it before, and have no need that
I should suggest it as an apology could it have served that
office, but would have made it for me yourself. In truth my Dear,
had you known in what anguish of mind I wrote the whole of
that poem, and under what perpetual interruptions from
a cause that has since been removed, so that sometimes I had
not opportunity to write more than 3 lines at a sitting, you
would long since have wondered as much as I do myself, that
it turned out anything better than mere Grub Street.

* My Cousin, give yourself no trouble to find out
any of the Magi to scrutinize my Homer. I can do without them,
and if I were not conscious that I have no need of their help
I would be the first to call for it. Where is your faith? Is it not
even upon my sleeve? Are you not horribly afraid that I sh^d.
humble you well for departing so wide from the principle of a
I tell you my beloved, anxious, precious friend, that I under-
-stand Homer as well as I understand Chevy Chase. And if I
do not prove it soon, call me Coxcomb for ever. I am ambitious
of the whole honour, I can not spare as much of it to any man, as
~~would~~ might be transmitted through the eye of a needle. Assure
yourself moreover, that I intend to be careful to the utmost line
of all possible caution both with respect to language and versifi-
-cation. I will do upon this subject all that you can wish me
to do. I will not send a verse to the Press that shall not have
undergone the strictest examination.

A Subscription is surely on every account the most
eligible mode of publication. When I shall have emptied the purses
of my friends and of their friends into my own, I am still free to
levy contributions upon the world at large, and shall then have
a fund wherewith to defray the expences of a new Edition. I long
for terms in which to thank you for your generous offer, and cannot
find them. — I have ordered Johnson to print the Proposals immediately,
and hope that they will kiss your hands before the week is expired.

113

George Colman, the Elder
1732–1794

Autograph letter signed, dated Gower Street, 27 August 1787, to Thomas Cadell. 1 p. 226 x 188 mm.

One of the greatest secular rewards of William Cowper's life was the fame that his poem *The Task* brought him, for upon its publication in 1785 many friends who had lost sight of him after he left London in 1763 resumed correspondence with him. Among these was George Colman, a boyhood friend from Westminster and a fellow member of the Nonsense Club, when nonsense was still the order of Cowper's day. Since they had last seen each other, Colman had become one of the most important men in the London theatrical world, a rival and friend of Garrick, a member of Johnson's literary club, friend of Walpole, Sir Joseph Banks and a long list of other notables. While Garrick prospered at Drury Lane, Colman ran Covent Garden with equal success between 1767 and 1774. He was also a playwright of some distinction and wrote in one genre or another for almost the entire length of his literate life. With Garrick he collaborated on what is perhaps his most famous play, *The Clandestine Marriage* (1766), and alone he wrote the popular plays *Polly Honeycombe, a Dramatick Novel in One Act* (1760) and *The Jealous Wife* (1761). The classical training he underwent at Westminster was not entirely lost, however, for he published well-respected editions of Terence and Horace, as well as a somewhat less Latinate drama entitled *Ut Pictura Poesis! or The Enraged Musicians* (1789). This was the last of his productions; he spent the final years of his life in madness. The letter to the publisher Cadell shown here concerns the publication of Colman's *Prose on Several Occasions* (1787).

Gower Street, Augt. 27. 1787. Dear Sir Supposing that you may by this time be able to form some opinion whether my little Collection is a marketable commodity, I should be much obliged to you to let me know whether it would be agreeable to you to take it entirely to yourself, & what you conceive to be the value of it. I have the utmost confidence in your candour & goodwill, yet I would by no means wish to make an improper call on either: & if it were not for a long & expensive illness, Garton's failure, & other disappointments, I would not trouble You on such a Subject. I am, Dear Sir, most Sincerely Yours G. Colman

Gower Street, Augt. 27. 1787.

Dear Sir

Supposing that You may by this time be able to form some opinion whether my little Collection is a market=able commodity, I should be much obliged to You to let me know whether it would be agreeable to You to take it entirely to Yourself, & what you conceive to be the value of it. I have the utmost confidence in your candour & goodwill, yet I would by no means wish to make an improper call on either: & if it were not for a long & expensive Illness, Garton's failure, & other disappointments, I would not trouble You on such a Subject.

I am, Dear Sir,

most sincerely Yours

G. Colman

James Macpherson
1736–1796

Autograph letter signed with initials, dated 19 February 1781, to Paul Benfield. 1 p. 226 x 183 mm.

In 1760 James Macpherson published in Edinburgh a slender volume entitled *Fragments of Ancient Poetry Collected in the Highlands of Scotland*, the preface to which confidently begins, "The public may depend on the following fragments as genuine remains of ancient Scottish poetry." The public was willing to concede its interest in these poetical fragments, but when Macpherson next published—his *Fingal, An Ancient Epic Poem* appeared in 1762—doubts about their antiquity began to occur in spite of reassurances by such eminent men as John Home, Hugh Blair and William Robertson. The debate over the authenticity of the Ossianic poems, called so after their supposed author, soon reached national proportions. Johnson roundly condemned them and, being challenged by Macpherson, wrote to him in very plain terms: "I thought your book an imposture from the beginning." A brief respite from this quarrel came when Macpherson traveled to Pensacola, Florida, as secretary to the colonial Governor. After his return to England he became a political writer, a career in which he prospered. He made his fortune when he became the London agent for an Indian nabob about 1781. The letter shown here was written to a colleague in India, the great peculator Paul Benfield. Edmund Burke later characterized Benfield as a "criminal who long since ought to have fattened the region kites with his offal," a clause which has the true Ossianic ring to it.

My dear Benfield, Nothing has happened here, worth your notice, since your departure. I wish you had, and I know not but you have, left, a greater latitude to your attorneys. They will, however, endeavour to fill up the vacuum, *in your instructions, without injuring you; and as much to your credit, as possible. One thing I must advise you, upon; and you are to treasure my advice, in your mind; "have patience'* yourself *and trust to the exertion of your friends, On the latter, you may depend implicitly. Your situation, in going out, is not quite to the wish of your friends; but it is much better, than they expected. You are a man of talents:—Your friends, I trust, are not very deficient; but you must trust more to the events of the times, than to the exertions of either. I shall write you, very fully, by* John, *who is to set out, day after to-morrow. I am, in the mean-time, My dear friend, Yours most affectionately J.M. Feb. 19*th 1781.

My dear Benfield.

Nothing has happened here, worth your notice, since your departure. I wish you had, and I know not but you have left, a greater latitude to your attorneys. They will, however, endeavour to fill up the _vacuum_, in your instructions, without injuring you; and as much to your credit, as possible. One thing I must advise you, upon; and you are to treasure my advice, in your mind; "have patience _yourself_ and trust to the exertion of your friends." On the latter, you may depend im:plicitly. Your situation, in going out, is not quite to the wish of your friends; but it is much better, than they expected. You are a man of talents:— Your friends, I trust, are not very deficient; but you must trust more to the events of the times, than to the exertions of either. I shall write you, very fully, by _John_, who is to set out, day after to-morrow. I am, in the meantime, My dear friend,

Yours most affectionately

Feb 19th 1780.

J. M.

EDWARD GIBBON
1737–1794

Autograph manuscript notebook containing expanded notes for his "Decline and Fall of the Roman Empire," written before 28 April 1783. 13 ff. 185 x 115 mm. MA 267.

In the first of the notes to appear in this manuscript volume, Gibbon writes, "There is some Philosophical amusement in tracing the birth and progress of error." He might have added that he employed the same techniques and found the same amusement in tracing the birth and progress of Christianity, a task essential to the design of the *Decline and Fall* but generally unwelcome to most contemporary readers. However, Gibbon did not approach lightly his skeptical examination of the early evidences of Christianity. He began Chapter XV ("The Progress of the Christian Religion") of Volume I in a defensive manner, distinguishing the means of the theologian from those of the historian: the latter, he remarked, "must discover the inevitable mixture of error and corruption, which [Religion] contracted in a long residence upon earth, among a weak and degenerate race of beings." When the first volume of the *Decline and Fall* appeared in 1776, Gibbon found himself obliged to defend his decidedly Continental conclusions before a nation that preferred (in Burke's words) the "rust of superstition." "Had I believed," he wrote in his *Autobiography*, "that the majority of English readers were so fondly attached even to the name and shadow of Christianity . . . I might, perhaps have softened the two invidious chapters . . . ."

This manuscript volume contains a series of annotations that amplify notes previously printed in the *Decline and Fall*. The page shown here concerns the story of the seven sleepers, a tale Gibbon seems to have enjoyed. In the thirty-third chapter of Volume III (for which this page provides a supplemental note), he observed that this "easy and universal belief, so expressive of the sense of mankind, may be ascribed to the genuine merit of the fable itself."

The pleasing and even Philosophical fiction of the seven sleepers who in the year 250 retired into a cave near Ephesus to escape the persecution of Decius, and who awoke one hundred and eighty seven years afterwards (see Asseman. Bib. Orient. Tom i p 338) has been received with universal applause. It is remarkable enough that this prodigy should be related by James Sarugi who was born only fifteen years after it is supposed to have happened; and who died Bishop of Batnæ in the year 521. (Asseman. Tom i p 289). From the legends and offices of the Church of Syria ~~it~~ the tale was soon adopted by the Christian World: by the Latins (Gregor Turon. de glor. Martyr. L i. C 95 passio ~~eodem~~ eorum, quam Syro *quodam interpretante in Latinum transtulimus) by the Greeks (Phot. Cod. 253) by the Russians, (Menologium Slavo-Russicum) and by the Abyssinians (Ludolf. p 436). Mahomet had probably heard it with pleasure when he conducted the camels of his mistress Cadigiah to the fairs of Syria. He inserted it in the Koran, and the story of the seven sleepers is related and embellished by the Arabs the ~~Per~~ Persians and all the nations who profess the Mahometan Religion. (Renaudot Hist Patriarch Alexandrin. p 38.39). . . .*

The pleasing and even Philosophical fiction of the seven sleepers who in the year 250 retired into a cave near Ephesus to escape the persecution of Decius, and who awoke one hundred and eighty seven years afterwards (see Asseman. Bib. Orient. Tom i p 338) has been received with universal applause. It is remarkable enough that this prodigy should be related by James Sarugi who was born only fifteen years after it is supposed to have happened; and who died Bishop of Batnae in the year 521. (Asseman. Tom i p 289). From the legends and offices of the Church of Syria the tale was soon adopted by the Christian World: by the Latins (Gregor Turon. de glor. Martyr. L i. C 95 passio eorum, quam Syro quodam interpretante in Latinum transtulimus) by the Greeks (Phot. Cod. 253) by the Russians. (Menologium Slavo-Russicum) and by the Abyssinians (Ludolf. p 436). Mahomet had probably heard it with pleasure when he conducted the camels of his mistress Cadigiah to the fairs of Syria. He inserted it in the Koran and the story of the seven sleepers is related and embellished by the Arabs the Persians and all the nations who profess the Mahometan Religion. (Renaudot Hist Patriarch Alexandrin. p 38-39) The seven sleepers who were discovered in a cave in Norway (Paul.

JOHN WOLCOT ("PETER PINDAR")
1738–1819

Autograph letter signed, dated 11 January 1800, to an unidentified recipient. 4 pp. 240 x 191 mm.

Peter Pindar is hardly a name to be reckoned with today, but there was a time when a poet like Burns could write to George Thomson and say, "The very name of Peter Pindar is an acquisition to your work," and then deferentially add, "Not that I intend to enter the lists with Peter: that would be presumption indeed." In the last quarter of the eighteenth century the means and accomplishments of satire were being seriously reconsidered; Cowper (once the schoolmate of Churchill) had come to doubt its moral efficacy, and Wordsworth, when asked in 1796 why he wrote no satire, replied, with some asperity, that "in all satires whatever the authors may say there will be found a spice of malignity." Pindar may at least be praised for his exuberant malignity and his willful neglect of John Brown's advice (from "An Essay on Satire occasioned by the Death of Mr. Pope"): "Be ever, in a just expression, bold,/ Yet ne'er degrade fair SATIRE to a Scold." Initially, Pindar's reputation arose from the loftiness of the subjects he chose to scold; his most ambitious satire was *The Lousiad: an Heroi-Comic Poem* (1785–95) about George III and a louse on his plate. But Pindar did not restrict his muse to royalty; his works take in a wide compass of contemporary celebrities: James Boswell and Mrs. Piozzi (*Bozzy and Piozzi, or the British Biographers*, 1786), Sir Joseph Banks (*Sir Joseph Banks and the Emperor of Morocco*, 1788) and William Pitt (*Hair Powder: A Plaintive Epistle to Pitt*, 1795) among many others.

This letter, signed "J. Wolcot," has the true Pindaric boisterousness, and reflects some of his subsidiary interests, particularly his love of music. (He recommends a music-master and mentions the violinist Giovanni Battista Viotti, who had been expelled from England on charges of political intrigue.) But the bulk of the letter is reserved for an affectionate invitation: "Do you never visit London? I have a beefsteak & a glass of Punch at all times at your service; with a longing desire to exchange old stories and go back to old times for my dear Friend we are not *chicken* . . . ."

[Starting with line 5:] Viotti is in England, but not suffered to to visit the Capital—he was a fool, and I think *merited his expulsion—He is really a wonder—the Jupiter of the* Crowds! *Do you never visit London? I have a beefsteak & a glass of Punch at all times at your service; with a longing desire to exchange old stories and go back to old times for my dear Friend we are not* chicken*—Longevity however is greatly in our power—Flannel, brandy & fire with decent eating & drinking (not* Aldermannic, *mind, for that is* inde-*cent), will in a great measure blunt the spicula of the poisons continually [illegible deletion] upon the Tap in that great Brewhouse called the Clouds.—* . . .

-ering Terms - but let his
Fingers speak for him —
as the Fiddle is his chief Instru-
-ment, you will be quite at
home with him — Viotti is
in England, but not suffered to
visit the Capital - because
a fool, and I think merited his
expulsion — He is really a
wonder - the Jupiter of the
Crowds! Do you never visit
London? I have a beefsteak
& a glass of Punch at all times
at your service, with a longing
desire to exchange old stories
and go back to old times

for my dear Friend we are
not chicken - Longevity however
is greatly in our power —
Flannel, brandy & fine with
decent eating & drinking (not
Aldermannic mind, for that is
indecent) will in a great
measure blunt the spicula of
the poisons continually ~~[illegible]~~
upon the Tap ~~[illegible]~~ in that great brewhouse
called the Clouds. —
once more let me, on the recom-
-mendation of my Friends the
Musical Ashleys, recommend to
your civilities & your Brothers
&c &c Mr Abbot & in return
be pleased to command every thing that can
be achieved in London
by my good
Friend yours J. Molioz

117

JAMES BOSWELL
1740–1795

Autograph letter signed, dated 2 and 6 April 1791, to William Temple. 8 pp. 225 x 185 mm. MA 981.

Boswell's *Life of Johnson* is as much the product of indolence and melancholy—eminently Johnsonian faults—as it is of exuberance and industry. As Boswell aged he came to a deeper understanding of the dark side of Johnson's character and the moral heroism that prevented him from succumbing to it. Once, it had been true that Johnson "had less enjoyment from [life] than I have," but by the time the *Life of Johnson* was being written, Boswell was forced to qualify this statement by adding that he also perceived "too much of reality in the gloomy picture." The letter, shown here, to his lifelong friend William Temple was written near the completion of the *Life*, and Boswell confessed to Temple what had long been apparent to both men: "I fear that my constitutional melancholy, which returns in such dismal fits and is now aggravated by the loss of my valuable wife, must prevent me from any permanent felicity in this life." Boswell's letters to Temple are among the most candid he wrote; and during Boswell's many crises, Temple offered encouragement (for which Boswell thanks him in this letter) or more plain-spoken truths like the one recorded in the *Journal* for 29 May 1790: "My friend Temple told me fairly that he had never seen any body so idle as I was." Thanks to the prodding of friends and his conscience, Boswell finally published the *Life of Johnson*—to the immediate acclaim of London—on 16 May 1791, the twenty-eighth anniversary of his introduction to Johnson in the bookshop of Thomas Davies.

The ninety-seven letters from Boswell to Temple in the Morgan Library were destined to be used as wrapping paper in a shop in Boulogne-sur-Mer in 1850 when they were recognized for what they were by an English visitor and saved for posterity. No one knows how many letters were destroyed as wrappings, but there are significant gaps in the correspondence. Today, the major archive of Boswell's manuscripts is in the Beinecke Library of Yale University.

[Starting with line 2 of recto page:] How delusive is this low spirited thought! But indeed I much fear that to a speculating and very feeling mind all that life affords will at times appear of no effect. When I recal the infinite variety of scenes through which I have passed, in my moments of sound sensation, I am elated; but in moments of depression, I either forget them all, or they seem indifferent.

My Life of Johnson is at last drawing to a close. I am correcting the last sheet, and have only to write an Advertisement, to make out a note of Errata and to correct a second sheet of contents, one being done. I really hope to publish it on the 25 current. My old and most intimate friend may be sure that a copy will be sent to him. I am at present in such bad spirits, that I have every fear concerning it—that I may get no profit, nay may lose—that the Publick may be dissappointed and think that I have done it poorly—that I may make many enemies, and even have quarrels.—...

what real advances have I made above that state! How delusive is this low-spirited thought! — But indeed I much fear that to a speculating and very feeling mind all that life affords will at times appear of no effect. When I recal the infinite variety of scenes through which I have passed, in my moments of sound sensation, I am elated; but in moments of depression, I either forget them all, or they seem indifferent.

My Life of Johnson is at last drawing to a close. I am correcting the last sheet and have only to write an Advertisement, to make out a note of Errata and to correct a second sheet of contents, one being done. I really hope to publish it on the 25 current. My old and most intimate friend may be sure that a copy will be sent to him. I am at present in such bad spirits, that I have every fear concerning it — that I may get no profit, nay may lose — that the Publick may be disappointed and think that I have done it poorly — that I may make many enemies, and even have quarrels. — Yet perhaps the very

one of my characteristical pamphlets upon this crisis. "An Appeal to the People" upon the threatened project of involving this country in a War with Russia in order to assist the Turks!

Approach thou like the rugged Russian Bear,
The arm'd Rhinoceros or Hyrcanian Tyger
Take any shape but that.

I am thinking to curtail my Poem on the Slave Trade and throw it into the World just before the great question comes on next Wednesday.

Pray let me know the subject of your intended Publication. Worthy Langton is in town.

Your little friend James is quite reconciled to Westminster School. He is grown a manly fellow. He I trust will be a prosperous Barrister.

There is no foundation for the match between Miss Palmer & Mr B. She is angry at me for talking of it. But I was only one of many. Let me hear more about Mr. Powlett. Best compliments & love to all with you. I ever am most affectionately yours J. B.

Hester Lynch Thrale Piozzi
1741–1821

Autograph manuscript, signed, of "Anecdotes of the late Samuel Johnson LLD during the last twenty Years of his Life . . . ," undated but written in 1785. 211 pp. 291 x 210 mm. MA 322.

Among the many peculiarities of *Anecdotes of the Late Samuel Johnson LL.D.* (published in 1786), not the least is the fact that it was written while the former Mrs. Thrale toured Italy with her new husband, Gabriel Piozzi, against whom Johnson had so vehemently and ineffectually protested. For years, Mrs. Thrale and her first husband, Henry Thrale, had provided Johnson with a measure of domestic comfort and almost familial attention in their home at Streatham Park. Johnson had occasionally thought of Mrs. Thrale as a potential biographer; he encouraged her to keep the "little Book" that became *Thraliana*, the source for *Anecdotes*, in which, after learning about Johnson's death, she wrote: "many a Joke we had about the Lives that would be published: rescue me out of all their hands·My dear, & do it *yourself* said he." Thankfully, her book forestalled no one, though it did provoke a just cry of inaccuracy from Boswell (who was himself liable to moments of similar creativity). The virtue of *Anecdotes* lies in its particular episodes and conversations, for in spite of her long friendship with Johnson, Mrs. Piozzi's attempts to characterize him in general terms seem surprisingly eccentric. Few men's minds have resembled less than Johnson's did "a royal pleasure-ground" or a "happy valley" with a "fit corner" for the "trim parterre" and the "antiquated ever-greens."

The pages shown here contain Johnson's memorable response to a friend who asked him if any man living could have written such a book as Macpherson's Ossian, and a reference to Boswell as Mr. B——. The diaries called *Thraliana* are now in the Huntington Library, San Marino, California.

[Starting near bottom of left-hand page:] When one talks of giving & taking the Lye familiarly, it is impossible to forbear recollecting the Transactions between the Editor of Ossian and the Author of the Journey to the Hebrides: it was most observable to me however, that Mr. Johnson never bore his Antagonist the slightest Degree of Ill:Will; he always kept those Quarrels which belonged to him as ~~an~~ ~~Auth~~ Writer, separate from those which he had to do with as a Man: but I never did hear him say in private one malicious Word of a publick Enemy, and of Mr. Macpherson I once heard him speak respectfully—tho' his reply to the Friend who asked him if any Man living *could have written such a Book? is well known, & has been often repeated—Yes Sir, many Men, many Women, and many Children. . . .*

I am now apprehensive for his general Health — he will lose
the Benefit of Exercise; Exercise! returns the Doctor, I
never heard that he used any; he might for ought I
know, walk *to* the Alehouse — but I believe he was
always *carried home again*. It was however unlucky
for those who delighted to echo Johnson's Sentiments —
that he would not endure from them today, what per:
:haps he had yesterday by his own Manner of treating
the subject made them fond of repeating; and I fancy
Mr. B— — has not forgotten, that though his Friend
one Evening in a gay Humour talked in Praise
of Wine, as one of the Blessings permitted by heaven
when used with Moderation, to lighten the Load of
Life, and give Men Strength to endure it; — yet
when in Consequence of such Talk, *he* thought fit
to make a Bacchanalian Discourse in its favour,
Mr. Johnson contradicted him ~~[illegible]~~ somewhat roughly
as I remember, and when to assure himself of Con:
:quest he added these Words — You must allow me Sir
at least that it produces Truth; — *in Vino Veritas* you
know Sir. — — — ~~that~~ replied Mr. Johnson, would be use:
:less to a Man, who knew he was not a Lyar when he
was sober. When one talks of giving & taking
the Lye familiarly, it is impossible to forbear

recollecting the Transaction between the Editor
of Ossian and the Authour of the Journey to the
Hebrides: it was most observable to me however,
that Mr. Johnson never bore his Antagonist
the slightest Degree of Ill: Will; he always kept
those Quarrels which belonged to him as a —
~~[illegible]~~ Writer, separate from those which he had
to do with as a Man: but I never did hear
him say in private one malicious Word of a
publick Enemy, and of Mr. Macpherson I once
heard him speak respectfully — — — tho' his reply
to the Friend who asked him if *any Man living*
could have written such a Book; is wellknown, &
has been often repeated — — — Yes Sir, many Men,
many Women, and many Children. I enquired of
him myself if this Story was authentick, and he said
it was: I made the same Enquiry concerning his
Acct. of the State of Literature in Scotland, which
was repeated up and down at one Time by every
body — — — how Knowledge was divided among the
Scots like Bread in abesieged Town, to every Man
a Mouthful, to no man a Bellyfull. This Story

119

HENRY MACKENZIE
1745–1831

Autograph letter signed, dated 22 December 1802, to Dr. James Currie. 3 pp. 253 x 205 mm.

Mackenzie's *Man of Feeling* begins in a most unsentimental manner, in mid-hunt, where a squire and a curate exchange the books they carry to provide paper for wadding in their shotguns. The fragmentary manuscript which the squire obtains recounts the history of Harley, the man of feeling, about which the squire remarks: "I was a good deal affected with some very trifling passages in it; and had the name of a Marmontel, a Rousseau, or a Richardson been on the title-page—'tis odds that I should have wept: But One is ashamed to be pleased with the works of one does not know whom." The squire was perhaps the only reader of *The Man of Feeling* to be embarrassed by its anonymity; Edinburgh readers bought out the first edition within a week of its appearance and happily paid the work "the tribute of some tears." *The Man of Feeling* is a novel in which narrative is sacrificed to emotion, as if Richardson had condensed *Clarissa* to a slim 268 pages and retained only the peaks of emotional turmoil. Not the least of the book's peculiarities is the fact that its author bears a greater resemblance to the hunting squire in the introduction than he does to the naïve and sentimental Harley. Nonetheless, when Mackenzie acknowledged his work, he was immediately dubbed "the man of feeling," probably the only Comptroller of Taxes ever to be thus designated.

After publishing three novels and several unsuccessful plays, and editing two influential periodicals, *The Mirror* and *The Lounger*, Mackenzie began to confine himself to his official duties and his important services of friendship toward the younger writers in Edinburgh. In this letter to James Currie, the author of a biography of Burns (whose career Mackenzie had substantially advanced), he remarks that "notwithstanding the partial Opinion of my Friends, Want of Ability as well as of Inclination disqualify me for resuming my Pen." Mackenzie remained active in Edinburgh's literary society until late in his life; in his journal Sir Walter Scott described him at the age of eighty, "on the very brink of human dissolution": "H.M. is alert as a contracting tailor's needle in every sort of business . . . and is the life of the company with anecdote and fun."

[Starting midway on verso page:] The Tragedy of the Spanish Father *I wrote, with great Rapidity, at a Time when I was not sufficiently aware of the difficulty of writing a Tragedy. There are, I think, (for I have not read it for a long time, I have now no Copy that is easily read) some good enough Strokes of high passion & of Tenderness in it; but probably Mr Kemble was right in his Judgment that it was not well adapted for the Stage. I rather think, however, that the principal Character was well enough adapted to him; proud & passionate to excess, & rowzed to madness by Resentment for his Injuries, by outraged Honor, & by dissapointed Tenderness, I recollect appropriating it at the Time to such an Actor as him, with a belief that that Character, at least would* tell *(as the Cant phrase is) in the Representation. There was certainly no female Personage worthy of his Sister. I am sorry to learn that the British Stage is likely to lose her for this Winter.*

Edinburgh *has suffered great Losses in literary Men. She has still a few who do her honor; & there are some young Men of very considerable Genius & Talents, who amuse themselves with Writing. Have you seen an* Edin^{r} Quarterly Review *published about Six weeks ago?. . .*

your Correspondence. Amidst the pastoral Scenery wh you mention on the Banks of the Annan & the Moffat, I was not insensible to ye Pictures it exhibited, or the Sentiments it excited; but on a Mind languid & worn down as mine is, this Dream of Delight & of Feeling is unproductive of any Effort to give it words. — The Visions float before the Mind, to be enjoyed not expressed — but I may save my Eyes when writing to you on this Subject; indeed on this Subject, those who are formed to understand it need no Words for ye purpose; to those who are not so formed, no words can convey the Idea.

The Tragedy of the Spanish Father I wrote, with great Rapidity, at a Time when I was not sufficiently aware of the difficulty of writing a Tragedy. There are, I think, (for I have not read it for a long time, & have now no Copy that is easily read) some good enough Strokes of high passion & of Tenderness in it; but probably Mr Kemble was right in his Judgment that it was not well adapted for the Stage. I rather think, however, that the principal Character was well enough adapted to him; proud & passionate to excess, & roused to madness by Resentment for his Injuries, by outraged Honor, & by disappointed Tenderness, I recollect appropriating it at the Time to such an Actor as him, with a Belief that that Character, at least, would tell (as the Cant phrase is) in the Representation. There was certainly no female Personage worthy of his Sister. I am sorry to learn that the British Stage is likely to lose her for this Winter.

Edinburgh has suffered great Losses in literary Men. She has still a few who do her honor; & there are some young Men of very considerable Genius & Talents, who amuse them=selves with Writing. Have you seen an Edinr Quarterly Review published about six weeks ago? if I thought it had not reached Liverpool, & knew how to send it, I should be glad to transmit it to you, as a Specimen of the Talents & Composition of the Young Literati of this City.

I delivered your Message to Lord Woodhouselee who desires his kind remembrance to you. He is now immersed in the laborious business of a Lord of Session, which like my Office admits of very little other Reading. — But a Letter from you, when you have leisure, will be a Sort of Reading of that peculiar Interest for which we always find Time & Eyesight. Believe me, with the most sincere regard, Dear Sir, Yr very faithful & most obedt Servant

H Mackenzie

Dr Currie, Liverpool

Richard Brinsley Sheridan
1751–1816

Autograph letter signed, dated 12 January 1776, to Robert Crispin. 2 pp. 237 x 192 mm.

On Saturday the twenty-first of September 1776, the Theatre Royal at Drury Lane opened a new season under new management with a prelude, *New Brooms!*, by George Colman the elder, *Twelfth Night* and a farce entitled *Miss in Her Teens* by the former actor/owner/manager of Drury Lane, David Garrick. The program in itself was hardly epoch-forming but the change in Drury Lane's ownership was. The Theatre Royal had been in Garrick's hands since 1747 and the coalition that purchased his half-share of the patent was organized by Richard Brinsley Sheridan, the best of the young playwrights. The letter illustrated here was written to Robert Crispin, one of the attorneys who was handling the complex negotiations between Sheridan, his partners and Garrick, who was asking £35,000 for his interest in Drury Lane. (Among the minor provisions of the agreement was the stipulation—freely offered by Sheridan and his friends—that Garrick retain his private box at the theater.) On his part, Garrick expressed contentment with the bargain that was struck and with the man who would attempt to replace him; to his former partner, Willoughby Lacy, he wrote, "Mr Sheridan is certainly a man of genius, & appears remarkably fair & open in his Conduct." Unfortunately, neither term of Garrick's compliment was quite fulfilled. Sheridan was indeed a man of genius, but he wrote only two more important plays after taking over Drury Lane: *The School for Scandal*, produced in May 1777, and *The Critic* (1779); and though he was fair and open, he also had a tendency to place his payments to Garrick last on his list of debts, so that within two years of selling his share in Drury Lane, Garrick was forced to press for settlement of the amount due him.

Sheridan's letters are widely distributed, but substantial numbers of them are preserved at Yale University and in the Royal Archives at Windsor Castle.

D^r. Sir, I have gone over the Draught with D^r. Ford, which appears extremely well calculated for the Purpose. I think relative to the moiety of ye Debts due from the Performers—which we are to take—it should not be as they shall stand on the 24th June, *but at their* present *amount—on our signing this Agreement—. we think likewise that the Term allow'd for us to take the Mortgage from M^r. Garrick, need only be* three months *(instead of a year) from the time of Lacy's giving notice that He does not mean to pay it off+should that be the case+as we wish to have it in our Power as soon as possible—& should certainly take it from G. directly. — We think it will not be worth while to stipulate anything relative to the Box given up to G. — I understand there is another mortgage on Lacy's share I suppose the Register will inform us whether Garrick's is not the first. —. . .*

R. B. Sheridan

D.r Sir,

I have gone over the Draught with D.r Ford which appears extremely well calculated for the Purpose. — I think rela=tive to the moiety of Debts due from the Performers which we are to take — it should not be as they shall stand on the 24th June, but at their present amount — on our signing the Agreement — we think likewise that the Term allow'd for us to take the Mortgage from M.r Garrick, need only be three months (instead of a year) from the time of Lacy's giving notice that He does not mean to pay it off — should that be the case — as we wish to have it in our Power as soon as possible — & should certainly take it from G. directly. — We think it will not be worth while to stipulate anything re=lative to the Box given up to G. — I under=stand there is another mortgage on Lacy's share — I suppose the Register will inform us whether Garrick's is not the first. —

I have added our Names &c. — & wish much M.r Wallis may have it as soon as possible — as G. goes from Town Sunday — & we hope to have matters finally adjusted on Tuesday Evening. —

I'll appoint a time for our meeting with M.r Ewart — on the Article which we are to sign with each other — which you'll be so good to have a Draught of.

I hope you are recover'd from your Indisposition — tho' the Weather is so much against going abroad, and there is no alteration in the Articles material enough to require our meeting.

I am, Sir,
Your very obed.t
R. B. Sheridan

Orchard Street
Jan 12.th 76.

Richard Brinsley Sheridan

121

THOMAS CHATTERTON
1752–1770

Autograph manuscript of "Sly Dick" and "A Hymn for Christmas Day," written ca. 1763–4. 4 pp. From the Collection of Mrs. Donald F. Hyde.

In April 1770 Chatterton left the attorney to whom he had been apprenticed in Bristol and set out for London, where he committed suicide four months later. He had come with the intention of transplanting his literary career to a more commodious setting, and in a letter to his mother and his old Bristol friends he wrote a premature, hopeful account of his success: "What a glorious prospect!... The poverty of authors is a common observation, but not always a true one. No author can be poor who understands the arts of booksellers—." Chatterton felt that he had fairly "dipped into" these arts, but he was soon starving, selling little and writing through the nights. Several periodicals, including the *Freeholder's Magazine*, did occasionally print his work, but it was not until seven years after his death that his most distinctive creations, the Rowley poems, were published. These were imitations of Middle English verse, supposed to have been written by one Thomas Rowley, a secular priest of Bristol. The literary men of London in the 1770s considered Chatterton a prodigy: "It is wonderful how the whelp has written such things," Johnson remarked. For the Romantics, who ignored his later work (which owes more to Churchill than to Chaucer), Chatterton became a rare eighteenth-century icon of the Imagination.

The two poems shown here are remarkable attestations to Chatterton's youthful ability, for they were written when he was eleven or twelve years old. The first, "Sly Dick," is merely an amusing fragment, but the second, "A Hymn for Christmas Day," displays a precocious mastery of the majestic idiom of Pope's "Universal Prayer."

Chatterton's manuscripts can be found principally in the Bristol Public Library and the British Library.

Sly Dick./ Sharp was the Frost, the wind was high/ And sparkling Stars bedeckt the Sky,/ Sly Dick in arts of cunning skill'd,/ Whose Rapine all his pockets fill'd,/ Had laid him down to take his rest/ And soothe with sleep his anxious breast./ 'Twas thus a dark infernal sprite/ A native of the blackest Night,/ Portending mischief to devise/ Upon Sly Dick he cast his Eyes,/ Then strait descends th'infernal sprite,/ And in his Chamber does alight:/ In visions he before him stands,/ And his Attention he commands;/ Thus spake the sprite—Hearken my friend/ And to my Counsels now attend,/ Within the Garrets' spacious dome/ There lies a well stor'd wealthy room,...

A Hymn for Christmas Day./ Almighty Framer of the Skies!/ O! let our pure Devotion rise,/ Like I~~n~~scence in thy Sight:/ Wrapt in impenetrable Shade/ The Texture of our Souls were made/ Till thy Command gave Light./ The Sun of Glory gleam'd the Ray,/ Refind the Darkness into Day,/ And bid the Vapors fly:/ Impell'd by his eternal Love/ He left his Palaces above/ To chear our gloomy Sky./ How shall we celebrate the day,/ When God appear'd in mortal clay:/ The mark of worldly scorn:/ When the Archangels heavenly Lays,/ Attempted the Redeemer's Praise/ And hail'd Salvation's Morn....

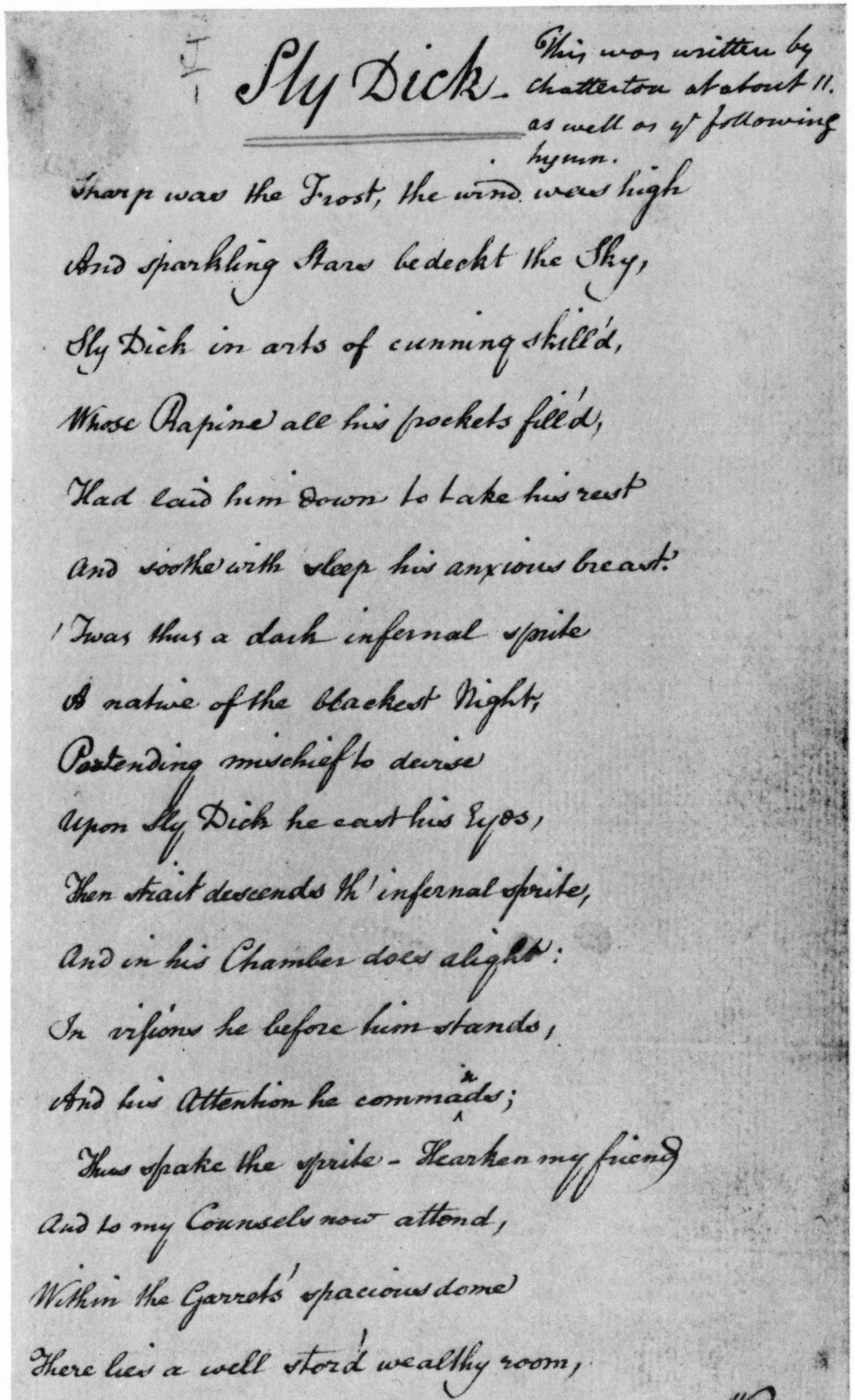

J/1

Sly Dick — This was written by Chatterton at about 11. as well as ye following hymn.

Sharp was the Frost, the wind was high
And sparkling Stars bedeckt the Sky,
Sly Dick in arts of cunning skill'd,
Whose Rapine all his pockets fill'd,
Had laid him down to take his rest
And soothe with sleep his anxious breast.
'Twas thus a dark infernal sprite
A native of the blackest Night,
Portending mischief to devise
Upon Sly Dick he cast his Eyes,
Then strait descends th' infernal sprite,
And in his Chamber does alight:
In visions he before him stands,
And his Attention he commands;
Thus spake the sprite — Hearken my friend
And to my Counsels now attend,
Within the Garrets' spacious dome
There lies a well stor'd wealthy room,

Well

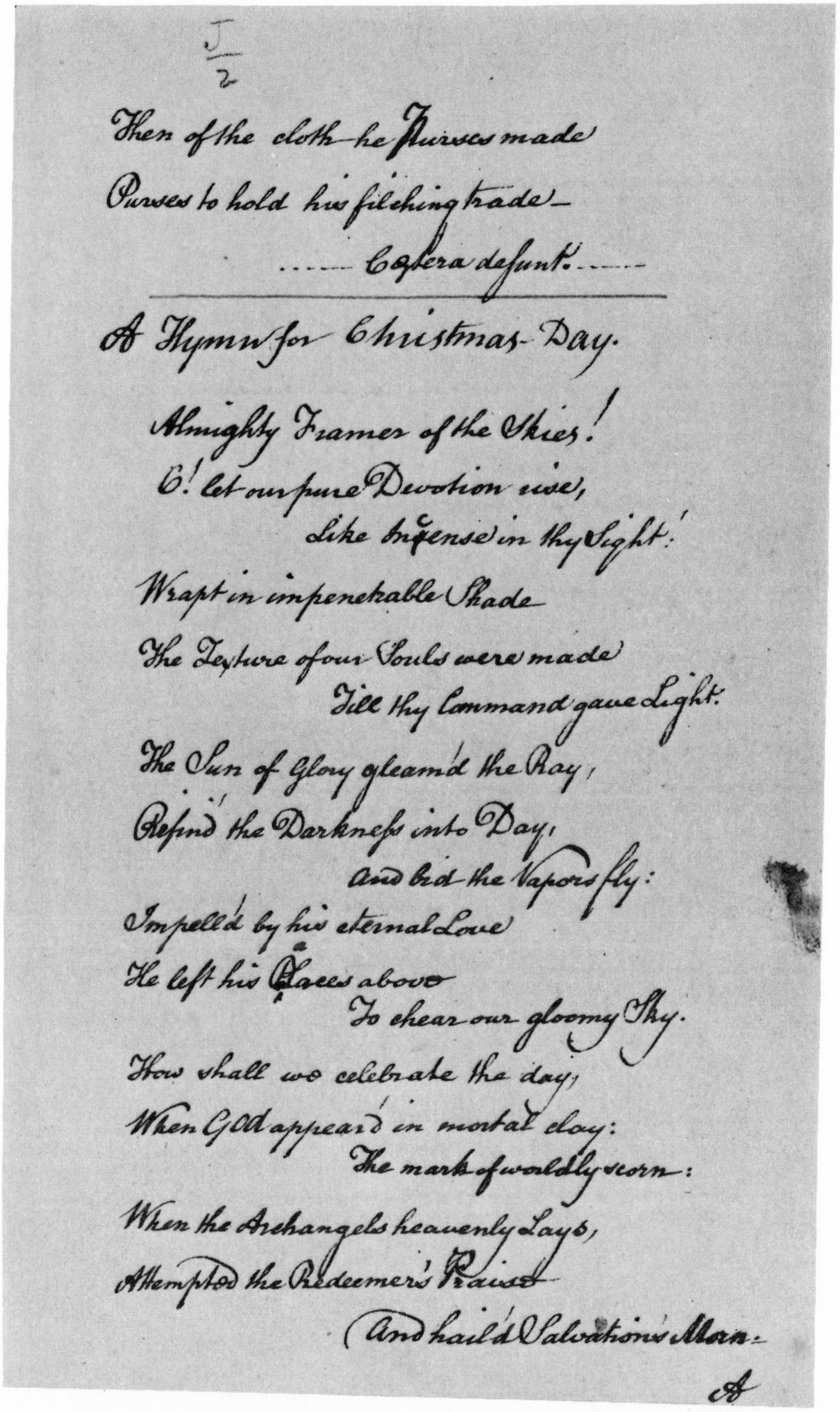

J/2

Then of the cloth he Purses made
Purses to hold his filching trade —
...... Cætera desunt. ......

A Hymn for Christmas Day.

Almighty Framer of the Skies!
O! let our pure Devotion rise,
Like Incense in thy Sight:
Wrapt in impenetrable Shade
The Texture of our Souls were made
Till thy Command gave Light.
The Sun of Glory gleam'd the Ray,
Refin'd the Darkness into Day,
And bid the Vapors fly:
Impell'd by his eternal Love
He left his Places above
To chear our gloomy Sky.
How shall we celebrate the day,
When God appear'd in mortal clay:
The mark of worldly scorn:
When the Archangels heavenly Lays,
Attempted the Redeemer's Praise
And hail'd Salvation's Morn.

A

Fanny Burney (Madame d'Arblay) 1752–1840

Autograph manuscript of an advertisement for the first edition of "Cecilia," dated July 1782. 1 p. 226 x 185 mm. MA 3391. Purchased as the gift of Constance Mellon Brown.

After Fanny Burney's entrance into the world with *Evelina* (1778) and the flurry of popularity that followed, the writing of her second novel, *Cecilia*, proved a disappointment to her. Instead of being a conspiratorial pleasure, as the composition of *Evelina* had been, it became a matter of public conjecture and a filial obligation, for her father, Dr. Charles Burney, kept her diligently at her task. Some of the tension created by the pressure of living up to her former success appears in this advertisement for *Cecilia*, written in July 1782. (It was apparently never used, for the sales of the book rapidly exceeded those of *Evelina*.) In her most formal Johnsonian manner (suitable to prose about the hopes and fears of an author) she writes: "the precariousness of any power to give pleasure, suppresses all vanity of confidence, & sends CECILIA into the world with scarce more hope, though far more encouragement, than accompanied her highly-honoured predecessor, EVELINA." *Cecilia* did bear the marks of its strained origin. Horace Walpole found it too long and some of its charaters "*outrés*"; in a letter of 1 October 1782 to Lady Ossory, he also observed that everyone in the novel is made to act precisely in character, "which is very unnatural, at least in the present state of things, in which people are always aiming to disguise their ruling passions, and rather affect opposite qualities, than hang out their propensities."

By far the most important collection of manuscripts by Fanny Burney is that in the Berg Collection of The New York Public Library, which includes incomplete manuscripts of *Evelina*, *Cecilia* and *Camilla*, as well as her diaries.

First Edition of Cecilia/ Advertisement./ The indulgence shewn by the Public to EVELINA, which, unpatronised, unaided, and unowned, past through 4 Four Editions in one Year, has [illegible deletion] encouraged its Author to risk this SECOND attempt. The animation of Success is too universally acknowledged, to make the Writer of the following Sheets dread much censure of temerity; though the precariousness of any power to give pleasure, suppresses all vanity of confidence, & sends CECILIA into the World with scarce more hope, though far more encouragement, than accompanied her highly-honoured predecessor, EVELINA. July 1782. VOL. I. A CECI-

First Edition of Cecilia

Advertisement.

The indulgence shewn by the Public to **EVELINA**, which, unpatronised, unaided, and unowned, past through Four Editions in one Year, has ~~[illegible]~~ encouraged its Author to risk this **SECOND** attempt. The animation of Success is too universally acknowledged, to make the Writer of the following Sheets dread much censure of temerity; though the precariousness of any power to give pleasure, suppresses all vanity of confidence, & sends **CECILIA** into the World with scarce more hope, though far more encouragement, than accompanied her highly-honoured predecessor, **EVELINA**.

July 1782.

123

George Crabbe
1754–1832

Autograph letter signed, dated 1 March 1828, to his son George.
3 pp. 235 x 188 mm. MA 2927.

Two years after Crabbe's death, Thomas Moore recalled how he and Samuel Rogers had once tried to induce Crabbe to talk about his first patron, Edmund Burke. The attempt was a failure, for Burke seemed to have left little impression; and to this sad fact, Moore added the observation that "the range of subjects, indeed, in which Mr. Crabbe took any interest was, at all times of his life, very limited. . . ." This limitation of subject matter and the limitation of technique that accompanied it made Crabbe a well-respected and, eventually, a well-remunerated poet. Certainly, his ascendance in social position (from being "one of those outcasts on the World" to chaplain to the Duke of Rutland) depended entirely on his poetical abilities, for he had, as Moore remarked, a "comparative inefficiency, as a member of society." In his verse Crabbe specialized in exploding the blissful traditions of pastoral poetry by portraying the tragedy that lurks in rural life. At first this was done in a manner general enough that Johnson could proclaim *The Village* (1783) to be "original, vigorous, and elegant." By the early nineteenth century, however, Crabbe had turned to a more detailed manner of description, which prompted Wordsworth to complain that "The Parish Register" (in *Poems*, 1807) was full of "matters of fact" and Hazlitt to assert, in a somewhat churlish spirit, that Crabbe "describes the interior of a cottage like a person sent there to distrain for rent."

The letter shown here, written to his son George late in Crabbe's life, is a fine familial epistle about duties at church, recent invitations and Crabbe's affection for one of his new granddaughters: "It is amusing to see the odd Expression of the Baby's Face at my white Head: She is not frightened but amused." Crabbe also mentions plans to perform a task he apparently undertook at several stages in his life, "to Overlook my writings of all kinds but especially the Versifications & to select & destroy as my Judgment—now impartial—may direct me. . . ."

[Starting midway, verso page:] We have Duty at Church All next Week except Saturday & most part of the week following but your Brother heeds not that kind of Employment nor will Accept my Assistence. We have a few Attendents on prayer Days, besides the Lads at School & the poor people 3 or 4 from the Workhouse. This is new and I am glad to see it.— I congratulate you on your Part at Church: It was a point worth your Exertion.

I have not forgotten our late Subject but have not felt disposed to write or even to methodise the few Thoughts that Occur to me: Still they are not forgotten.—

I want, very much, to Overlook my writings of all kinds but especially the Versifications & to select & destroy as my Judgment—now impartial—may direct me & I often say to Myself, If deferred now, can I reasonably expect ~~my~~ more Leisure or even greater Inclination. I must spur up myself for the Task. Have you not lost a Vol. of Shakespear? the 10th Macbeth &c. I have it & will lay it by— . . .

I know not whether Mr Bowles comes to you or not and it may be you do not know certainly but if you do I will be glad of the Information before the Time. I had some Thoughts of Writing to him but doubted whether it would be perfectly correct.

It is with great Pleasure I hear that all are well with you and I hear of no Complaints here. We had Invitations to Mr Tovells but I begged Leave of Absence on Account of Indisposition & was excused I hope as three of the Family went. They all returned Losers at Cards, & I think if everybody could lose It would not be a bad Thing, but I confess it is a Resource for those who cannot or will not think or exchange their Thoughts when they do.

We have Duty at Church All next Week except Saturday & most part of the week following but your Brother heeds not that kind of Employment nor will accept my Assistance. We have a few Attendants on prayer Days, besides the Lads at School & the poor people 3 or 4 from the Workhouse. This is new and I am glad to see it. — I congratulate you on your Seat at Church: It was a point worth your Exertion.

I have not forgotten our late Subject but have not felt disposed to write or even to methodise the few Thoughts that Occur to me: Still they are not forgotten. —

I want, very much, to Overlook my Writings of all kinds but especially the Versifications & to select & dispose as my Judgment — now impartial — may direct me & I often say to myself, If deferred now, can I reasonably expect more Leisure or even greater Inclination. I must spur up myself for the Task. Have you not lost a Vol. of Shakespeare? the 10. Macbeth &c. I have it & will lay it by —

This is more than I have written for some Time past & it is well for me that I am prepared with Good Friday & Easter-Sunday Sermons, for my Head does not permit me to methodise my Ideas. Remember me affectionately to all my little ones and their Mama: I feel great Desire to see them all Again, & that is my great Inducement, for Company I could have here if I desired it, but I have not Caroline's & though my little Girls here are for their Times as good as can well be expected, They are not very Conversable: It is amusing to see the odd Expression of the Baby's Face at my white Head: She is not frightened but amused. — We were all invited to Mr Webber's Tomorrow but declined Going: I had two Reasons: One it was in Passion Week — How those former Observances wear Away, not from a different mode of Thinking as some Dissenters, but from much less pardonable motives. — Give me a Line or two, if it be convenient to you & when I say that I would go to no Home except yours be assured that All but the Going is pleasant to your affectionate Father Geo Crabbe.

William Godwin
1756–1836

Autograph letter unsigned, dated 5 September 1800, to Samuel Taylor Coleridge. 4 pp. 224 x 184 mm. MA 1857.

In 1793 Godwin published *An Enquiry Concerning the Principles of Political Justice*, a work which set such an ideal standard of radical zeal that it proved to be a trap for its philosophically unvigilant readers. Hazlitt provides the best description of the way in which human beings naturally lapse from "the stern sense of duty" engendered by the spirit of revolution and preached by Godwin: "Two persons agree to live together in Chambers on principles of pure equality and mutual assistance—but when it comes to the push, one of them finds that the other always insists on his fetching water from the pump in Hare-court, and cleaning his shoes for him." Godwin, too, fell from his lofty standard. Having proscribed marriage and familial bonds in *An Enquiry*, he was married to Mary Wollstonecraft in March 1797. Their daughter, Mary Shelley, records an anecdote about how some of her father's inconsistencies, such as his desire to be addressed as William Godwin, Esq., were received by a younger generation of radicals: "I remember Shelley's unspeakable astonishment when the Author of Political Justice asked him half reproachfully why he addressed him 'Mr G." But if Godwin lapsed, his followers lapsed with him. Coleridge, once an admirer, wrote in *The Watchman* for 2 April 1796, "I do consider Mr. Godwin's Principles as vicious; and his book as a Pander to Sensuality. Once I thought otherwise. . . ."

By 1800, however, Coleridge encountered Godwin (whom his young son Hartley called Mr. 'Gobwin') regularly in literary society, and though amused by "the pedantry of atheism" began to correspond with him. Godwin was the elder man, but it was Coleridge who wielded the more effective intellectual influence, so much so that Godwin eventually adopted a mild theism. His expressions of affection for Coleridge in the letter shown here are sincere, if wooden. To his long diatribe on the legal profession, Coleridge responded, "I swell out my chest, & place my hand on my heart, & swear aloud to all that you *have* written, or shall write, against Lawyers & the Practice of the Law." Godwin's host at the time he wrote this letter was James Philpot Curran, an Irish judge and well-known orator.

[I feel myself a purer, a simpler, a more] unreserved & natural being in your company than ~~it~~ in that of almost any human creature. Certainly if your invitation had reached me in Dublin, I should without a moment's hesitation have obeyed it. But I imagined you were still in Somersetshire, &, if it had been so, I think I should have taken courage to beat up your quarters with the fall of the leaf: but unhappily I do not now feel myself authorised, either in the economy of money or time, to add to my ~~return~~ recent dissipation a second excursion to the amount of six hundred miles. . . .

The observations I made of him convinced me more fully than ever, how incalculable a misfortune it is for a man to be devoted to the profession of a lawyer. I know not whether you entirely coincide with the opinions I have published on that subject: but, if you do not, I must nevertheless believe, that, had you seen what I saw, you would have become a convert. Pope says, "How sweet ~~on~~ an Ovid was in Murray lost!" but, if I am not mistaken, a greater than Murray is here! . . .

unreserved & natural being in your company than ~~it~~ in that
of almost any human creature. Certainly, if your invitation
had reached me in Dublin, I should without a moments hesitation have obeyed it. But I imagined you were still in Somersetshire, &, if it had been so, I think I should have taken
courage to beat up your quarters with the fall of the leaf: but
unhappily I do not now feel myself authorised, either in the
economy of money or time, to add to my ~~column~~ recent dissipation a second excursion to the amount of six hundred miles.

I began a letter to you from Dublin, which, if
sent, would have been addressed to Stowey, but it was laid aside,
& never completed. I was well satisfied with my excursion to
Ireland. I liked it as a foreign country, &, though the difference between that island & my own may not be very great, it
is still something, & to me, who never before strayed more
than 150 miles from this metropolis, was sufficiently discerni-
ble. I was much pleased with the character of the man whose
invitation has drawn me thither, & the eminent situation he
holds in the judgment of his countrymen gave me every opportunity of access to & intercourse with persons on that side
of the water, whose reputation had most impressed my feeling
& excited my curiosity on this. In the letter I began to you
from Dublin, I occupied myself among other things in attempting a character of my host, Mr. Curran; & indeed a
chief reason why the letter was never finished, was because,
having once left it imperfect, I began to discern new traits in
the character of the man, which gradually increased my dissatisfaction with the sentiments with which I had commenced
it. The observations I made of him convinced me more fully than
ever, how incalculable a misfortune it is for a man to be devoted to the profession of a lawyer. I know not whether you entirely
coincide with the opinions I have published on that subject; but,

if you do not, I must nevertheless believe, that, had you seen what
I saw, you would have become a convert. Pope says, "How sweet
~~#~~ an Ovid was in Murray lost!" but, if I am not mistaken, a
greater than Murray, is here! – Curran is, as he himself assured me,
& as closer observation led me to believe, constitutionally of a gloomy,
choleric & atrabilaire turn of mind, habitually turned to comment
upon himself & his actions, & to regard his efforts & story with dissatisfaction, as the abortion of a friend to his country & mankind. He
is strongly imbued with enthusiasm & zeal: but the dissatisfaction I
have mentioned has led him for the most part to take refuge in
humour, frolic & drollery, so that superficial observers take him rather for a buffoon, than a melancholy man. Having once fallen into this pursuit, his imagination, which is more various & untired
than I almost ever witnessed in a human being, comes in aid of
the project, gives elevation to his facetiousness, & adorns his jeems
with several attributes of the most genuine wit. Must not this
strange distortion of character have been in a great degree th[illegible]
consequence of his profession? a profession, base & lying, ve-
nal of tongue, prodigal of falshood, factitious of passion, so-
phistical, thorny, the natural & unappeasable adversary of tru[illegible] could
a less powerful cause have generated the dissatisfaction I describe?
Must it not be greatly owing to the same cause that (while a
production, a speech, I read of his in Ireland, convinced me that
he was of the first order of logicians) I found him superficial
in ~~minute~~ investigation, & unaccustomed to analysis in relation to
the natures of things, at the same time that he shrunk from no discussion, & was perhaps beyond any one I ever conversed with, patient
of opposition?

It was not however merely the men of Ireland, that
at once excited, & gratified my curiosity: I was delighted with the
features of the scenery. I traversed the mountainous & romantic
county of Wicklow in almost all directions; & I am almost afraid
to forfeit my character with you as a man of taste, when I add,
that, having on my return surveyed, with some carefulness of leisure,

125

William Blake
1757–1827

Autograph letter signed, undated, but written 12 September 1800, to John Flaxman. 2 pp. 195 x 163 mm. MA 2618. Gift of Miss Tessie Jones in memory of her father Herschel V. Jones.

At the end of the eighteenth century, a time of stridently millennial language, the customary banalities of life were often weighed against a sense of imminent apocalypse. For some poets, like Cowper, apocalypse implied a dreaded dissolution of being, which led him to speak of it as a thing apart, but Blake regarded it as a familiar promise, renewed constantly in his daily life. In this letter to the sculptor John Flaxman, written in September 1800, Blake alludes to the immediate visionary present and an appointment to call on Mrs. Flaxman as if they were events on consecutive leaves of his calendar; and he apologizes for the poem he includes in this letter by suggesting that "As the time is now arrivd when Men shall again converse in Heaven & walk with Angels I know you will be pleased with the Intention & hope you will forgive the Poetry." The verse epistle, "To My Dearest Friend John Flaxman," provides a parallel history of Blake's "lot in the Heavens," where he is blessed by visions of Milton, Ezra, Isaiah and Shakespeare, and his "friends upon Earth," a succession that includes Flaxman, Fuseli and William Hayley. Blake concludes "that Seeing such visions I could not Subsist on the Earth/ But by my conjunction with Flaxman," but Flaxman, like the rest of his "friends upon Earth," was subject to what Blake called "the Doubts of other Mortals," doubts that strained to the breaking point many of Blake's friendships with men of subordinate genius.

The major collection of poetical manuscripts by Blake, including the Rossetti notebook, once in the possession of Dante Gabriel Rossetti, is in the British Library.

To My Dearest Friend John Flaxman/ these lines/ I bless thee O Father of Heaven & Earth that ever I saw Flaxmans face/ Angels stand round my Spirit in Heaven. the blessed of Heaven are my friends upon Earth/ When Flaxman was taken to Italy. Fuseli was giv'n to me for a season/ And now Flaxman hath given me Hayley his friend to be mine. such my lot upon Earth/ Now my lot in the Heavens is this; Milton lovd me in childhood & shewd me his face/ Ezra came with Isaiah the Prophet, but Shakespeare in riper years gave me his hand/ Paracelsus & Behmen appeard to me. terrors appear'd in the Heavens above/ And in Hell beneath & a mighty & awful change threatend the land/ The American War began All its dark horrors passed before my face/ Across the Atlantic to France. Then the French Revolution commencd in thick clouds/ And My Angels have told me. that Seeing such visions I could not Subsist on the Earth/ But by my conjunction with Flaxman who knows to forgive Nervous Fear/ I remain for Ever Yours/ William Blake/ Be so kind as to Read & then Seal the Inclosed & Send it on its much beloved Mission

328

My Dearest Friend

— It is to you I owe All my present Happiness
It is to you I owe perhaps the Principal Happiness of
my life. I have presumed on your friendship in
staying so long away & not calling to know of your
welfare but hope, now every thing is nearly completed
for our removal to Felpham that I shall see you
on Sunday as we have appointed Sunday afternoon to
call on Mrs Flaxman at Hampstead. I send you
a few lines which I hope you will Excuse. And
As the time is now arrived when Men shall again
converse in Heaven & walk with Angels I know
you will be pleased with the Intention & hope
you will forgive the Poetry

To

To My Dearest Friend John Flaxman
these lines

I bless thee O Father of Heaven & Earth that ever I saw Flaxmans face
Angels stand round my Spirit in Heaven. the blessed of Heaven are my
friends upon Earth
When Flaxman was taken to Italy. Fuseli was given to me for a season
And now Flaxman hath given me Hayley his friend to be mine. such
my lot upon Earth
Now my lot in the Heavens is this; Milton lovd me in childhood &
shewd me his face
Ezra came with Isaiah the Prophet, but Shakespeare in riper years gave
me his hand
Paracelsus & Behmen appeard to me. terrors appeard in the Heavens above
And in Hell beneath & a mighty & awful change threatend the Earth
The American War began All its dark horrors passed before my face
Across the Atlantic to France. Then the French Revolution commenced
in thick clouds
And My Angels have told me. that seeing such visions I could not subsist
on the Earth
But by my conjunction with Flaxman who knows to forgive Nervous Fear

I remain for Ever Yours
William Blake

Be so kind as to Read & then Seal the Inclosed & send it on its
much beloved Mission

William Blake

The Pickering or Ballads Manuscript, autograph manuscript unsigned, written ca. 1807. 22 pp. 185 x 120 mm. MA 2879. Gift of Mrs. Landon K. Thorne.

Blake closes one century and opens another; he provides not only the most imaginative auguries of the future of English poetry but also the most radical and cogent criticism of what came before. Against an empirical, Anglican, mercantile nation—whose philosophy was contained in a work he called "An Easy of Huming Understanding by John Lookye"—Blake raised a cry of revelation and prophetic faith: "They mock Inspiration & Vision. Inspiration & Vision was then & now is & I hope will always Remain my Element, my Eternal dwelling Place. How can I then hear it Contemnd without returning Scorn for Scorn?" Blake reserved most of his scorn for his shorter poems. His long visionary works articulate a redemptive landscape in which "The Expanding Eyes of Man behold the depths of wondrous worlds . . . & one Sun Each morning like a New born Man issues with songs & Joy Calling the Plowman to his Labour & the Shepherd to his rest." The poems in the manuscript shown here fall between these two extremes. They are not so much satiric or prophetic as gnomic, indicating in few words the boundaries of this world and the infinite contours of Blake's "Eternal dwelling Place." Chief among them is "Auguries of Innocence":

God Appears & God is Light
To those poor Souls who dwell in Night
But does a Human form Display
To those who Dwell in Realms of day.

This manuscript is called the Pickering Manuscript after a former owner, B. M. Pickering, who bought it in 1866. It includes ten poems written between 1800 and 1804 and transcribed in fair copy by Blake in 1807 and is the unique source for seven of them.

Auguries of Innocence/ To see a World in a Grain of Sand/ And a Heaven in a Wild Flower/ Hold Infinity in the palm of your hand/ And Eternity in an hour/ A Robin Red breast in a Cage/ Puts all Heaven in a Rage/ A dove house filld with doves & Pigeons

The Grey Monk

I die I die the Mother said
My Children die for lack of Bread
What more has the merciless Tyrant said
The Monk sat down on the Stony Bed

The blood red ran from the Grey Monks side
His hands & feet were wounded wide
His Body bent his arms & knees
Like to the roots of ancient trees

His eye was dry no tear could flow
A hollow groan first spoke his woe
He trembled & shudderd upon the Bed
At length with a feeble cry he said

When God commanded this hand to write
In the studious hours of deep midnight
He told me the writing I wrote should prove
The Bane of all that on Earth I lovd

My Brother starvd between two Walls
His Childrens Cry my Soul appalls
I mockd at the wrack & griding chain
My bent body mocks their torturing pain

Thy Father drew his sword in the North
With his thousands strong he marched forth

Thy Brother has armd himself in Steel
To avenge the wrongs thy Children feel

But vain the Sword & vain the Bow
They never can work Wars overthrow
The Hermits Prayer & the Widows tear
Alone can free the World from fear

For a Tear is an Intellectual Thing
And a Sigh is the Sword of an Angel King
And the bitter groan of the Martyrs woe
Is an Arrow from the Almighties Bow

The hand of Vengeance found the Bed
To which the Purple Tyrant fled
The iron hand crushd the Tyrants head
And became a Tyrant in his stead

Auguries of Innocence

To see a World in a Grain of Sand
And a Heaven in a Wild Flower
Hold Infinity in the palm of your hand
And Eternity in an hour
A Robin Red breast in a Cage
Puts all Heaven in a Rage
A Dove house filld with Doves & Pigeons

Robert Burns
1759–1796

Autograph letter signed, dated 29 October 1788, to Mrs. Frances Dunlop. 4 pp. 332 x 200 mm. MA 46.

Writing to George Thomson in October 1794, Burns described his "glorious recipe" for writing songs: "I put myself on a regimen of admiring a fine woman; & in proportion to the adorability of her charms, in proportion you are delighted with my verses." Burns's politics, his drinking and the conjunction of fine women and song bedeviled his reputation during his lifetime and well into the next century, raising doubts as to whether the Scottish national poet was the author of the pious "Cotter's Saturday Night" or the randier bard who wrote "Tam o'Shanter." Mrs. Dunlop, to whom Burns sent this letter, was a firm, if conventional, friend who felt an occasional hesitation before sallying into battle on Burns's behalf. In the letter she wrote in response to the one shown here, she remarked, "I am sometimes almost ashamed to attempt your defence. A gentleman told me with a grave face the other day that you certainly were a sad wretch, that your works were immoral and infamous. . . ." Like John Stuart Mill discovering Wordsworth, Mrs. Dunlop first read Burns during a period of dejection, found solace in the Kilmarnock volume (*Poems, chiefly in the Scottish Dialect* [1786]) and took the surest way to the poet's warm heart by ordering six copies of that work. To Mrs. Dunlop, Burns wrote more letters than he did to any other person, and in spite of the incongruities in their friendship, it lasted nearly ten years. In his farewell letter to her, written eleven days before his death, Burns recalled: "With what pleasure did I use to break up the seal [of her letters]! The remembrance yet adds one pulse more to my poor palpitating heart!"

The letter shown here includes two poems written at the extremes of Burns's temperament. The first fragment, which he called "The Poet's Progress, an embryotic Poem in the womb of Futurity," is part of a longer, bitterly satiric poem, written in English, about the defenselessness of a poet in the brutal world of bookselling. The second poem, published in *The Scots Musical Museum*, is a lovely song about a minister's daughter named Jean Jaffray.

The collection of Burns letters in the Morgan Library is the largest in the world.

But O thou cruel Stepmother and hard,/ To that poor, senceless, naked thing—A Bard!/ A thing unteachable in worldly skill,/ And half an idiot too, more helpless still.—/ No heels to bear him from the opening dun;/ No claws to dig, his hated sight to shun:/ No horns, but those by luckless Hymen worn,/ And those, alas! not Amalthea's horn.—/ His dart satyric, his unheeded sting;/ And idle fancy's pinion all his wing:/ The silly sheep that wanders, wild, astray,/ Not more unfriended, and not more a prey.—/ Vampyre Booksellers drain him to the heart,/ And butcher Critics cut him up by art.——

. . .

I gade a waefu' gate yestreen,/ A gate, I fear, I dearly rue:/ I gat my death frae twa sweet een,/ Twa lovely een o' bony blue.—

'Twas not her golden ringlets bright;/ Her lips like roses wat wi' dew:/ Her heaving bosom, lily-white,/ It was her een sae bony blue.—

But O thou cruel Stepmother and hard,
To that poor, fenceless, naked thing—a Bard!
A thing unteachable in worldly skill,
And half an idiot too, more helpless still.—
No heels to bear him from the opening dun;
No claws to dig, his hated sight to shun:
No horns, but those by luckless Hymen worn,
And those, alas! not Amalthea's horn.—
His dart satyric, his unheeded sting;
And idle fancy's pinion all his wing:
The silly sheep that wanders, wild, astray,
Not more unfriended, and not more a prey.—
Vampyre Booksellers drain him to the heart,
And butcher Critics cut him up by art.—

Critics, appall'd I venture on the Name;
Those bandits that infest the paths of Fame:
Bloody Dissectors, worse than ten Monroes;
He cuts to teach, they mangle to expose.—
His heart by causeless, wanton Malice wrung;
By Blockheads daring even to madness stung;
Torn, bleeding, tortur'd, in th' unequal strife,
The hapless Poet flounces on thro' life:
Till fled each Muse that glorious once inspir'd,
Extinct each ray that once his bosom fir'd;
Low-sunk in feeble, unprotected age,
Dead even resentments for his injur'd Page,
He feels no more the ruthless Critic's rage!
So, by some hedge, the generous Steed deceas'd,
To half-starv'd, snarling Curs a dainty feast;
By Toil & Famine wore to skin & bone,
Lies, senseless of each tugging bitch's son.—

Thus far only have I proceeded, & perhaps I may never again resume the subject.—I must mention one caution to you, Madam, with respect to these verses; I have a remote idea that I may one day use them as instruments of vengeance, & consequently I will hide them like a Conspirators dagger.—I mean this, lest you might inadvertantly mention them, or acknowledge them as your old acquaintances, should you meet with them anonymously in a Newspaper.—I need not add that I allude to a certain Bookseller's connection & mine.—

How do you like the following song, designed for an Air composed by a friend of mine, & which he had christened, "the blue-eyed lassie."

I gade a waefu' gate yestreen,
A gate, I fear, I dearly rue:
I gat my death frae twa sweet een,
Twa lovely een o' bony blue.—
'Twas not her golden ringlets bright;
Her lips like roses wat wi' dew;
Her heaving bosom, lily-white,
It was her een sae bony blue.—
She talk'd, she smil'd, my heart she wyl'd,
She charm'd my soul I wist na how;
And ay the stound, the deadly wound,
Cam frae her een sae bony blue.—
But spare to speak, & spare to speed;
She'll aiblins listen to my vow:
Should she refuse—I'll lay my dead
To her twa een sae bony blue.

Robert Burns

Autograph letter signed with initials, undated, but written in September 1793, to George Thomson. 22 pp. 255 x 207 mm. MA 50.

Between 16 September 1792 and 12 July 1796 (nine days before his death) Burns wrote fifty-six letters—containing more than one hundred songs—to George Thomson, the editor of *A Select Collection of Original Scotish Airs for the Voice* (1793–1818). Burns's enthusiastic response to Thomson's plan for *A Select Collection*, which included contributions from Peter Pindar, Ignaz Pleyel and eventually Haydn and Beethoven, arose partly from his desire to see his songs presented in a more elegant format than *The Scots Musical Museum* (to which he had also contributed ballads) but mainly from the pleasure he took in composing songs to fit traditional airs: "Ballad-making is now as compleatly my hobby-horse, as ever Fortification was Uncle Toby's; so I'll e'en canter it away till I come to the limit of my race. . . ." As the project advanced and the burden of work increased (Peter Pindar withdrew from his part of the bargain in August 1793) Burns merely threw himself more exuberantly into his task, for which he would not accept payment. Thomson must have been somewhat awestruck by the fertility and openhandedness of the man whose knowledge of traditional ballads he had tapped, but Burns's evident genius did not deter him from offering naïve criticism and, ultimately, from altering many of Burns's songs and manuscripts after his death. Luckily, all of Burns's letters to Thomson have survived and are preserved in the Morgan Library.

In the remarkable letter illustrated here, Burns comments on a list of seventy-five ballads that Thomson wished to include in *A Select Collection* and adds one more, "Auld Lang Syne": "The air is but mediocre; but the following song, the old song of the olden times . . . is enough to recommend any air—." Burns never acknowledged this song as his own (though most scholars agree that it is), neither here nor in a letter to Mrs. Dunlop written almost five years earlier which also includes a copy of "Auld Lang Syne" and Burns's remark: "Light be the turf on the breast of the heaven-inspired Poet who composed this glorious Fragment!"

One Song more, & I have done.—Auld lang syne—The air is but mediocre; but the following song, the old Song of the olden times, & which has never been in print, nor even in manuscript, untill I took it down from an old man's Singing; is enough to recommend any air—

Auld lang Syne—/ Should auld acquaintance be forgot,/ And never brought to mind?/ Should auld acquaintance be forgot,/ And days o' lang syne?

Chorus/ For auld lang syne, my Dear,/ For auld lang syne,/ We'll tak a cup o' kindness yet,/ For auld lang syne—. . .

Page 18.

the Museum — "I had a horse, & I had nae mair:"
It is a charming song, & I know the story of
the Ballad. —
One song more, & I have done — Auld lang syne —
The air is but mediocre; but the following song, the
old song of the olden times, & which has never been
in print, nor even in manuscript, untill I took it
down from an old man's singing; is enough to
recommend any air —

Auld lang syne —

Should auld acquaintance be forgot,
And never brought to mind?
Should auld acquaintance be forgot,
And days o' lang syne?

Chorus

For auld lang syne, my Dear,
For auld lang syne,
We'll tak a cup o' kindness yet,
For auld lang syne —

We twa hae run about the braes,
And pu't the gowans fine;

But

Page 19.

But we've wander'd mony a weary foot,
Sin auld lang syne! —
For auld lang &c. —

We twa hae paidlet i' the burn,
Frae mornin sun till dine:
But seas between us braid hae roar'd,
Sin auld lang syne. —
For auld &c. —

And there's a hand, my trusty fiere,
And gie's a hand o' thine;
And we'll tak a right guide-willie waught,
For auld lang syne —
For auld &c. —

And surely ye'll be your pint-stowp,
And surely I'll be mine;
And we'll tak a cup o' kindness yet,
For auld lang syne.
For auld &c. —

Now

129

Matthew Gregory Lewis
1775–1818

Autograph poem, "On the failure of her Royal Highness's efforts to reclaim a worthless Object of her bounty," signed with initials, dated 26 February 1803. 1 p. 184 x 113 mm. MA 3093.

M. G. Lewis has the awkward distinction of belonging to that small set of authors who are seemingly ill-matched with their creations. Lewis' personal virtues were numerous—Lord Holland called him "sincere, affectionate, and generous"—and his conspicuous social faults were hardly diabolical; after a visit by Lewis in November 1813, Byron described him as "a good and good-humoured man, but pestilently prolix and paradoxical and *personal*... his vanity is *ouverte*... and yet not offending." At the age of nineteen, while he was an attaché of the British embassy in The Hague, Lewis wrote *The Monk: A Romance*, which brought him immediate notoriety. *The Monk* is a tale as labyrinthine and lugubrious as the convent tomb in which one of its characters is imprisoned; furthermore, it had the reputation of being obscene, anticlerical and utterly fascinating. Unfortunately, its many critics were often unable to peer beyond the author's familiar nickname, "Monk" Lewis, so that when he died he was excoriated as "a reckless defiler of the public mind" who "knew in his soul that he was compounding poison for the multitude...." About *The Monk*—which in the nearly two centuries since its publication has lost little of its power—one may say what Leslie Stephen said about Lewis' monodrama *The Captive*, which was performed just after this poem was written and allegedly threw its audience into hysterics: "It may be read with impunity."

Lewis' secondary literary fame as a poet derived from his "excellent ear and a command of elegant language." Much of his poetry, however, was of an occasional nature, written for members of the nobility by whom, as Sir Walter Scott observed, he was unduly intrigued. This poem of solace was composed for Frederica, the Duchess of York, after one of the objects of her bounty, an "unworthy Elf," had relapsed into the ways of guilt and misery.

The manuscript of *The Monk: A Romance* is in the Wisbech and Fenland Museum, Cambridgeshire.

On the failure of her Royal Highness's efforts to reclaim a worthless Object of her bounty.

The Wretch to guilt and misery flies,/ And royal Frederica sighs/ Oër gracious plans defeated:/ Yet think not, Princess, for yourself/ *[Though lost be that unworthy Elf]/ Your object not compleated.*

For, long ere this, to heavenly climes,/ Your wish to turn his soul from crimes,/ Has made its blest ascension;/ And in that book, which Angels read,/ The leaf, which would have held your deed,/ *Is filled by your* intention. *M. G. L. February 26th 1803.*

1

On the failure of her Royal Highness's efforts to reclaim a worthless Object of her bounty.

The Wretch to guilt and misery flies,
and royal Frederica sighs
O'er gracious plans defeated:
Yet think not, Princess, for yourself
[though lost be that unworthy Elf]
Your object not compleated.

For, long ere this, to heavenly climes,
Your wish to turn his soul from crimes,
Has made its blest ascension;
and in that book, which Angels read,
The leaf, which would have held your deed,
Is filled by your intention.

M. G. L.

February 26th 1803.